THE NATURAL HISTORY
OF THE GARDEN

THE
NATURAL HISTORY
OF THE
GARDEN

Michael Chinery

with illustrations by

Marjorie Blamey
Anthony Orford
Denys Ovenden
Gordon Riley

COLLINS
ST JAMES'S PLACE, LONDON

William Collins Sons & Co Ltd
London · Glasgow · Sydney · Auckland
Toronto · Johannesburg

First published 1977
Reprinted 1978
© Michael Chinery, 1977
ISBN 0 00 219606 9
Filmset by Jolly and Barber Ltd., Rugby
Made and Printed in Great Britain by
William Collins Sons & Co Ltd Glasgow

Contents

Colour Plates

Preface

ONE of the first things that a gardener learns on taking over a garden for the first time is that he or she does not have vacant possession. The garden is shared by a vast array of uninvited guests, both plant and animal, many of which positively compete with the gardener and are only too ready to take control as soon as his vigil is relaxed. Many of the garden animals are very small and inconspicuous, and some are beautifully camouflaged as a protection against their enemies. Many others come out only at night, when the air is cool and moist and their soft bodies are in no danger of drying up. Nevertheless, during the course of a year's work in the average garden, whatever that may be, the gardener will come across many of these creatures, as well as the more conspicuous day-flying birds and butterflies. He or she will also have to contend with numerous uninvited plants – the weeds – digging or pulling them up and perhaps secretly admiring their tenacity and their powers of regeneration.

The aim of this book is to enable the gardener to recognise some of the commoner and more obvious of these guests and invaders, to help him or her to know why the creatures have chosen to live where they do, and to explain what they are doing there. It is *not* intended to be a pest control handbook, although the text points out those creatures against which some form of control measures are desirable.

Acknowledgements

I wish to thank the numerous friends and colleagues who have helped in the preparation of this book. My thanks go in particular to Mr John Sankey, Mr Harold Oldroyd, and Dr Ian Yarrow who all gave much advice on the selection of species for inclusion in the book. Mr Ian Gould also gave helpful advice. John Sankey provided a number of specimens for the artists, and in this context I also wish to thank Mrs Frances Murphy and Mr John Parker of the British Arachnological Society. Dr June Chatfield kindly provided some snails, and Janet Dawson of the Leicester Museum kindly lent a number of insects for painting. Several friends allowed me to examine their gardens and sheds for interesting 'creepy crawlies' while deciding just what creatures do live in gardens, and my thanks are also due to the many people whose gardens have been surreptitiously examined from the garden gate or through holes in the hedge. In this way, I was able to get a good idea of the commonest and most troublesome weeds.

I am extremely grateful to the artists, who have done a superb job on the plates and the text figures. Most of the paintings have been done from living specimens, and particular thanks go to Gordon Riley and his family who have cheerfully accepted and nurtured slugs, spiders, caterpillars, and numerous other creepy crawlies while the paintings were being done. My own family has also put up with an assortment of creatures in the house, and my wife even accepted an array of spider webs in the porch while I was working on the book. My thanks to them all.

Finally, my thanks go to Sheila Kinsey and Margaret Horne, who transformed my untidy thoughts into neat pages of typescript.

Michael Chinery
Hundon, Suffolk

CHAPTER I

A Place to Live

MANY of the older books on gardening divided the uninvited animal inhabitants into 'friends' and 'foes' of the gardener, a distinction which was based entirely on the feeding habits of the animals concerned. Carnivorous creatures, which feed on other animals, were considered friends, while all plant-eating forms were treated as enemies. It is now considered old-fashioned to talk in this way, because we know so much more about the animals' habits and we know how many of them fit into the complex web of life. Each species has a part to play in the balance of nature, and the removal of any species may lead to changes in the community as a whole. There are, nevertheless, some animals which are less desirable in the garden than others and against which the gardener usually wages some kind of warfare. These are the pests, and they include the familiar aphids – the greenfly and blackfly. Some of the garden creatures, on the other hand, are very useful. Ladybirds, for example, consume large numbers of aphids, and no gardener would get very far without the assistance of the humble earthworm. But the great majority of garden creatures are completely neutral to the gardener's interests: they neither help nor hinder and they use the garden merely as a place to live.

You have only to walk around any country or suburban area to see that the majority of British homes have some sort of garden, and if you take your walk on a summer evening or at the weekend you will see that the majority of occupiers put some effort into their gardens. They may not all actually enjoy it, but many of them do, as shown by a recent survey which put gardening high on the list of recreational activities in Britain. Dr D. G. Hessayon, writing in *The Garden Book of Europe,* estimates that there are 14.5 million home gardens in the United Kingdom, and, taking his estimated average size of 2,000 square feet, this amounts to a total garden area of about 670,000 acres. Our gardens as a whole are thus extremely important reservoirs of wild-life.

As well as covering a very large area, our gardens are very varied, with numerous different habitats in which plants and animals can settle down. Area for area, a garden is one of the richest of all places in terms of the variety of plant and animal life. This applies to small town gardens as well as to country cottage gardens. The richness is, of course, due mainly to the activity of the gardener himself. He grows as many different kinds of plants as he can in the available area, including decorative plants, plants to eat, and hedging plants to give him privacy. Each kind of plant supports several kinds of animals, and each of these in turn provides food for various carnivorous or predatory animals. The gardener also creates several other habitats by building sheds and walls, by erecting fences and laying paths, by digging out fish ponds, and by piling up the inevitable rubbish heap. All of these features, most of which are present in our hypothetical average garden, provide shelter and sometimes food for numerous animals. They also provide footholds for many of our native and introduced plants, which then arrive and contribute even more to the variety, both in themselves and through the additional animal life which they support.

Many factors affect the type and numbers of wildlife in a garden, and one cannot expect all gardens to have the same kind of inhabitants. The type of soil, the age of the garden and its location, and the treatment meted out by the gardener are the major factors involved in determining the wildlife population. The soil is very important because it controls the kinds of plants, both wild and cultivated, that can grow in the garden, and the plants, being the primary producers of food, determine what animals can live there. Soil also affects some of the animals directly. Many snails, for example, need a certain minimum concentration of lime in the soil if they are to make their shells properly. These snails are absent from gardens on sandy soil.

Air pollution is another factor influencing garden wildlife, and it makes itself felt both directly and indirectly. Its direct effects include the blackening of leaves and the clogging of their pores with soot. This can sometimes kill trees and shrubs, and thus drive out the insects and other animals that feed on them. The effect is especially marked among the evergreens, whose leaves are not renewed each year and are, therefore, subjected to greater amounts of pollution then the deciduous species. Air pollution is detrimental to lichens and many mosses as well, and we find few of these simple plants in industrial regions. Animals are also affected by the smoke and other poisons of the air, and indirect effects are brought about by the effect of pollution on the soil. Sulphur dioxide and other acidic gases are washed down by the rain and produce measurable increases in the acidity of the soil, thus reducing bacterial activity and decreasing the fertility. Gardens in industrial regions thus tend to be much poorer in wildlife than those in less polluted areas.

The age of a garden also has a great effect on the abundance of wildlife. Animals, as we have seen, depend ultimately on plant life for their food, and animal life cannot therefore establish itself until the plant life has arrived. A new plot, with a layer of topsoil if you are lucky and a pile of clay and rubble if you are not, will support very few residents other than microscopic organisms. There may be a few worms, and a few spiders thriving on passing insects, but not many other creatures will be able to make a living in the garden at this stage. Colonisation takes place gradually. The gardener introduces his chosen plants, and weed seeds arrive on the breeze or are dropped by passing birds. Insects and other animals visit the garden from neighbouring habitats and, if conditions are suitable, they take up residence. It takes many years, however, for a garden to become really fully populated, and a garden cannot really be said to be mature until it supports fully grown shrubs or trees. On this basis, a great many of Britain's gardens are immature, especially those on our numerous new housing estates. But this does not mean that these gardens are barren; they just don't support such a variety of wildlife as an older and more mature garden.

The location of a garden has a considerable effect on the speed at which it is colonised. A garden in the middle of a new housing estate will be populated much more slowly than a single cottage garden on the edge of a wood or a meadow, simply because the animals take longer to reach it. This applies especially to the earth-bound creatures, such as the slugs and woodlice, but it is also true of some of the insects. In time, however, as long as the two gardens are on similar soil and in the same part of the country, and as long as air pollution does not interfere, the town garden and the country garden will acquire a very similar *resident* population. The word resident is important because gardens receive many visitors, especially birds and insects, which pass through from time to time without feeding there regularly. Although the location, within a given geographical area, may not have much effect on the resident garden animals, it certainly does control the visitors. A country garden, surrounded by fields and hedgerows, will obviously see more butterflies and other insects than a similar garden in a town. It will also get more bird visitors. This makes it rather difficult to say just what is a garden animal and what is not. A book of this kind obviously cannot include all the creatures that visit a garden, but the ones which I have chosen to describe are all either common residents of the garden or regular visitors. Before leaving geography, it

13

must also be pointed out that there is a marked difference in climate between the south and the north of the British Isles. This difference has a marked effect on the distribution of our animals.

Far fewer species of insects and other invertebrates are found in Scotland than in England. The Scottish gardener cannot, therefore, expect to find such a variety of animals as his English counterpart, but the discrepancy is not as great in the garden as it is in the wild. The artificial conditions of the house and garden have allowed many southern species to move far further north than they could have done otherwise.

The gardener himself is, of course, a prime factor controlling the wildlife in the garden. The gardener who never ventures down the path without his hoe and his aerosol can will have a far less interesting garden, though a tidier and possibly more productive one, than the gardener who, like myself, is a little less fussy. Gardens obviously mean different things to different people, but some gardeners derive just as much pleasure from seeing the blue tits and the red admirals, or even an unusual species of earwig, as from pulling a fresh lettuce or climbing the trees to gather the apples.

Household pets also have a marked effect on the wildlife of the garden, and of the neighbouring gardens as well. This is especially true of cats, of which there are thought to be about 6 million in Great Britain. These animals discourage birds from visiting the garden, and they also keep down the numbers of small mammals such as mice and voles. But such is the intricate web of life in a garden, that the reduction of one group of animals leads directly to the increase of others. Loss of the birds, for example, brings about a marked increase in the insects on which they feed. Economically, therefore, cats may be a bad thing, because many of the insects are pests. On the other hand, a cat can be useful if it keeps the birds away from the peas and the currants. This is a simple illustration of the fact that it is difficult, if not impossible, to decide whether an animal is good or bad for the gardener. The cat and mouse relationship can have even further ramifications. Reduction in the numbers of field mice will allow more of the gardener's peas and beans to germinate, as well as allowing more weeds to spring up, and it may also lead to an increase in the number of bumble bees. The latter pollinate the flowers while probing for nectar, and so seed production may also increase. Charles Darwin, whom we shall meet again in connection with the earthworms, was the first to point out this relationship. He showed that the field mice attack bumble bee nests and destroy the young bees and, because bumble bees are the main pollinators of clover, he explained that more cats meant fewer mice, more bumble bees, and more clover seed.

The size of a garden has less effect on its wildlife than either age or treatment, although it is obvious that a small garden cannot support so many plants and habitats as a larger one. We can not all have a garden to match that of Buckingham Palace, but it is interesting to record some of the discoveries made there during a special investigation by members of the British Entomological and Natural History Society.

The Palace garden covers some 39 acres and, screened off by a good wall, it gets relatively little disturbance other than that caused by normal gardening activity. In particular, there are no cats. These facts, combined with the great variety of habitats provided by the trees and shrubs and the lake, make it a haven for birds. A total of 61 species was recorded during the period of the investigation, and 21 of these were found nesting in the grounds. The spider experts found 57 species of spider, while the entomologists discovered 343 species of butterflies and moths – more than a tenth of all the species so far discovered in the British Isles – and 90 kinds of beetles. Taking into consideration the constant gardening and weeding that goes on, and the Palace's situation in the heart of London, the investigators found a remarkably large flora and fauna in the garden, even for a garden extending to 39 acres. It must be pointed out, however, that this survey was conducted by a team of expert naturalists, who knew where to look and who were able to distinguish between many very similar creatures.

The average garden will obviously support fewer plants and animals than one of royal proportions, merely because it embraces fewer habitats, but it will still yield more than enough creatures to keep the gardener busy if he should choose to study those he finds. In my own small, but admittedly rather untidy garden I have found representatives of 18 orders of insects (not all residents), and I know that I would find three more groups if I were to search the mice and birds for fleas and lice. I have also recorded 15 kinds of butterflies in the garden, seven species of mammals, and 24 kinds of birds. Add to these the scores of less obvious 'creepy-crawlies' that wander over the plants or through the soil and you will soon see that even a small garden has plenty of life in it.

The origin of pests

The difficulty of dividing garden creatures into friends and foes has already been mentioned, but there are, nevertheless, a number of plants and animals which are definitely not on the side of the gardener. These are the pests. Your dictionary may define a pest as any destructive or troublesome organism (living thing), but the emphasis should be on the word troublesome. Wood-boring beetles tunnelling through a dead tree trunk in the woods are certainly destructive, but they are not troublesome and they are not regarded as pests. Not until they move into our homes and attack our furniture and timber do they become troublesome and really merit the title of pest. The same is true in the garden: the pests are those creatures which are sufficiently numerous to compete with us and harm our crops and possessions. On this basis, many of our garden weeds are also pests, but we usually restrict the word to our animal opponents.

The gardener whose cabbage leaves are reduced to skeletons by caterpillars, or whose apples always seem to have maggots in them, might be forgiven for thinking that these insects were created just to feed on his crops. But this is, of course, untrue: the insects were in existence long before man even evolved, let alone began his horticultural activities. They fed on various wild plants and, by definition, could not be regarded as pests. Why, then, did they turn their attention to our fields and gardens? The answer is simple: men started to grow the plants that the insects liked, and they grew large quantities on relatively small areas. The insects found these artificial habitats very suitable, and they had to spend very little time and energy hunting for food. As a result, large populations built up and the creatures became pests. Large populations of this kind rarely build up under natural circumstances because there are rarely any such pure stands of single plant species. The insects are then, perforce, more scattered. An individual plant may support a fairly high population, but these creatures may not spread much to other plants of the same kind because of the 'dilution factor' – the food plants are interspersed with other species and not so easily reached. There is, however, another more important factor at work here. The other plant species, as well as passively denying food to the pest animal, may harbour animals which actively destroy it. It is as well to bear this diversity factor in mind when planning a garden: retain all hedges as living reservoirs of birds and ladybirds, and don't plant all your cabbages in one patch. It has been shown on several occasions that gardens with plenty of diversity yield far more than one-crop gardens, or require far less insecticidal treatment to produce the same yield. The separation of crops into little patches is not always practical in a small garden, but similar results

PLATE 1: **Weeds.** 1 Dandelion 38; 2 Curled dock 36; 3 Petty spurge 35; 4 Groundsel 25; ▶
5 Chickweed 25; 6 Herb Robert 35; 7 Enchanter's nightshade 41; 8 Ground elder 42;
9 Broad-leaved willowherb 41; 10 Rosebay willowherb 41; 11 Black nightshade 34.

can sometimes be obtained by rotating the crops. Growing the same crop year after year on the same patch of soil allows pests to build up in the soil. They hibernate there during the winter and wake up in the spring to find a nice new crop waiting for them. But if you rotate your crops, by planting cabbages, for example, where you last grew potatoes, the potato pests will wake up to find nasty cabbage roots. A few may be able to make their way to nearby potatoes, but most will die. This crop rotation also helps to maintain the fertility of the soil, because each crop has different require-ments and the drain on the soil is not so constant.

The above remarks have been confined to 'home-grown' pests, but imported pests can be even more serious. These are animals that have been brought into the country, deliberately or acciden-tally, and have spread themselves around because there are no natural enemies to control them. The majority of these pests have entered the country with imported plants, and this is the reason for our strict regulations covering the importation of plants. Many other, apparently harmless animals have arrived in this way. They have not been able to invade the complex wild communities of our countryside, but they have managed to establish themselves in and around our houses and gardens, where the artificial conditions – notably the extra warmth – are to their liking. Animals of this kind are often called synanthropes, a name which simply means 'with man'. They include several species of woodlice, centipedes, and spiders. The common house-sparrow is also markedly synan-thropic.

The origin of weeds is discussed in the next chapter.

Identifying garden creatures

The animal kingdom is divided up into about thirty major groups called phyla. Several of these groups contain only microscopic creatures, and several more are found only in the sea. Only five of the phyla are likely to be seen in the garden, although another half dozen phyla are probably there in the form of microscopic animals. The five groups normally seen are: the backboned animals or vertebrates (phylum Chordata), the slugs and snails (Mollusca), the roundworms (Nematoda), the earthworms and potworms (Annelida), and the arthropods (Arthropoda). The last group is a very large one and it contains a wide range of 'creepy-crawlies' – insects, spiders, woodlice, centipedes, and many others. All of them have bodies which are divided up into segments, and their

◀ PLATE 2: **Weeds.** 1 Scarlet pimpernel 34; 2 Fat hen 33; 3 White deadnettle 38; 4 Red deadnettle 29; 5 Stinging nettle 37; 6 Shepherd's purse 27; 7 Common fumitory 32; 8 Prickly sowthistle 27; 9 Long-headed poppy 30; 10 Nipplewort 26.

legs all have several joints. The name arthropod actually means 'jointed foot', although many young arthropods have no legs.

The most common backboned animals of the garden are the birds and the small mammals, such as the shrews and voles. Lizards and snakes may appear from time to time in certain gardens, while frogs and toads may be resident if your garden boasts a pond. These backboned animals are all fairly easy to recognise, but the other garden creatures – the invertebrates or animals without backbones – may present problems. Many of them are lumped together by the gardener and called insects if they have legs, worms or snails if they don't. The following simple key will help you to put most of the animals you find in your garden into their correct groups. Further information can then be found in the appropriate section of the book.

Key to the common groups of garden animals (Invertebrates)

Having found an animal that you wish to identify, start at the beginning of the key and read the two alternative descriptions in clue number one. Decide which one fits your animal and then move on to the clue whose number is given on the right. Follow this procedure again until you arrive at the name of the group to which your animal belongs.

1 Animal without legs   2
  Animal with legs   7

2 Animal long and hair-like   Roundworms (p. 69)
  Animal not hair-like   3

3 Animal with no sign of division into rings or segments   4
  Animal clearly divided into rings or segments   5

4 Soft-bodied animal with coiled shell into which the body
    can be withdrawn when disturbed   Snails (p. 71)
  Soft-bodied animal with no shell, or with only a tiny shell
    at the hind end   Slugs (p. 78)

5 Tapering white or greyish animal – a maggot – often found
    in rotting material   Fly larvae (p. 154)
  Animal not fitting this description   6

6 Grey or brownish leathery creature found in soil: a number
    of small lobes spreading star-like from hind end of body
                      Leatherjackets (Crane-fly larvae) (p. 163)
  Cylindrical animal, generally pinkish or white, with
    numerous segments and no visible out-growths
                      Earthworms and Potworms (p. 60)

7 Very small greyish animal with pink claws, almost as large
    as the body, at the front   False Scorpions (p. 220)
  Animal not like this   8

8 Animal with three pairs of legs: often with wings
               Adult and some young insects (p. 106)
  Animal with more than three pairs of legs   9

9 Animal with four pairs of legs   10
  Animal with more than four pairs of legs   12

10 Body divided into two fairly distinct regions: often making
    silken webs   Spiders (p. 195)
  Body not clearly divided into two regions   11

11 Legs usually very long in comparison with body: 2nd pair
    of legs always the longest   Harvestmen (p. 214)
  Very small, rounded or pear-shaped body: legs relatively
    short   Mites (p. 221)

12 Flattened or domed oval animal with seven pairs of legs
                       Woodlice (p. 83)
  Longer and more slender animal or, if squat, it has more
    than seven pairs of legs   13

13 All legs alike   14
  Front three pairs of legs horny and jointed: hind legs soft
    and stumpy
    Caterpillars of butterflies and moths (p. 133) and sawflies (p. 184)

14 Quick-moving brownish animal with many pairs of legs:
    one pair on each body segment   Centipedes (p. 90)
  Generally slower moving: often black and shiny: two pairs
    of legs on each segment   Millipedes (p. 99)

CHAPTER 2

Weeds and Other Plant Guests

OUR gardens are continually being invaded and colonised by wild and uninvited plants. Some of these invaders, such as the mosses and lichens that perch on walls and tree trunks and fill cracks in the garden path, are harmless guests and have little effect on either us or our crops, but many others spring up in the cultivated ground and compete to a greater or lesser extent with our flowers and vegetables. These are the weeds. They include the grasses that invade the herbaceous border, the dandelions and groundsel in the vegetable plot, and the bindweed threading its way through the shrubbery. The fastidious gardener, who likes nothing but the best grasses on his lawn, also considers the little daisy to be a weed, although he might admire the same species when it flowers on the village green. This dual standard is the basis of the accepted definition of a weed, which is that a weed is a plant growing where it is not wanted.

One often hears gardeners bemoaning the fact that the weeds always come up before the crops push their way through the soil, and one hears many complaints that the only things growing in the garden are the weeds. It is almost as if the weeds do this just to be awkward, but rapid growth and tenacity are the natural attributes of the weeds. They are in fact, the very essence of weeds, for without such features a plant would not be able to invade the garden and become a weed in the first place.

Weeds can be divided into two main categories: small, quick-maturing species, often with several generations in a year, and perennial species with tough underground parts that survive from year to year and defy nearly all attempts to get rid of them. The quick-maturing annuals or ephemerals include such plants as the chickweed and shepherd's purse and they can be scattering their seeds when only about six weeks old. Constant vigilance is thus necessary to keep these weeds under control: miss even one or two young plants hidden under a cabbage leaf before you go away for your holiday, and you may well come back to find that they have already scattered their seeds. Some of these seeds will lay dormant in the soil for many years and a batch will germinate every time you

20

turn the soil over, so the garden will never be completely free from these annual weeds. The perennial weeds include larger and tougher plants, such as docks and couch grass. Although they may be less numerous than the annual weeds, they are even more difficult to keep under control because of their amazing powers of regeneration. Any small piece of root or rhizome left in the soil can grow into a new plant, and so careless digging of these weeds may actually result in greater numbers. Annual and perennial weeds nearly all produce very large numbers of seeds.

Garden weeds usually look unsightly because many are of irregular growth and they spring up haphazardly between the neatly planted crops, but if this were their only fault the gardener would have no need to worry about them. Unfortunately their behaviour is much more sinister. Weeds compete with the crops for light and air, and their roots all compete with each other for water and minerals in the soil. The competition is very one-sided, however, for the roots of many weeds actually produce poisons which inhibit the growth of neighbouring roots and thus ensure that the weeds always get the lion's share of the nutrients. In addition, the weeds often harbour pests and diseases which can spread to the crops. The gardener must thus fight an unending battle to keep down the weeds. The hoe is his greatest ally in this battle, but chemical weedkillers are useful in some situations, such as the lawn and the garden path.

The origin and spread of weeds

Our annual weeds are plants with a fairly low tolerance to competition, especially in their early stages, and they are normally found only on disturbed ground where their rapid growth enables them to establish themselves ahead of other species. They rarely manage to invade mature communities. The perennial weeds are much better able to deal with competition and some, such as the bindweeds, actually thrive on it because they simply climb up their competitors. But these perennials still need fairly open soil in which to establish themselves as seedlings and they are largely confined to disturbed areas such as roadside verges and waste ground when they are not growing in our gardens. The natural habitats of our weeds would therefore seem to be the sand dunes, cliffs, and rocky hillsides where the soil is unstable and fresh patches are continually being exposed. Some of our common garden weeds certainly do occur in such situations and, with their highly efficient dispersal mechanisms, it is easy to understand how they spread over the land as soon as man began to cultivate it and provide them with suitable conditions. When once they had reached cultivated land, their high seed production and tenacity ensured that they remained there to plague us through the ages.

Although many of our garden weeds are native plants, a good many others are aliens which have been introduced over the centuries and which have established themselves to a greater or lesser extent. Many of these have arrived accidentally as impurities in imported seed and other crops, but some were deliberately introduced to gardens and have since escaped and spread across the country. This is always a danger with introduced plants because, even if they are very well behaved at home, they can become more vigorous or even aggressive in a new environment and they can very soon become serious weeds. A good example is the Bermuda buttercup, a South African relative of the wood sorrel which is now a serious pest in the bulb fields of the Scilly Isles. The little yellow oxalis is another relative that sometimes becomes a weed in British gardens. It is a native of southern Europe, but it has become well established on cultivated ground, especially on rock gardens and other stony places. It is best known in its purple or brown-leaved form, but there is also a green-leaved variety. Usually growing as an annual plant, it scatters numerous seeds from the long, pod-like fruits which follow the yellow flowers.

Yellow oxalis

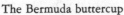

The Bermuda buttercup

As I have already pointed out, and as every gardener knows only too well, constant vigilance is necessary to keep a garden free from weeds because a new population springs up within a few days of the ground being cleared. Many of these new weeds come from seeds which were lying dormant in the soil, just waiting for the gardener to bring them up to the surface before germinating, but many others come in from outside and it is worth considering the various routes by which these weeds reach the garden. Most of them arrive in the form of seeds and the majority of them are simply blown along by the wind.

The little parachutes that bear away the fruits of dandelions and groundsel are very well known, but many other small fruits and seeds travel by air even without the benefit of wings or parachutes. Birds and other animals also transport weed seeds. Hooked fruits, such as those of cleavers or goose-grass (page 32), are easily carried in the fur of small mammals, while birds swallow numerous small seeds and scatter them in their droppings. Plants with juicy fruits are habitually dispersed in this way. Some seeds may be crushed and digested, but some pass through unharmed and actually benefit from the process because their coats are softened and germination is thus easier. In addition, the droppings provide valuable nutrients. Plantains, groundsel, dandelions, and chickweed are among the common weed species which have been grown from the droppings of various birds. And we must not forget the gardener himself, for he is probably responsible for bringing many weeds into the garden without realising it. The manure that we avidly dig into the soil whenever we can get it often contains the seeds of various grasses and other plants – though I am not suggesting that we should forgo the benefits of the manure in order to avoid a few extra weeds. Compost heaps also contribute weeds to the garden in the form of seeds and roots or rhizomes. It is true that a well-made compost heap should generate enough heat to kill the weeds in it, but in my experience the average gardener's compost heap is not very well made and it always contains living weeds. The answer here is to make better compost heaps, according to the instructions in numerous gardening books, and not, as one sees all too often, to put the garden rubbish in the dustbin or to burn it. This results in an enormous loss of organic matter which is so necessary for good soil structure.

The gardener also introduces weeds to his garden when he brings in shrubs and other plants, for the soil around these inevitably contains some weed seeds, but he probably introduces the majority of weeds on his person. Hooked and sticky fruits and seeds cling to human clothing just as easily as they do to animal fur, and one often carries home an assortment of 'burrs' attached to socks and trousers after a country walk. Trouser turn-ups, now happily out of fashion, also collect numerous loose seeds and Sir Edward Salisbury, a leading authority on weeds and alien plants, once raised more than 300 plants from the debris taken from his turn-ups. More than twenty species of weeds were represented in this sample. Muddy shoes also carry numerous weed seeds, often a very long way. A picnic down by the river or in the woods might result in several pairs of muddy shoes coming home to be scraped and cleaned in the garden, and this could lead to the appearance of several unusual weeds.

Before we go on to look at some of the commoner weeds in detail, it is worth pointing out that not all gardeners have to contend with the same weeds. Although weeds are generally unspecialised plants and able to grow more or less anywhere, many do have distinct preferences concerning the soil. Gardens on light, sandy soil will thus generally contain a different assortment of weeds from gardens on the chalk or on heavy clay. The types of weeds occurring in a garden also depend to some extent on its location. A town or suburban garden hemmed in by other well-kept gardens and by barren bricks and mortar will obviously stay freer of weeds than a similar garden in the country which is surrounded by fields and verges producing millions of seeds to the acre, but don't think that the town gardener can throw away his hoe. We have already seen that weeds can travel in surprising ways and over large distances, and wherever you make your garden, you can be sure that some of the weeds will find it.

Weeds, like beauty, are to some extent in the eye of the beholder: a plant regarded as a weed by one gardener may be cherished by another. The lawn daisy is one of the best examples: I don't mind daisies on the lawn at all, and I certainly don't go to the bother of digging them up or poisoning them, but nor do I go to the other extreme and guide my lawn mower around each patch of their flowers. Some plants originally introduced as decorative species can also become almost 'weeds'. In some areas they may remain well-behaved, but in different soils or under

Bear's breech

24

different climatic conditions they may become aggressive and try to take over the garden. A good example is the bear's breech or acanthus, a handsome, spiky plant from southern Europe.

ANNUAL WEEDS

The weeds that fall under this heading are those that complete their life cycles in one year or less. Some of them germinate in the autumn and scatter their seeds and die in the following summer, but most of them germinate in the spring after the seeds have lain dormant in the soil for the winter. Some of the common weeds, such as the groundsel and the shepherd's purse, can be seen in flower at any time of the year in the milder regions. Plants with these very short life cycles, sometimes as little as six weeks, are often called ephemerals.

Annual meadow grass (Plate 3) is the small, bright green grass that springs up very rapidly as soon as the hoe lies idle for more than a few days. It is one of the few common annual grasses and the only one likely to be seen in the garden. Its rather triangular flower heads can be seen at any time of the year, springing up from the flower or vegetable beds or from small cracks in the garden path. Annual meadow grass is abundant on roadside verges and lawns and its seeds have no difficulty in finding their way to the freshly dug ground.

Common **chickweed** (Plate 1) is a very abundant weed whose bright green, oval leaves very soon cover freshly dug soil. It is often so frequent in rows of peas that it threatens to swamp the peas themselves. The little white flowers each produce about ten seeds, but the plants produce several flowers every day for several weeks and each plant probably scatters some 2,500 seeds during its lifetime. The leaves are loved by birds, including domestic chickens, and these animals play a large part in scattering the seeds. Many seeds are carried away on the bird's feet, and others pass unharmed through the digestive tracts. Some of them germinate right away, but others get buried and some of them are known to survive for more than 25 years, so it is doubtful if the garden soil is ever really free of chickweed. It has been estimated that an acre of soil may contain over 5 million chickweed seeds at any one time. But don't worry: they won't all germinate together, and even if they do you can always harvest the chickweed instead of your vegetables. Cooked in butter, it makes a tasty dish of 'greens' to accompany your roast beef.

Groundsel (Plate 1) is one of our commonest weeds and its little yellow flower tufts and fluffy heads of 'parachutes' must be familiar to all gardeners. The plant can be seen in flower at any time of the year. The average plant produces about 1,000 seeds, and these are scattered very efficiently by the wind. There is also a 'back-up' mechanism which ensures dispersal even under wet conditions when the parachute will not work: the little fruits become gummy when they are wet and they stick to birds and animals, including the gardener. Many of the fruits also pass unharmed through birds digestive tracts and they are scattered far and wide by this means. They germinate very rapidly and the plants produce three or more generations in a year. Like the chickweed, with which it is often associated, the groundsel is generally commoner and more aggressive on the heavier soils. Its leaves frequently bear bright orange patches which are the spore-bearing regions of a rust fungus that attacks the plant.

The garden supports several plants with yellow, dandelion-like flowers. They all belong to a group known as composites, because each flower head is really composed of numerous tiny flowers all packed tightly together. The group also includes the groundsel, the daisies, and the thistles. Some are annuals and some are perennials. One of the commonest of the annuals, especially on the heavier soils, is the **nipplewort** (Plate 2). Its seeds germinate in the autumn or the spring and the seedlings often cover the ground with their more or less heart-shaped leaves. The branched flowering stem rises up in May or June and it carries rather more triangular or diamond-shaped leaves, the lower ones of which are often broken up into several leaflets at the base. The nipple-shaped buds which give the plant its name are densely clustered at the top of the stem at first, but differential growth of their individual stalks causes them to become widely separated before the pale yellow flowers open. The plant is in flower from June until well into the autumn, but the flowers open only in fairly warm and bright weather. The leaves were once eaten as salad, but they are rather bitter and I cannot recommend eating nipplewort as a means of controlling it in the garden.

The **sowthistles** are fairly tall bristly or prickly plants with clusters of dandelion-like flowers and with abundant milky juice in their stems. Two annual species occur commonly in the garden – the smooth sowthistle and the prickly sowthistle. The **smooth sowthistle** is a greyish green plant with rather soft spines on the leaf margins. The leaves themselves are deeply divided or lobed on the lower part of the plant and the terminal lobe is large and triangular. Higher up on the plant the leaves are less divided, but they all clasp the stem with sharply pointed flaps. The pale yellow flower heads can be seen throughout the summer, and so can the fluffy fruits, but the gardener would be well advised to cut down the plants before they flower if he does not want them to spread. When once the flowers have opened, the sowthistles have the unusual ability to mature and release their seeds even after the plants have been cut down. A pile of these weeds can thus be just as dangerous as the standing crop in terms of seed potential. The seeds germinate in the autumn or spring and most specimens are dead within a year, but some plants are biennials and they take two years to mature and scatter their fruits.

The **prickly sowthistle** (Plate 2) is a much more robust and spiny plant than the smooth sowthistle and its main stem is much more prominent, although both species may reach heights of five feet or more. Its leaves are a deeper shade of green and less deeply divided than those of the smooth sowthistle and they clasp the stem with rounded instead of pointed flaps, but the plants are otherwise very similar. A third sowthistle sometimes occurs in the garden, but it is a perennial and it is known as the creeping sowthistle because of its wide-ranging underground stems. Its flowers are much larger and much deeper yellow than those of the annual species, and its flower stalks are clothed with sticky yellow hairs.

The **cabbage family** contains several important agricultural weeds, including the infamous charlock. It also includes many of the characteristic plants of waste land and roadsides, but relatively few are regularly found in the garden and only the shepherd's purse can really be called a common garden weed. These cruciferous weeds are important to the gardener, however, because they can and do act as reservoirs for the pests and diseases of our cultivated brassicas, such as cabbages and other greens, swedes, and radishes. The abominable cabbage aphid (see page 123) will survive quite happily on shepherd's purse, for example, while several other cruciferous weeds play host to the club root fungus that deforms and eventually kills the roots of our cultivated species.

Shepherd's purse (Plate 2) is an extremely variable weed which gets its name from the vaguely purse-shaped seed pods and the flat, yellowish seeds that sit inside them rather like coins. The plant produces a rosette of leaves at ground level and these may be weakly lobed or deeply dissected. The flowering shoot or inflorescence is flat-topped at first and the little white flowers are crowded together, but it elongates as the outer flowers give way to the seed pods and the ripe fruits are fairly well separated. Although little beetles and other insects visit the flowers, self-pollination takes place before the flowers even open. The plant does not therefore depend on good weather and insects for setting its seeds and this is one reason for its success as a weed. It can flower and scatter its seeds quite happily in the middle of winter and it can thus pass through three or even four generations in a year. The summer generation grows so quickly that the plants often start to scatter their seeds before they are six weeks old. With an average seed production of about 2,000 seeds per plant, it is easy to see how the shepherd's purse has become such a common weed. The seeds become sticky when they are wet and many are carried about on the feet of birds and gardeners. Many more are carried internally by birds and deposited far from their original homes. Most of them germinate fairly soon after ripening, but buried seeds can remain alive for many years and a new crop of shepherd's purse may well come up every time the soil is turned over. **Hairy bittercress** has little white flowers similar to those of shepherd's purse, but its leaves are completely broken up into little leaflets and its seed pods are long and slender.

Annual wall rocket or wall cress has bright yellow flowers. It arrived in Britain from southern Europe in the 18th century. Since then, its prolific seed production has enabled it to spread to many parts of these islands, although it is usually found only on the lighter soils. It is commonly found on and around old walls, where it obtains both warmth and good drainage. The crushed leaves emit a rather strong and unpleasant smell and the plant fully deserves the alternative name of stinkweed which is given to it in some areas. Leaves and stems are all hairless. A large perennial relative is often

Annual wall rocket

28

found in the same situations, but it can be distinguished by its rather woody base and also by the seed pods: those of the annual wall rocket are longer than their stalks when ripe, but those of the perennial species are shorter than their stalks.

Hedge mustard (Plate 4) is the only other yellow-flowered crucifer commonly found in the garden, but even then it is generally seen only in the more neglected corners. It is much more common on waste land. When mature, it is a much-branched and rather bushy plant with wiry flowering stems. The flowers are very small and the seed pods are pressed very closely to the stem. Like annual wall rocket, hedge mustard sometimes behaves as a biennial and takes two growing seasons to flower and shed its seeds.

The **red deadnettle** (Plate 2) is a common weed of gardens and waste places and, like most other members of the mint family, it is very strongly scented. The plant flowers from March to October, but it is at its best in the spring, just when we are preparing our seed beds. It is tempting to leave a few clumps of this rather attractive plant for our own enjoyment and that of the numerous bumble bees that visit it, but this temptation should be resisted if you don't want to spend all summer pulling up the hairy little seedlings. The fruits possess oil-filled outgrowths which attract ants, and the latter drag them all over the garden on the way back to their nests. The oily outgrowths often break off on the way and the ants then abandon the fruits with their seeds inside. Ants are thus important distributors of deadnettle seeds, although they are effective only over short distances.

Seeds that germinate in the spring and summer produce fairly small plants, but those that germinate in the autumn produce a number of creeping shoots during the winter and early spring and they develop into fairly large clumps. It is these clumps that look so attractive in the spring. **Henbit** is a very similar plant to the red deadnettle, but its leaves are much more rounded. The tubular parts of the flowers are also much longer than those of the red deadnettle, protruding noticeably from the surrounding bracts and giving the impression that the flowers are about to fall. The white deadnettle is a perennial plant and is described on page 38.

Several kinds of **speedwell** grow as weeds in fields and gardens and some of them are known as birdseyes because of the prominent white 'eye' in the centre of the blue or mauve flower. Some are annual plants and some are perennials. The **common field speedwell** is a sprawling and somewhat hairy annual which is also known as Buxbaum's speedwell and Persian speedwell. It is a native of western Asia and it did not arrive in Britain until early in the 19th century, but it has spread so successfully that it is now the commonest speedwell of fields and gardens. Much of its increase has been due to the carriage of its seeds in grain and hay, but ants are probably responsible for scattering the plant around the garden. Large plants may yield up to 7,000 seeds and even if the ants eat some of these there are still plenty left to produce the next generation of plants. There are usually two generations in a year.

The common field speedwell carries its long-stalked flowers singly in the axils of its leaves and it shares this habit with the two **ivy-leaved speedwells**. The latter, one with blue flowers and one with lilac flowers, are quite similar to the common field speedwell in habits, but their leaves have longer stalks and they are shaped very

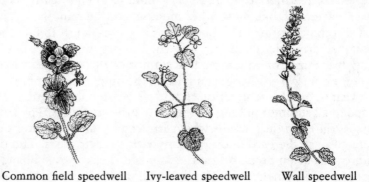

Common field speedwell   Ivy-leaved speedwell   Wall speedwell

much more like ivy leaves. The **wall speedwell** is a more erect plant, with oval leaves and very small blue flowers carried in leafy clusters at the tops of the stems. It grows on the drier soils and on old walls. Germander speedwell and slender speedwell are both perennials and are described on pages 40 and 41.

The large group of plants known as **umbellifers** is well represented in the garden by both weeds and cultivated plants. The latter include carrots, parsnips, true parsley, and numerous other herbs, while the weeds include cow parsley (page 47), ground elder (page 42), and fool's parsley. All have either white or yellow flowers which are massed together in flat or domed heads called umbels. **Fool's parsley** is a rather poisonous annual which got its name from its vague similarity to true parsley. It can be fatal to humans and it is has certainly caused many deaths in the past through being mistaken for true parsley, but gardeners are unlikely to make this mistake today because our cultivated parsley strains usually have densely curled leaves, much more robust than those of the fool's parsley. The latter also has a slightly greyish stem, finely grooved and much smoother than that of true parsley. There is no possibility of confusion when the plants are in flower because fool's parsley has white flowers and true parsley has yellow flowers. Fool's parsley can be distinguished from other white-flowered umbellifers by the

Fool's parsley, showing the characteristic 'beards' hanging down from the white flower heads

long bracts that hang down beard-like from the flower clusters. **Hemlock** (Plate 4), long famed as a source of poison, is rather similar to fool's parsley in many ways, although it lacks the bearded umbels and it usually bears prominent purple spots on its stems. It generally grows near water and sometimes occurs in gardens bordering streams.

Knotgrass or irongrass is not a grass, but a member of the dock family. It gets its name from the prominent joints on the stem which suggest a series of knots. Knotgrass is a sprawling plant that enjoys bare ground and it commonly invades drives and paths as well as bald patches on the lawn. Unlike most annuals, it has tough and wiry stems with marked powers of regeneration, and it is therefore little affected by mowing or by trampling. Its extensive root system, which goes down to depths of three feet or more in dry soils, provides sufficient nourishment for the damaged stems to send out new shoots with little delay. Clusters of little pink or green flowers are borne at the bases of the oval leaves throughout the summer and the seeds that they scatter normally germinate in the following spring. Some germinate in the first autumn, however, and thus get a good start if the winter is mild. **Redshank** is a close relative of knotgrass which often appears in moister gardens. Its pink or white flowers are carried in dense spikes springing from the axils of the

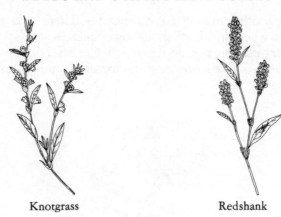

Knotgrass   Redshank

lanceolate leaves. The latter usually have a prominent dark mark in the centre.

Cleavers or goosegrass (Plate 4) is the plant that small children love to throw at each other or to drape surreptitiously on each other's backs so that it sticks to their clothing. Look at the plant under a lens and you will see that it is covered with tiny hooks. It is these hooks that catch into clothing, although their real function is, of course, to help the weak-stemmed goosegrass to climb over its competitors and reach the sun. This it does very well, shooting up through the hedge and rapidly swamping the fruit bushes if given the chance. Cleavers is especially common and vigorous on the heavier soils and often produces stems six feet long in such places. Very small white flowers are produced during the summer and they give rise to small round fruits which are clothed with the same hooked hairs that cover the stems and leaves. The fruits are thus very easily dispersed by animals, including humans who carry them around on socks and other clothing.

The **common fumitory** (Plate 2) is easily recognised by its finely divided, greyish and rather waxy leaves and by its slender pink flowers. The latter are in evidence throughout the summer on the top of the rather weak stems. Each flower gives rise to a heart-shaped fruit containing a single seed, but there are numerous flowers on a plant and the total seed production is quite appreciable. The seed coat is rather oily and the seeds are eagerly sought by ants. Some of the seeds are eaten by the ants, but others are lost or abandoned on the way to the nest and so the ants play some part in scattering the fumitory around the garden, as they do with the speedwells and the deadnettles. Fumitory is particularly common and troublesome on the lighter soils: on heavier soils its

PLATE 3: **Weeds.** 1 Prostrate pearlwort 43; 2 Couch grass 47; 3 Annual meadow grass 25; 4 Creeping buttercup 42; 5 Greater plantain 43; 6 Germander speedwell 40; 7 Field or common bindweed 43; 8 Ground ivy 38; 9 Common daisy 40; 10 Greater bindweed 45; 11 Creeping thistle 40.

4

rather frail body tends to get swamped with more vigorous weeds.

Poppies are primarily weeds of the open fields, but their small seeds are very easily scattered by the wind and they readily invade gardens and waste ground. They are especially abundant on the lighter soils, but by no means confined to them. The four bright red petals and the mass of black stamens easily identify the poppies, but there are actually two common species – the common or field poppy and the long-headed poppy. The common poppy has an urn-shaped seed capsule and often has black blotches at the bases of its petals, whereas the long-headed poppy (Plate 2) has a much more elongated capsule and never has black blotches. Although the flowers produce no nectar, they produce abundant pollen and they are much visited by bees. The insects run round inside the flowers and draw bunches of stamens between their legs to scrape off the pollen. The latter is then packed into the pollen baskets (see page 172). Poppy flowers last only for a few hours, after which the petals fall and the seed capsule grows rapidly. When ripe, it reveals a ring of small pores around the rim and the slightest breeze is enough to sway the stem and flick out some of the numerous seeds. If you don't want to perpetuate your poppies, have them up early or at least remove the heads as soon as the petals have fallen: leave them until some of the capsules are ripe and you will scatter seeds no matter how careful you are.

The seeds of the long-headed poppy normally germinate in the autumn, but those of the common poppy generally sprout in the spring. Some of the seeds delay germination for a year or two, however, so there is always a reserve supply. Deeply buried seeds can probably survive for a century or more and then spring to life when they are brought to the surface. This explains the abundance of poppies in new gardens and on roadside verges recently created from old fields. It also explains the sudden appearance of sheets of poppies in fields after deep ploughing or drainage operations. Such sights were common a century ago, but farmers now keep poppies under control by using selective weedkillers on their crops. The common poppy and the long-headed poppy are both widely distributed in the British Isles but, except possibly in the north, the common poppy is the more abundant.

Fat hen (Plate 2) is one of the most characteristic plants of disturbed ground, whether it be the garden, the roadside, or the farmyard. It is a rather inconspicuous plant and it seems able to merge in with all kinds of vegetables in the garden: even the keen gardener often misses it when it lurks among his cabbages or

◀ PLATE 4: **Hedgerow weeds and others.** 1 Cow parsley 47; 2 White bryony 45; 3 Cleavers 32; 4 Hemlock 31; 5 Traveller's joy 46; 6 Hedge mustard 29; 7 Hedge woundwort 47; 8 Woody nightshade 46; 9 Elder 46; 10 Wild rose 44; 11 Bramble 46.

potatoes. Some of the seeds germinate in the autumn, but most of them sprout in the spring when the rows of vegetable seeds are beginning to come through. The greyish leaves of the seedlings can be distinguished very easily by their mealy appearance. This is caused by a coating of tiny globular hairs, which are so close together in the young and unexpanded leaves that the leaves appear almost white. The stem of the mature plant is often tinged with red, but even then the fat hen remains rather inconspicuous, for its flowers are small and green and they are carried in little clusters among the uppermost leaves. The little black seeds are scattered largely by birds. The closely related red goosefoot sometimes occurs in gardens, especially if these have recently been treated to a load of farmyard manure. Red goosefoot likes very rich soil and it grows abundantly round manure heaps and silage pits, so its seeds are very likely to be distributed with the manure. Its stems are redder than those of fat hen and its leaves lack the mealy covering.

The **scarlet pimpernel** (Plate 2) is usually unmistakable because of its brilliant red flowers, but it does sometimes produce flowers with various shades of purple and even blue. The plant is primarily a weed of the corn fields and their edges, but it crops up quite regularly in gardens, especially those on the lighter soils. The flowers can be seen from May to October, but they normally open only in warm and sunny weather. They close up at the approach of cloud and rain and the plant has thus earned itself the alternative name of poor man's weather-glass.

Black nightshade (Plate 1) is a particularly troublesome weed on rich soils because, like the stinging nettle (page 37), it has a liking for high concentrations of nitrogen in the soil. It very often occurs around the compost heap and I always find it growing among my runner beans and peas, where it takes advantage of the manure and compost placed in the trenches during the winter. Black nightshade is a bushy, but rather weak plant that often straggles over the ground. Its white star-like flowers with prominent conical clumps of stamens indicate its close relationship to the potato. The flowers are followed by shiny black berries in the autumn and, like all other parts of the plant, these berries are poisonous.

Another scrambling annual which often occurs on waste ground and neglected gardens is the **black bindweed**. A relative of the docks, and not a true bindweed, it has rather insignificant pinkish flowers on slender spikes arising from the main stems. Given the opportunity, the black bindweed will readily climb up a fence or other neighbouring support, but it does not often grow in the hedge because it needs full light and rather disturbed ground.

Black bindweed

Petty spurge (Plate 1) is the bright green little plant that springs up all over the garden and that covers our hands with milky juice when we pull it up. The seedlings appear in late spring and summer and the plants produce their very small and inconspicuous flowers from June to November. There are no petals and the male flower consists simply of a single stamen to scatter pollen. The female flower consists merely of a three-celled ovary or seed case. Each female flower is usually surrounded by a number of male flowers and a cluster of yellowish leaves. Small beads of nectar are produced around the flowers and they are sufficient to attract little flies and beetles for the purposes of pollination. The seeds are thrown out of their cases when ripe and they are probably scattered around the garden by ants which are interested in the oil-containing bodies attached to them.

Most of the weeds described so far will occur, if only briefly, in even the best kept gardens, but **herb robert** (Plate 1) is very much a plant of the unkept garden. It flourishes on poor, rocky soil and it often establishes itself on broken paths and walls. Its leaves turn red in the late summer and it is then a very attractive sight. The scent given out by the crushed leaves will tell you that the herb robert is a relative of the cultivated geraniums, or pelargoniums to give them their proper name.

PERENNIAL WEEDS

The perennial weeds are those species that live for several years. Their aerial parts usually die down in the autumn, but their extensive underground systems remain alive and, using food stored up during the summer, they send up vigorous new shoots in the following spring. Some of these weeds possess only roots under the ground, but many of them also have creeping stems called rhizomes. These travel horizontally through the soil and send up aerial shoots at intervals. They grow very rapidly and a single plant can cover several square yards in a single season. These rhizomatous plants are very difficult to remove from the garden because every little piece of rhizome left in the soil can grow into a new plant. Many of the roots also have remarkable powers of regeneration and it is not usually enough simply to pull up the tops of the plants: small pieces of root left in the soil can throw up new shoots, but roots do not usually spread through the soil in the way that rhizomes do.

The **docks** are among the most objectionable garden weeds because of their enormous seed production and their complete unwillingness to surrender to the gardener in the annual tug-of-war. The thick, branched tap roots go down to depths of three feet or more and they anchor themselves so firmly that they defy most people's efforts to yank them out. There is often complete stalemate in the contest, but more frequently the root snaps just under the surface, sending the gardener flying backwards and leaving the lower part of the root ready to send up a new crown of leaves and shoots. Deep digging may bring up most of the root in light soils, but this is not always possible and the best way to get rid of an established dock then is to cut off the crown as soon as it appears. The plant will not give up at once, but it will gradually get weaker and the leaves will be smaller each time until it finally dies. The wise gardener, of course, does not let things get to this stage and hoes up the little seedlings as soon as they appear.

The **curled dock** (Plate 1) is the most frequent species in the garden and it can be recognised by the crinkly edges of the leaves and by the way in which the leaf blade narrows gradually towards the stalk. The flowering stem is not greatly branched, but it is densely packed with red-tinged, greenish flowers which are so numerous that a plant may well scatter 30,000 seeds in a single season. Little 'wings' on the fruits allow them to be blown about by the wind and, with a germination rate of about 80 per cent in good light, it is not surprising that this dock is a common weed. Those seeds that get washed down into the soil and away from the light can survive quite happily in a dormant state and more than half of them can germinate after fifty years, so the gardener should never let this or any other dock flower in or near the garden. The **broad-leaved dock** is also very common in the garden. The mature plant is more robust than the curled dock, with a much-branched stem and very broad leaves, but plants that have been weakened by cutting back are generally much smaller and so great is their urge to reproduce themselves that they often send up unbranched flowering stems only a few inches high. These small plants can be distinguished from the curled dock, however, by the shape of the leaves. The lower ones are more or less heart-shaped at the base, and the upper leaf blades are squared off.

Most gardeners probably consider the **stinging nettle** (Plate 2) an even more objectional weed than the dock, particularly in view of the alleged value of the latter in soothing the stings of the nettle, but I think more good can be said of the nettle than of the dock. Both can be eaten, but the stinging nettle is a much better and more versatile vegetable. Stinging nettles enjoy loose soil with plenty of nitrogen in it and they are thus very characteristic of disturbed ground where man has dumped rubbish. Patches often develop in

The annual nettle, a smaller relative of the stinging nettle with somewhat more rounded leaves. It is common on cultivated ground, and male and female flowers are carried on the same plant. The sting of the annual nettle is less powerful than that of its larger cousin, but it acts in just the same way, with large stinging hairs (shown enlarged) on leaves and stems

hedgerows and at the bases of old and crumbling walls, and the plants readily spring up around the compost heap. Long yellow roots anchor the plant securely in the soil and creeping stems spread out just under the surface of the soil so that one plant can cover a relatively large area. Stems and leaves all carry stinging hairs which can be identified by the little reservoirs of formic acid at the base. Each hair has a very brittle cap of silica which snaps off when we brush against the plant and exposes a minute hypodermic needle. Further pressure drives the needle into the skin and forces the acid up the hollow hair and into the wound. Grasping the nettle firmly is often less painful than brushing against it because the firm grip bends the hairs over and prevents the acid from passing along them. The pollen-producing male flowers are grouped into long greenish catkins, but the female flowers, which are carried on separate plants, are very small and inconspicuous. Pollen is blown from the male catkins by the wind and, along with grass and plantain pollen, it is a major cause of hay fever during June and July. On the credit side, however, the nettles provide food for the caterpillars of some of our most attractive butterflies (see page 260). These caterpillars, together with various colourful weevils (page 193) and other insects that feed on the leaves, are quite unaffected by the stinging hairs. The nettle also plays host to a little midge which induces the formation of little red galls on the leaves.

The **deadnettles** are in no way related to the stinging nettle but they get their name from the marked similarity in the shape of the leaves. This is especially true of the **white deadnettle** (Plate 2), which often grows among the stinging nettles but which is easily distinguished by its square stem (a feature which it shares with the other members of its family) and by its white flowers from which children like to suck the sweet nectar. Bumble bees are also fond of the deadnettle, whose stamens and stigmas are neatly arranged to brush against the backs of visiting bees and thus ensure cross pollination. Each tubular flower produces four little fruits which, like those of the red deadnettle (page 29), are scattered around the garden by ants. The white deadnettle forms large clumps through the growth of prostrate shoots that spread out at about ground level and take root at intervals. Both kinds of deadnettle are fairly hairy, although they have no stinging hairs, and this makes them somewhat resistant to herbicidal treatment because the sprays cannot wet the leaves properly.

Ground ivy (Plate 3) is another strongly scented member of the deadnettle family that often smothers the ground underneath hedges and shrubberies. Its kidney-shaped leaves often take on a very deep purplish tinge, and the plants sometimes bear large red galls that are due to the presence of ant-like insects called gall wasps.

The **common dandelion** (Plate 1) is one of the brightest of our spring flowers and one which is much admired when it clothes the roadside verges with gold, but it is not a plant which should be tolerated in the garden. With its immense seed production and aggressive nature, it can very soon swamp our cultivated plants and it can also make unsightly patches on the lawn. When growing in good light on the lawn, the leaves press themselves down on to the ground and the root contracts to pull them down even more firmly. The result is that the dandelion rosette kills off the grass underneath it and we have to put up with the weed or else a bald patch for a time. But the dandelion does not always grow as a flat rosette. Transplant a rosette from the lawn to a patch of dense herbage, or merely let the grass grow up around it, and the plant will gradually assume a new form: the leaves will no longer hug the ground and they will grow obliquely upward to compete with the surrounding plants. The leaves will also grow much larger than they did when spreading out on the lawn. In addition to this plasticity of the individual, there are a great many strains of dandelion which differ in the size and shape of the leaves and the bracts around the flower heads. This variability stems from the plant's unusual method of reproduction. Although flowers are freely visited by bees and other insects, the seeds are formed without fertilisation and there is never any mixing of genetic material from two plants. Any changes or mutations that occur during the formation of a seed will be inherited by all of its offspring and thus lead to numerous distinct strains.

Each seed is enclosed in a little fruit which is topped by the familiar 'parachute'. There are, on average, about 180 of these fruits in a head or 'clock' and they are carried away by the wind when they are dry. The seeds germinate rapidly and cover the ground with pale green, spoon-shaped leaves which usually lack the teeth so characteristic of the older leaves. This is the time to attack, before the plants produce their long and very tough tap roots. When once the latter have developed, the removal of a dandelion becomes a difficult task. Even if it is cut off six inches below ground level, it is still capable of producing new shoots and sending them up to form an even denser clump of leaves. Continual removal of these new leaves will weaken the plant, and the leaves can be used in salads if you are desperate, but far better to remove the dandelion seedlings and grow lettuces in the first place.

The flowers of the **coltsfoot**, also known as coughwort and claywort, are often confused with those of the dandelion, but the

Coltsfoot

pinkish scales on the stem will easily distinguish it. The coltsfoot also flowers very early in the spring, before many dandelions are out, and the flowers always appear before the heart-shaped leaves. Coltsfoot is very much a plant of roadsides and other disturbed areas, especially on the heavier soils, but it will often spring up on garden paths and its underground stems will spread it very quickly through the garden if it is not removed.

The **daisy** (Plate 3) is the most familiar of the lawn weeds, although not all gardeners think of it as a weed. The flowers are certainly very attractive when they open to greet the sun in the morning, and the attraction is not completely lost when they go to bed at night and draw their pink-tipped florets into a tight bunch around the golden disc. Like the dandelion, the daisy forms leaf rosettes which press down on to the ground and suppress competition, but the daisy has the added advantage (for itself) of several short creeping shoots which spread out and produce new rosettes around it. The daisy patch thus grows larger and larger. Birds distribute the little seeds on their feet, and ants also carry them about because they have a high oil content (see page 29). If you really don't like daisies on your lawn, you can treat them with a spoonful of sulphate of ammonia. This will kill the plants and then break down to fertilise the soil and help the grass to re-establish itself. The same treatment can be used to get rid of dandelions and plantains (page 43).

Thistles are mostly weeds of fields and waste land and the only one which bothers the gardener at all is the **creeping thistle** (Plate 3), a species which often invades bonfire sites and other patches of burnt ground. It can be recognised by its pale, strongly scented flowers and by its spineless stems. The flowers on any one plant are generally either male or female and so not all plants bear fruit, but the thistle makes up for this with its phenomenal powers of vegetative spread. The creeping roots go down nine feet or more in open soils and they produce horizontal branches capable of growing 40 feet in a single year. The plants can thus form extensive clumps, and this weed is very difficult to control when once it has established itself.

The commonest of the perennial speedwells is the **germander speedwell** (Plate 3), a rather hairy plant which sprawls over the ground and roots at the nodes so that it gradually carpets large areas. It is particularly common in hedgebanks, but the seeds are carried by ants and they often find their way into the garden. Germander speedwell is easily distinguished from the common annual species (page 30) because its flowers are carried in groups

instead of singly. The **slender speedwell** is a mat-forming perennial with mauve flowers and rather rounded leaves. A native of Asia
Minor, it was originally introduced to European gardens as a rock
plant, but it has now made itself thoroughly at home here and it is

Slender speedwell

spreading quite rapidly. It is especially common as a lawn weed.
The plant rarely sets seed in the British Isles, but the creeping stems
readily break up and small pieces are easily carried to fresh pastures
by the wind and by birds.

The attractive **rosebay willowherb** or fireweed (Plate 1) was
once grown as an ornamental plant and as a lure for bees, but it is
such an aggressive plant that most gardeners now treat it as a weed.
Its natural habitats include woodland margins and rocky hillsides,
but it is particularly fond of burnt ground and it is called fireweed
because of its rapid invasion of fire-damaged land. Few other plants
can match its tolerance of unweathered ashes. Many bombed sites
were covered with the plant after the war, and seedlings will soon
spring up on an abandoned bonfire patch in the garden. Colonisation of new habitats takes place by way of the abundant fluffy seeds
– more than 100,000 may be produced by a single plant in the
summer – and the effectiveness of the dispersal can be seen by the
way in which plants often grow perched high up on cliffs and walls.
When once the seedlings have become established they send out
rhizomes which grow rapidly through the soil, and so a single plant
soon covers a large area.

The **broad-leaved willowherb** (Plate 1) is primarily a weed of
shrubberies and shady gardens. Although each plant may have only
a few flowers open at any one time, it flowers for much of the
summer and produces large numbers of seeds. The plant also
spreads by means of abundant creeping stems just above or just
below the surface of the ground. Broad-leaved willowherb is very
often accompanied by the **enchanter's nightshade** (Plate 1), which

41

is a member of the willowherb family and not a true nightshade at all. Its extensive rhizomes creep through the soil and send up numerous shoots of rather dark, red-tinged leaves. The plant thus forms large patches. The little white or pale pink flowers have only two petals, but each is deeply lobed so that there appear to be four. Whereas the willowherb fruits split open and release their fluffy seeds, those of the enchanter's nightshade do not. They contain only one or two seeds and they are clothed with little hooks. The latter readily catch in the fur of voles and other small mammals and the seeds are carried away.

If there are any more troublesome weeds than **ground elder** or goutweed (Plate 1), I have no wish to meet them. After fighting the plant for nine years in my own garden, I am only just beginning to get the upper hand and I think I would hesitate to buy another house with a garden full of this obnoxious weed. It is a relative of the fool's parsley (page 30), as can be seen by looking at the flowers, but no self-respecting gardener should let this pest flower. It doesn't actually produce many seeds, but by the time it gets to the flowering stage the plant will have grown a vigorous crop of under-ground rhizomes, and these are what make the weed so difficult to eradicate. They can add three feet to their length in a single season and they become so densely intertwined that trying to dig them up is almost like trying to dig into layers of wire netting. They can be dug out with effort but numerous pieces remain behind and very soon throw up a new crop of bright green leaves. Continual pluck-ing of these new shoots will weaken and kill the plants, but the job has to be done almost daily and if any leaves are missed they will soon start sending food down to replenish the rhizomes. Treatment with herbicides doesn't do much harm to the plant either, unless you go the whole hog and poison the ground with a total weedkiller such as sodium chlorate. Unfortunately, this method prevents your growing anything at all for several months. Another method of control which I have used with some success in parts of my own garden is to turn the area into grass by regular mowing, with or without the addition of grass seed. Ground elder cannot stand mowing and it soon declines. After a couple of years the ground can safely revert to flower beds or vegetables. Ground elder, also known as farmer's plague, was probably brought into Britain by the Romans, who used it as a vegetable and as a cure for gout.

The common garden buttercup is the **creeping buttercup** (Plate 3), which can be recognised by its long creeping stems or stolons. These grow rapidly over the surface of the ground, rooting at the joints and producing a large colony of inter-connected plants which may exceed five feet in diameter. Such colonies are very difficult to remove from the herbaceous border when once they are established. The creeping buttercup is especially abundant on moist and heavy soils.

Despite its attractive funnel-shaped flowers, the field **bindweed** or convolvulus (Plate 3) is a real nuisance in the garden because of its rapid growth and its ability to swamp all the smaller cultivated species or to climb up the larger ones. It is especially troublesome on the heavier soils, where its creeping underground stems and its extensive root system are very difficult to extract in anything approaching entirety. The flowers are visited by numerous insects and are often full of thrips (page 128). Each flower produces only a few seeds, but heavy seed production is not necessary for a plant with such a vigorous method of vegetative spread. The greater bindweed, which is the one with large white flowers, is described on page 45.

The **pearlworts** are small moss-like plants with narrow, hairless leaves and very small white or greenish flowers. Two species are common in the garden – the annual pearlwort and the prostrate pearlwort (Plate 3). The latter is a perennial plant which forms very low-growing mats on paths and other areas of bare ground. It also invades the lawn and the rockery, especially in the damper parts. Annual pearlwort also grows on paths, but it prefers the drier areas. It forms loose tufts which, like the mats of the perennial species, are very resistant to trampling. Both species produce minute seeds which are so light that two million would not weigh an ounce. These seeds are easily scattered by the wind and many of them find their way to the tops of walls and buildings where they grow in association with various mosses (see page 50).

The **plantains** are very familiar plants of the roadside, and they often spread into the garden. The greater plantain (Plate 3) generally establishes itself on drives and paths, and also on the lawn, especially if the latter is subjected to heavy wear and liable to develop bald patches here and there. The rosettes of tough, broad leaves remain below the level of the mower blades and they can survive any amount of trampling. The species will also appear in any patch of garden which is left idle for more than a short while, especially if the ground has previously been well trodden. In such situations, the leaves generally grow upwards and, if left alone, the plants send up a number of leafless flowering spikes. The individual flowers are very small and rarely noticed, even when the brownish stamens are hanging from them. Many of the seeds are scattered by goldfinches (page 233), which seem to enjoy swinging on the dried stems later in the year.

Gardens on the chalk and other lime-rich soils also support the hoary plantain, easily distinguished by its greyish, downy leaves. It also has a much more obvious flower spike, fringed with a mist of large, pinkish stamens. The narrow leaves of the ribwort plantain easily separate it from the other two species. **Ribwort plantain** is one of our commonest plants and it is abundant in all kinds of grassy

Ribwort plantain, with blackish brown flower spikes and creamy white anthers hanging from the flowers. The leaves vary from almost oval to strap-shaped and they may be downy or hairless

places and waste land, but it is generally less common in gardens than the greater plantain. It has a conspicuous flower spike, with a ring of white stamens scattering their pollen to the breeze. As in all plantains, the lowest flowers on the spike always open first, and they are finished long before the uppermost flowers open. The ring of stamens thus gradually moves up the flower spike during the flowering period.

WEEDS OF THE HEDGE

Many plants enjoy the shelter provided by a hedgerow, and some actually make use of the hedgerow plants by climbing up them. Whether we consider these invaders to be weeds or not depends very much on the type of hedge and its situation. A tall hawthorn hedge surrounding a country garden is enhanced by a cloak of wild roses (Plate 4) in June, and again by the brightly coloured hips in the autumn, but the same wild roses would not be welcome in a suburban privet hedge. The type of hedge may also influence the weeds directly. Deciduous hedges are always much weedier than evergreen ones, because dense evergreen hedges cut off both light and water and make the ground below quite unsuitable for weed growth.

The **greater bindweed** (Plate 3) is one of the most attractive of the hedgerow climbers and, if it were not such an invasive species, it would undoubtedly be welcome in the garden for the sake of its beautiful white flowers. The fast-growing, twining stems and the large heart-shaped leaves readily smother hedges and shrubs in the summer, and they weaken the plants by denying them light for making food. Like its smaller cousin, the field bindweed (page 43), the greater bindweed possesses deep underground rhizomes and roots, and it is very difficult to eradicate.

The **white bryony** (Plate 4) is not a nice climber to have on the garden hedge because of its very poisonous berries. The plant, which sends new shoots up from the roots each year, can always be recognised by its dull and hairy leaves and by its unusual tendrils. The latter are tightly coiled to form 'springs' between the stems and the supports to which they cling. Gale-force winds do not damage the bryony because the springy tendrils stretch and contract as the plant sways, and there is little danger of the tendrils snapping. The **black bryony** is a quite different plant, easily distinguished by its shiny, heart-shaped leaves and by the lack of tendrils. Black bryony climbs by coiling around neighbouring stems in a clock-wise direction.

The bryonies are herbaceous plants, but there are also a number of woody climbers which invade our garden hedges. **Ivy** is perhaps

Black bryony, with shiny red berries and slender spikes of pale green flowers which appear throughout the summer

the most frequent of these, and it also covers walls when it gets the chance. The fact that it is just as happy on old walls as on trees and bushes indicates that the ivy is not a parasite – it does not take food from the supporting plants – but it does weaken them if it gets too dense by depriving them of light and carbon dioxide, two of the vital requirements for the food-making process of photosynthesis.

Ivy showing the two leaf shapes and (right) the climbing roots emerging from the stem

In the absence of suitable supports, the ivy is content to creep along the ground, and it is often to be found carpeting the hedge bottom as well as struggling up through the branches. It climbs by means of special roots which grow out from the stems and attach themselves to the supports. Ivy growing on the ground or in the lower part of the hedge has pointed, star-shaped leaves, but the upper stems bear much more rounded and shinier leaves. The flowers appear in October and, although not very obvious to our eyes, they are very attractive to wasps and many other insects which take their fill of nectar by day and night. Other woody climbers commonly found in the hedge include brambles and traveller's joy, both illustrated on Plate 4. The elderberry (Plate 4) also invades hedges, especially where they have been damaged, and its rapid growth makes it something of a weed because it shades out some of the other shrubs.

Woody nightshade or bittersweet (Plate 4) is most often to be found in neglected hedges and shrubberies and on waste ground, where it is easily recognised by its purple star-shaped flowers. These are in evidence throughout the summer, and so are the drooping clusters of poisonous berries which are green at first and then pass through yellow and orange before becoming bright red.

Many herbaceous weeds may grow at the bottom of the hedge, but the hedge woundwort and the garlic mustard or jack-by-the-hedge are especially characteristic of such situations. **Hedge**

woundwort (Plate 4) can easily be mistaken for a deadnettle or even a stinging nettle when the shoots are immature, but the beetroot-coloured flowers readily identify it later in the year. **Garlic mustard** is a member of the cabbage family, as shown by its four well-separated petals, and it gets its name from its strong smell of garlic. Like many other members of the family, it is basically a biennial, but little buds often develop on the roots and produce new plants each year, so the species appears to be perennial. Large patches develop in sheltered hedgerow situations.

The more neglected hedgerows usually harbour a number of white-flowered umbellifers. Two of the most common are the cow parsley and the hogweed, both of which are also known as keck. **Cow parsley** (Plate 4) is a slightly downy plant with bright green, much divided leaves. Its hollow stems often have a purplish tinge, especially when young, and little boys love to use them as pea-shooters in the spring. The 'peas' are the unopened flower buds of the hawthorn. The white flowers of the cow parsley are extremely attractive, fanning out in delicate heads which have given the plant such local names as Queen Anne's lace and lady's needlework. The whole plant has a rather pleasant aromatic smell and it makes a nice addition to soups and omelettes, but make sure that you know your umbellifers before trying them in any recipes, for many of these plants are very poisonous. Cow parsley could be confused with fool's parsley (see page 30), but the little 'beards' on the latter should distinguish it when in flower. It is also a smaller plant and it is not at all downy. Upright hedge parsley is another very similar and very common hedgerow plant, but it flowers in late summer, long after the cow parsley flowers have finished.

Hogweed is also known as cow parsnip, and its young shoots are good to eat, but do make sure of your identification before trying them. The hogweed is a much stouter and hairier plant than cow parsley, and its leaves are not finely divided. Its flowers are also much larger and, like those of most umbellifers, they are very attractive to hover-flies (page 156), sawflies (page 183), and many other insects.

The only really troublesome grass which springs up in the garden is the **couch grass** or twitch (Plate 3). With its long, creeping underground stems, it can invade a garden very rapidly from the verge or the hedge or from the neglected garden next door. Sharply-pointed rhizomes spread through the soil and throw up slender tufts of leaves here and there on the way. Neighbouring tufts often merge with each other and form dense clumps three or four feet high. The slender flowering spikes appear in July and

August and they can be distinguished from those of **rye grass** because the spikelets are arranged with their broad sides against the main axis. The seed production of couch grass is not high, but the plant more than makes up for this with the tenacity of its wiry rhizomes. The couch grass is found on all kinds of soil, but it is most

Rye grass (*left*) and couch grass

Cocksfoot grass

troublesome on the heavier land. The rhizomes can be pulled out more easily from the lighter soils.

Regular mowing of the lawn keeps down the coarse grasses and maintains the turf in good condition, but there are always those awkward corners and the areas around the bases of trees where the mower cannot go. Here, unless we are diligent with the shears, there is an opportunity for the coarser grasses to establish themselves. Couch grass may spring up, but one of the most common species in such situations is **cocksfoot grass**, so called because of the resemblance of its flower spike to the spreading toes of a chicken. If unchecked, this grass will form a dense clump. The young shoots are very flattened and pale, and the grass is easily recognised in this way if it is not in flower. Some of the true lawn grasses, such as meadow grass and rye grass, also manage to flower around the bases of the trees, where their heads are not being continually cut off. Meadow grass is a taller and usually somewhat greyer version of the annual meadow grass described on page 25. Rye grass, which is commonly included in lawn seed mixtures because it stands up to plenty of wear, sends up wiry stems whose alternating spikelets are arranged with their narrow sides against the main axis. Even the mower does not always deal with these wiry stems, and they can often be seen sticking up from a newly mown lawn.

If we leave aside the various mosses that invade our lawns (see page 53), the only non-flowering plant that regularly becomes a weed is the common or field **horsetail** (Plate 5), which is a relative of the ferns. The plant appears in early spring, when brownish shoots looking not unlike asparagus tips push their way up through the soil. These are the fertile shoots of the plant and each bears a 'cone' at the top. Dust-like spores are released by the cones and scattered by the wind. The green shoots of the horsetail appear a little later and resemble miniature fir trees to start with. They have no true leaves, for the whorls of green needles are actually branches. Horsetails are very difficult to get rid of when once they have established themselves, because they possess underground rhizomes which spread through the soil at considerable depths. The rhizomes also bear numerous small tubers which are easily detached when the ground is disturbed and which readily grow into new plants. Horsetails occur on all kinds of soils, but they are found mainly where the soil surface remains damp in early spring. The damp conditions are necessary for the development of the spores and the subsequent production of young horsetail plants. Well dug gardens are not likely to be invaded, but horsetails may well be persistent in new gardens formed on what was previously waste land.

Ferns and mosses

Shady walls, especially old ones with crumbling mortar, provide footholds for many small plants. We find several grasses and other flowering plants in such places, but the most characteristic species are non-flowering plants, whose spores are very easily carried up on to the walls by air currents. The **maidenhair spleenwort fern** (Plate 5) and the **wall rue** are common on walls in many parts of the country. Wall rue does not look very much like a fern when we see the leaves sprouting out from the gaps between stones or bricks,

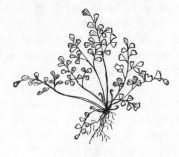

Wall rue   Rusty-back fern

but we can appreciate its nature as soon as we turn over a leaf and see the little brown spore capsules on the lower surface. The **rusty-back fern** is another common wall-living species, getting its name from the coating of reddish brown scales on the undersides of the leaves. Although it is by far the most drought-resistant of our ferns, it is more abundant in the west of the country where the rainfall is greater. It is completely absent from some eastern areas. The **common polypody** also grows on damp walls, especially if there is a coating of moss through which its roots can grow, but it is most often found perching on rough bark and in the forks of trees. These wall-dwelling ferns all have some resistance to drought, but they cannot survive on really exposed south-facing walls and they are always at their best on the shady sides where there is always some moisture.

Numerous **mosses** can be found on old walls and tree trunks, usually on the shady sides or in places where they are regularly splashed with water, for these little plants have no waterproof coats and few have any resistance to prolonged drought. As well as clinging to walls and tree trunks, the mosses clothe rocks and stones and also manage to make a living in the small cracks between paving stones. Many of them also live on bare soil. Together with the lichens (see page 54), they are important colonisers of bare places, for few natural surfaces are too smooth to deny a foothold for their simple roots. When once they are established, they begin to trap dust around themselves and, as the older parts rot, they build up a thin layer of soil in which grasses and other plants can take root.

The mosses reproduce themselves by scattering minute spores. These are formed in cylindrical or urn-shaped capsules which are carried up above the leaves on slender stalks. Unripe capsules are protected by pointed hoods, but these fall off as the capsules ripen and the wind then scatters the spores. Upon reaching a suitably moist place, each spore puts out a branching thread called a pro-tonema, and this produces a number of buds. Each bud then grows into a new plant and, because there are always lots of buds close together, the mosses always grow in little clumps right from the start. Some form tightly packed cushions, while others form looser mats, but this clustering habit is of great value because each clump can hold water rather like a sponge. The delicate leaves do not dry out even if there is no rain for several days, and so the mosses can survive on the tops of walls and even on roofs as long as the climate is reasonably moist. Because they have no deeply-penetrating roots, the mosses can do no direct harm to the walls on which they grow, and they do a great deal to beautify plain brick walls. The only possible harm they can do is to trap the seeds of larger plants which might then damage the brickwork with their roots, but a regular inspection will allow you to remove these plants before they reach a damaging size.

A typical moss capsule, showing the hygroscopic teeth which control the opening of the capsule and ensure that the spores are released only in dry weather, when they are most likely to be blown away

The small size of the mosses means that lenses and microscopes are generally necessary for their identification, but some of the garden dwelling species are fairly easy to recognise. One of the commonest of the wall-living species is the **wall screw moss** (Plate 5). It forms neat little tufts up to two inches in diameter on the tops of walls and, like most other wall-dwelling mosses, it also establishes itself on concrete paths and undisturbed piles of stones. Its stems are no more than about half an inch high and the leaves are bright green, but little hairs on the leaf tips sometimes give the whole tuft a greyish appearance, especially when dry. The spore capsules are cylindrical and they are carried upright on reddish stems throughout the spring. Each capsule has numerous tiny teeth which twist tightly together in wet weather and give the plant its name of screw moss. Wall screw moss is one of the earliest colonisers of both brick and stone walls, and it is often joined by the **grey cushion moss** (*Grimmia pulvinata*). The leaves of this species are dark green, but the cushions appear grey because each leaf ends in a long white hair. The capsule stalks are short and strongly curved and the oval capsules are almost hidden among the leaves.

Cracks between bricks and paving stones are often filled with a very silvery moss that also overflows on to the surface and makes neat little cushions. This is the **silvery thread moss** which can be recognised very easily by its shiny appearance and also by the way in which the leaves are packed tightly around the stems. Like the grey cushion moss, this species also makes itself at home on old roofs and even on stone window sills. Walls which have accumulated a fair amount of soil on the top or on ledges usually support *Bryum*

Silvery thread moss

capillare, which might look rather like the wall screw moss at first sight. It is a much more robust plant, however, and it is easily distinguished by its drooping, pear-shaped capsules. These are bright green when immature in the spring, but they become brown when they are ripe.

Undoubtedly the most prominent of the mosses on the garden wall is the **silky wall feather moss** (Plate 5), which covers large areas with a cloth of golden green. The long, creeping shoots are sharply pointed and the golden tinge is especially noticeable near the tips. In moist conditions the stems cling tightly to the wall, but they curl up in dry weather and they are then able to survive quite long periods without rain. This moss is also abundant on rockery stones, particularly if they are made of limestone, and on the bases of tree trunks. But, beautiful as it is, it should not really be allowed to adorn your apple trees because, like the lichens, it provides winter shelter for various insect pests. The **rough-stalked feather moss** (*Brachythecium rutabulum*) and the similar, but smaller *B. velutinum* often grow with the silky wall feather moss and they might be confused with it at first. The leaves of the *Brachythecium* species are much broader, however, and the plants are easily distinguished when their horizontal spore capsules are present. The silky

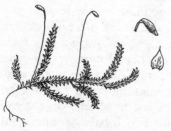

Rough-stalked feather moss

Common cord moss

wall feather moss is not particularly keen on producing capsules, but when they do appear they are always upright.

The rough stalked feather moss also invades the lawn if it is sufficiently moist, but mosses cannot withstand much competition and they should be no problem in a well-kept lawn. Regular mowing stimulates the grasses to produce an abundance of spreading shoots which crowd out the mosses, but don't be tempted to put the cutters too low in order to make your lawn into a billiard table; this will only produce bald patches and open the way for a further invasion of mosses and other weeds. If your lawn is badly affected by moss, you can easily treat it with a proprietary moss killer, but good drainage is also necessary if you wish your lawn to be kept free of moss.

The old-fashioned cinder paths which one still finds in some cottage gardens often become covered with a velvet-like carpet of **common cord moss** *(Funaria hygrometrica)*. This short, yellowish green species is very characteristic of burnt ground and it will soon appear on a bonfire site or around a permanent ash pit. It can often be recognised from a distance because, if it is at all common, its orange capsules and stalks appear to cover the ground with a sheet of flame when they are ripe. *Leptobryum pyriforme* often grows with *Funaria,* but it can be distinguished by its much longer leaves and by the fact that its capsules ripen in late spring. *Funaria* does not produce ripe capsules until late summer. Both species regularly invade greenhouses.

Damp paths, especially those around a garden pond, may well support some flat and rather leathery plants looking like seaweeds. These are liverworts and they are close relatives of the mosses. Most of the liverworts actually look very much like mosses, but the flat species that we find around the pond are very distinct. One of the commonest species is the **crescent cup liverwort** *(Lunularia cruciata),* whose spreading lobes bear crescent-shaped cups full of little detachable buds called gemmae. These gemmae are washed out of the cups by rain and each can grow into a new plant. *Lunularia* thus spreads very rapidly in suitable habitats. It is often

The crescent-cup liverwort

something of a nuisance in greenhouses, where it revels in the warmth and frequently clothes the ground and the flower pots. Out of doors, it is more common in the south of the country and it is possibly a species which has been introduced from the Continent.

The so-called **common liverwort** (Plate 5) is found in the same places as the previous species, but it can be distinguished by the gemmae cups which resemble miniature crowns. In the spring it can be recognised even more easily by the stalked reproductive organs, but these are not to be confused with the spore capsules of other liverworts. All mosses and liverwort produce male and female organs, but they are normally embedded in the bodies of the plants. Male cells are released and they swim in the film of water that usually covers the plants. They eventually reach the female cells and join with them. Not until this has happened does the spore capsule begin to grow. The common liverwort is unusual in that its male and female organs develop on separate plants and are carried on umbrella-like structures. Fertilisation takes place in the normal way, but the spore capsules then develop on the undersides of the female 'umbrellas'. The spore capsules of all liverworts are spherical and much simpler than those of the mosses. When the spores are ripe the capsules split into four valves, which then fold back so that their white insides form conspicuous little 'stars' standing up above the plants. The leafy or moss-like liverworts can always be distinguished from the true mosses in this way.

Garden lichens

Anyone who has looked at an old wall will have seen the more or less circular patches of orange or grey lichens that coat the bricks and stones. These lichens are the hardiest of all plants, able to survive extremes of temperature as well as prolonged drought. A south-facing wall gets surprisingly hot on a summer day – often hot enough to make you take your hand away – and yet the lichens survive. Old walls running from east to west often support completely different floras on their two sides. The north face, which remains cool and shady, may be covered with mosses and ferns, while the south face will carry nothing but lichens. The plants grow extremely slowly, but they also seem to grow at a fairly constant rate and the size of their patches has been used as a guide when dating old buildings.

A lichen (pronounced *liken*) is actually a dual plant, consisting of a fungus and an alga living in partnership. Each kind of lichen consists of a particular fungus and a particular alga, and the fungus is never found alone. The lichen-forming algae can live by themselves, however. They are minute green plants and, together with other single-celled algae, they form the green or greyish green powder that coats damp walls and tree trunks. Most algae are aquatic plants, however, and they include all the seaweeds and the blanket weed that often chokes our ponds.

The fungus partner forms the bulk of the lichen, and the alga exists as scattered cells or groups of cells near the surface. Both partners are involved in the important business of getting food. The fungus absorbs rainwater, and acids from its branching threads dissolve minerals from the rocks or from the dust that gets trapped around the plant. The alga, meanwhile, is busy converting the water and carbon dioxide into sugars which both partners can use. It is undoubtedly this joint effort that makes the lichens such hardy plants, able to withstand such adverse conditions. The plants are, nevertheless, unable to survive in polluted air, and lichens are generally rather rare in towns.

Lichens can be divided into three main groups – crustose, foliose, and fruticose. The crustose lichens form extensive crusts on walls and rocks, and there is rarely any obvious lobing of the plant, although the crust may be split up into numerous small hexagonal areas. These lichens cannot usually be removed from the substrate without breaking them. Foliose lichens form spreading patches which adhere closely to the substrate by means of root-like threads, but the plants are fairly clearly divided into leaf-like or finger-like lobes. They occur on rocks and walls, on tree trunks, and also on the ground. Fruticose lichens are attached to the substrate only at the base and they often look like miniature bushes. Many of them live on the ground, but in moist environments they clothe rocks and trees as well. Crustose and foliose lichens are the most resistant to drought.

From time to time the fungus partner produces spore-bearing cells at the surface. The spores are then released and they blow away in the wind. Many lichens produce their spores in brightly or boldly coloured patches which probably attract flies and other insects. In such cases, the movement of the insect may cause the spores to be fired out. Many will be trapped on the insect and thus carried to distant pastures. The spores belong only to the fungus partner and, although they will germinate by themselves, they will not develop very far unless they come into contact with the right kind of alga. Then they will form new lichens. There is also another and possibly more important method of reproduction, involving the production of minute bodies called soredia. These flake away from the surface and, unlike the spores, they contain both fungus and alga. They can thus grow directly into new lichens.

Ochrolechia parella (Plate 5) is one of the commonest crustose lichens on both brick and stone walls. It forms large grey patches which are always edged with white, and its spore-bearing patches (apothecia) are pinkish brown discs with prominent margins. *Lecanora campestris* is a similar species, but its white margin is much less prominent and its apothecia are much darker. *Lecanora muralis* (Plate 5) forms conspicuous rosettes on bricks and mortar. The edges of the rosettes are broken up into numerous very slender lobes. This species is very often accompanied by *Xanthoria aureola* (Plate 5), one of several common bright orange species. As well as colonising bricks and mortar, these lichens form a most attractive decoration for the rather drab asbestos sheds and garages that are so common today. Unfortunately, it takes quite a few years for the slow-growing lichens to make their presence felt.

Several lichens, including the dog lichen (Plate 5) and other species of *Peltigera*, grow on the ground. The dog lichen is most likely to be found among the grass on shady paths, especially where the soil is sandy or where the path has been made up with cinders.

Tree trunks support numerous foliose lichens, and in humid regions the bark can be completely hidden by these greyish green lodgers. One of the commonest species is *Hypogymnia physodes,* a pale grey species with rather inflated and very smooth lobes. The apothecia, when present, are reddish brown. There are many other very similar species.

As a final example of garden lichens, we must look at the pixie-cup (Plate 5), which is probably the most familiar to gardeners because of its eye-catching shape. It grows on walls and tree stumps, but perhaps the most likely place in which the gardener will see it is on the rockery, where it coats the rocks and the undisturbed ground around them. The cups and their stalks are completely covered with powdery soredia. *Cladonia pyxidata* is a shorter species with broader cups, but it is otherwise very similar.

Toadstools and other fungi

Gardeners and non-gardeners alike are always horrified to see toadstools springing up around the base of a fence or toolshed, because this means, quite literally, that the rot has set in. The fungi are central figures in nature's army of scavengers, lurking every-where and waiting for an opportunity to attack dead organic mater-ial – and our garden timbers are fair game. Distressing as it may be to see our property being attacked in this way it is worth remembering that the fungi are only doing their job. In nature, they play a vital role in breaking down dead material and returning the goodness to the soil.

Wherever toadstools spring up in the garden, you can be certain that there is some organic material close at hand – perhaps an old tree root or a buried plank, some dead leaves, some animal dung, or even an old boot: all are acceptable to numerous kinds of fungi. Unlike most plants, the fungi have no chlorophyll and they cannot make food for themselves. They have to attack and break down or digest existing organic material, and then absorb the nourishment for themselves. In this respect, the fungi are more like animals than plants, and, although they are clearly plant-like in structure, many biologists now consider that they are neither plants nor animals.

Although the majority of fungi are saprophytes, meaning that they get their nourishment from dead material, a good many of them attack living organisms and are therefore parasites. Some of them cause serious plant diseases, such as wheat rust, club-root of brassicas, potato blight, and various mildews.

The most familiar fungi are the umbrella-like toadstools, but there are many other types. Some form ear-like lobes on wood or on the ground, others form cups and pustules, while the bracket fungi form shelf-like projections on tree trunks. Many other fungi exist as fluffy moulds. But, whatever the appearance of the fungus, it is important to realise that the visible parts are usually only a small fraction of the complete fungus. The bulk of the fungus exists as a mass of fine threads ramifying through the substrate, and the aerial parts are usually just the reproductive parts. Like the mosses and ferns, the fungi reproduce by scattering minute spores, and these are formed on or in the aerial parts. The typical toadstool has numerous radiating gills underneath the cap, and the spores are carried on the surfaces of these gills. Some other fungi have numerous pores under the cap, and the spores are formed on the linings of these pores. Most moulds bear spore capsules at the ends of their aerial threads and scatter the spores from there. These capsules are very easily seen in the pin moulds (*Mucor* spp) which grow on rotting fruit and old bread. All fungi produce immense numbers of spores and, being scattered by the wind, the spores get everywhere. They are also very resistant to heat and drought and they can wait patiently for the right conditions to come along. Fungi thus spring up without warning wherever suitable substrates occur.

One of the commonest species that sprouts from the bases of fences and sheds is the leathery fungus called **candle snuff** (Plate

5). Like all fungi, it revels in damp situations and it will not attack dry wood. Timbers in contact with the ground should always be treated with fungicide to prevent infestation with this and other fungi. Remember that the removal of the visible parts of the fungus does nothing to cure the problem, for the bulk of the fungus is inside the wood. Many small umbrella-like toadstools occur in similar situations, and they also grow on small twigs and other pieces of wood left lying around the garden. Two very common species, which will be noticed for their extreme daintiness if for nothing else, are *Mycena galopus* (Plate 5) and the little bluish *M. corticola*.

While pulling up the old pea sticks or tidying the hedge, the gardener will almost certainly come across twigs covered with beautiful pink spots. These belong to a fungus called **coral spot** (Plate 5), which attacks dead twigs of many kinds. The same fungus also produces dark red cushions on the twigs at certain times of the year. The pink spots and the red cushions produce different kinds of spores.

Stereum purpureum is one of the commoner bracket-forming fungi found in the garden, and it is one that we can definitely do without, for it is the cause of silver-leaf disease in plums and

Stereum purpureum

cherries. It sometimes attacks apple trees as well. The fungus enters through wounds in the bark and, by blocking the water-carrying tissues, it causes the leaves of the affected branches to become silvery. Vigorous trees sometimes recover from the infection, but the affected branches usually die and the spore-producing bodies appear on the bark. They form rather tough crusts, from which the brackets protrude horizontally. The spore-producing layers are lilac coloured when young, but they become grey as they get older. Infected trees can be saved by removing affected branches as soon as the silvering of the leaves is noticed and by painting the cut surfaces to prevent the entry of more spores. Purple stains on the cut surfaces indicate that the fungus is present in the wood, and further cutting back will then be necessary.

It is obviously not possible to cover all the garden fungi and other plant guests in a book of this kind, but we must mention the familiar 'fairy rings' on the lawn. Several toadstools form rings, but one of the commonest is *Marasmius oreades*. This species is good to eat and it tastes like the cultivated mushroom, but, as with all fungi, it is important to make sure of its identity before getting out the frying

Fairy-ring fungi (*Marasmius oreades*) (see also Plate 5)

pan. *Marasmius oreades* can be recognised by its shape, by its slightly pinkish tinge, and by its very tough and elastic stems. The ring-shaped nature of its colonies is easy to understand if we consider the methods of growth and feeding of the fungus. A few spores may invade the lawn at a certain point, and the threads of hyphae will begin to spread out in all directions. Toadstools may not be formed yet, but the organic matter in the soil at the original point will soon be exhausted. The threads will die off there and so a ring will be left around the original point. The threads will continue to spread outwards, but not inwards because the food material is exhausted. Toadstools will crop up from time to time, and the ring will get larger each year because of the outward growth of the threads. Dead hyphae in the centre of the ring will gradually decay and release food materials back into the soil, and these will allow the grass to grow more strongly. We thus get a ring of toadstools surrounding a circle of dark green grass. There may also be a ring of dark grass just outside the toadstools. This is caused because the fungal threads there are breaking down organic material and some of it is being absorbed by the grass roots. In the immediate vicinity of the toadstools, however, there may be a ring which is devoid of grass, because the dense fungal threads in this region starve the grass roots of air and moisture. *Marasmius oreades* always produces such a bare ring, but not all ring-forming fungi act in this way.

CHAPTER 3

The World of the Worm

'It may be doubted whether there are any other animals which have played such an important part in the history of the world as these lowly organised creatures.' Charles Darwin: *The Formation of Vegetable Mould Through the Action of Worms* (1881)

READING the above words for the first time, the gardener might well be surprised that Darwin was referring to the humble earthworm which is unearthed nearly every time we put fork or spade to work. The worm is so common that the gardener, unless he happens to be an angler as well, never gives it a second look and rarely troubles to think what it is up to in the soil. And yet it is the very abundance of the worm that contributes so much to its importance. There is very little experimental proof that worms are beneficial in the garden, because very few experiments have been carried out, but biologists are all agreed that Darwin was right. The worm does play a very important role in the soil, and it is probably true to say that the soil we know today would never have been formed without the action of earthworms.

A mature earthworm, showing the distinct rings or segments and the swollen saddle or clitellum. The latter is concerned with egg-laying and is not a scar showing where the animal has been cut in two

Although Darwin's book was the first major work on the subject of earthworms, the animals were attracting attention long before Darwin's day. Another famous Englishman, Gilbert White, had looked carefully at them during the 18th century and, as a result of his observations, he was able to write in 1777: '. . . men would find that the earth without worms would soon become cold, hardbound, and void of fermentation; and consequently sterile. . . .' Let us now take a closer look at the earthworms themselves and see just how they do affect the soil.

The earthworms, together with the leeches and several other groups of aquatic worms, belong to the phylum of animals called the Annelida. This name means 'ringed' and refers to the conspicuous rings or segments of the body. Within the Annelida, the earthworms are placed in a group known as the Oligochaeta, a name which means 'few bristles' and which refers to the fact that, compared with the marine bristleworms, the earthworms are not very bristly. There are, in fact, four pairs of small bristles on the lower half of almost every segment. They are not easy to see, but you can feel them very easily by running a finger gently from back to front along the underside of the worm. The bristles help the worm to move.

All of our 25 native species of earthworms belong to the family Lumbricidae but, as we shall see, they do not all live in normal soil. They are all cylindrical animals, somewhat pointed at the front end and rather flattened at the rear. The number of body segments varies from species to species, but a mature *Lumbricus terrestris* (few earthworms ever receive common names) usually has about 150 segments. The worms may have a blue or green sheen on them, but the basic colour is pink or reddish brown. This is caused by the red blood flowing very near to the surface of the body. Worms have no lungs with which to breathe, and nearly all of their life-giving oxygen is absorbed into the blood through the skin. Most of the larger worms that are unearthed in the garden have a distinct band around the body about one third of the way along from the front end. It involves several segments and is often a different colour from the rest of the body. Known as the clitellum or saddle, it is involved in egg-laying (see page 65) and it indicates that the worm is mature. It is sometimes thought to be a scar showing where a worm has been chopped in half and then grown together again, but this is an erroneous belief. Worms can grow new head and tail ends if they are mutilated, but two halves cannot grow together again, and worms cut near the middle usually die.

The earthworm has a simple brain, but it has no distinct head and it has no eyes or other obvious sense organs. The whole body surface is sensitive to light, however, and the worm exposed by the gardener's fork soon burrows back down into the soil if it manages to escape the ever-present robin and blackbird. Prolonged exposure to sunlight is fatal to the animal. Movement is brought about by two sets of muscles acting in conjunction with the bristles and the pressure of the body fluids. The worm's passage is lubricated by a plentiful supply of mucus secreted by the skin, but the animal is almost helpless on a smooth surface because it can find no purchase for its bristles.

The movements of the earthworm are surprisingly powerful:

hold one in a closed fist and you will be amazed at the force with which it thrusts its snout between your fingers. This is, of course, very necessary for the worm, which spends its life tunnelling through the soil and forcing its way between the soil particles. This tunnelling activity is one of the worm's major contributions to the fertility of the soil. The tunnels form an extensive network in the soil, especially in the upper nine inches or so where the majority of plant roots are, and they allow air to circulate freely among the roots. At the same time, they allow excess water to drain away. As well as helping the plant roots directly, this aeration encourages the decay of dead material and the release of nitrates and other plant foods into the soil.

The majority of earthworms are to be found in the top nine inches or so of the soil under normal conditions, but they can descend to much greater depths when necessary. During very cold or very dry weather the larger worms can be found several feet beneath the surface, where they are unaffected by the climatic conditions. Two of our earthworm species go into an enforced state of suspended animation during the summer months. This obligatory rest is called a diapause and the worms coil themselves up in a chamber at the bottom of a burrow. Deep digging in the summer often brings up the resting worms and even this rough treatment often fails to arouse them from their slumbers. Several of our other worms can go into similar sleep, but it is not a necessary part of their lives.

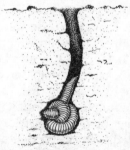

A tightly coiled earthworm in its diapause rest

The other major contribution of the earthworm stems from its feeding activity. Earthworms feed largely by swallowing soil and digesting the decaying plant and animal material that it contains. They are especially attracted to regions in which the soil has a high content of organic matter, and this explains their abundance under compost heaps. Numbers are also increased in such places by the fact that a high organic content brings about an increase in the rate of reproduction. Many of the worms' tunnels are actually formed as a result of the soil being swallowed, but what the worms do with the soil they have swallowed is equally important.

We are all familiar with worm casts, and we probably curse them from time to time when they make the lawn too unsightly, but they are signs that the worms are busy with their vital ploughing activities. The worm casts consist of soil that has been swallowed at lower levels and passed through the bodies of the worms before being voided at the surface. In fact, only two of our earthworms – *Allolobophora longa* and *Allolobophora nocturna,* the same two species that go into diapause during the summer – normally make surface casts, but these two are very common and casts are abundant in most gardens between October and May. The other earthworms void their soil in the upper reaches of their burrows, but, whether the soil is deposited on or just under the surface, the worms still perform a very valuable ploughing action. Rainwater washes minerals down into the lower regions of the soil, out of reach of the majority of plant roots, but the worms then bring the mineral-rich soil up again and make the minerals available to the plants once more.

This ploughing action is not so obvious or important in a garden plot which is dug over each year, but it is very important under a lawn or meadow. Worms are more abundant in such places in any case, because food is more plentiful, disturbance is at a minimum, and enemies are less able to penetrate the ground. The effect of the worm population can be clearly seen after only a few years. If you dig down into your lawn you will find that the uppermost layer is almost stone-free, and you may find two or three inches of stone-free soil under a very old lawn. This sorting of the soil is a direct result of the worms' activity, because they cannot swallow particles more than about 2mm in diameter. Only the finest soil is thus brought to the surface layers, and the stones gradually sink to lower levels as the finer material is mined from under them and deposited on top.

Charles Darwin was particularly interested in worm casts and their role in burying objects left on the surface. He collected worm casts from known areas of land over a period of a year and found that they totalled some ten tons per acre. He also put down layers of chalk and ashes and investigated the rates at which they were covered by the worm casts. From observations carried out over a period of thirty years, Darwin concluded that earthworms bury objects at a rate of about one inch every five years. Modern naturalists feel that this is an exaggeration, but perhaps Darwin had some very hungry worms in his part of Kent! The rate would certainly drop after a while, when the objects had sunk below the level of greatest worm activity. The stones lying around the outer edge of Stonehenge now appear to be sinking at a rate of no more than eight inches per century. Whatever rates are involved, we can be certain that both the cast-forming worms and the non-casters contribute to the burial of objects and ancient buildings by undermining them and depositing the excavated material around or on top of them.

Many gardeners hate to see worm casts on their lawns and seek ways to get rid of them. By all means brush the casts off the grass if you wish, bearing in mind that they are rich in minerals, but resist the temptation to use a worm killer. By killing the worms you may swap a healthy lawn with a few worm casts for a poorly drained one with mossy patches and coarse grasses. If you are a bowls or croquet addict and must have a lawn without worm casts, try dressing the surface with ammonium sulphate. This fertiliser discourages worms from visiting the surface, but it has less effect on those that stay below and the drainage of the lawn is not seriously impaired.

Although they are beautifully adapted for life in the soil, the earthworms are not entirely confined to a subterranean existence. If you venture out into your garden on a summer evening, when the air is warm and damp, you may catch glimpses of them emerging from their burrows and searching for food or for each other. A red light will help you to see them without upsetting them, but you will have to walk very carefully. The worms are very sensitive to vibrations and a heavy footstep will send them shooting backwards into their tunnels. The animals very rarely leave their tunnels completely: the hind end generally remains anchored in the burrow and the front region can be pulled in very rapidly if need be.

Lumbricus terrestris is the worm that you are most likely to see on the surface, although several other species do come out in this way. Listening quietly by the hedge or the herbaceous border, you may actually hear the worms nosing about among the leaves and dragging them down into their burrows. The worms show distinct preferences for certain kinds of leaves, thus indicating that they have an efficient sense of taste. They are particularly attracted to the tips of the leaves, and nearly all the leaves are drawn into the burrows tip first. The worms gradually nibble the tips away and leave the rest of the leaves lining the burrows. The leaves gradually rot away and enrich the soil, so here we have yet another valuable contribution by the earthworm.

PLATE 5: **Flowerless plant guests.** 1 Common horsetail 49, a sterile shoot without spores, b fertile shoots; 2 Maidenhair spleenwort fern 49; 3 Wall screw moss 51; 4 Silky wall feather moss 52; 5 *Lecanora muralis* 56; 6 *Ochrolechia parella* 56; 7 *Xanthoria aureola* 56; 8 *Peltigera canina* 56; 9 Common liverwort 54; 10 Pixie-cup lichen 56; 11 Coral spot fungus 58; 12 Candle snuff fungus 57; 13 *Mycena galopus* 58; 14 Fairy ring toadstool 59.

6

If leaves are not available on the surface, the worms will scour the ground around their burrows for other small pieces or organic matter which they can suck up. Worms surfacing on gravel paths and other stony areas may have to clear the stones away before they can find food, and this is the probable explanation for the little conical piles of gravel that can often be seen in such places. Going out at night, you may be able to see a worm using its tubular snout like a vacuum cleaner to pick up the little stones and deposit them in a pile around the entrance to its burrow.

Earthworms, when mature, contain both male and female sex organs, but they must still pair up before they can lay eggs. Most worms pair in their tunnels, but *Lumbricus terrestris* normally pairs on the surface. Neighbouring worms come out of their burrows on damp nights and, still with their tail ends in the ground, they lie close together and cover themselves with mucus. This position may be maintained for several hours, during which time each worm receives sperm from the other. This sperm is stored in a special sac and the worms separate. Each one later lays its eggs. The outer skin of the saddle secretes a membrane which becomes detached and forms a loose 'collar' around the saddle. Eggs then pass into the membrane and the worm begins to wriggle out of it backwards. On the way over the front part of the body, the membrane receives some of the sperm from the other worm and the eggs are fertilised. When it is free of the worm's body, the membrane becomes sealed up at the ends and it forms a protective cocoon for the eggs. The latter are nourished by a fluid albumen contained in the cocoon and the little worms – usually only one in *Lumbricus terrestris* – emerge sometime between one and five months later. They are complete with all their segments when they hatch, but they still have as much as 18 months to wait before they are mature. Captive worms have been known to live for more than ten years, but the animals are unlikely to reach such a ripe old age in the wild where numerous enemies are waiting to snap them up.

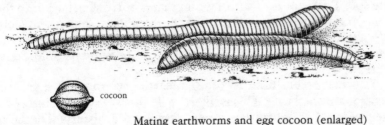

cocoon

Mating earthworms and egg cocoon (enlarged)

The enemies of earthworms

The major enemy of the earthworm is the mole, which is more fully described on page 247. Living almost entirely under the ground, the mole takes an immense number of earthworms, and during the winter it eats little else. Laboratory experiments suggest that a mole of average size probably eats at least fifty earthworms every day. The moles also store earthworms in time of plenty, biting off the front end and leaving them in special chambers in the soil. Removal of the front end prevents the worms from escaping, but if the mole does not return to its larder the worms eventually grow new heads ends and crawl away.

Moles are not particularly important enemies of the worms in our gardens because cultivation processes usually deter the moles from taking up residence. More important garden predators include shrews, hedgehogs, and various birds. The shrews (see page 246) catch their worms both under the ground and on the surface, especially among the leaf litter at the bottom of a hedge. Hedgehogs also find worms among the leaf litter, but they take mainly those worms that come out and lie on the surface at night. Blackbirds, thrushes, starlings, and several other garden birds feed eagerly on earthworms and, as we are always being told, it is the early bird that gets the worm. Shy of the light, the worms normally retreat into their burrows at daybreak, but some of them fail to make it before the first birds are abroad. But worms are not just a breakfast dish for the birds. Our feathered friends are never far away when the gardener is digging, and they are very good at digging for themselves. You will often see a bird walking over the lawn and stopping here and there to cock its head on one side to listen. It is picking up slight sounds from beneath the surface and then, suddenly, in goes its beak. It may emerge with a leather jacket (page 163) or a beetle, but it may catch a large worm and then a battle begins. Anchored by its bristles, the worm is no easy victim, and the bird must exert a considerable force to pull the worm from the soil. Try it yourself with a worm that is burrowing back into the soil – you will be surprised just how difficult it is to pull it out. Very often the bird has to be content with just a part of the worm, for the earthworm will often break in two before relaxing its hold on its burrow.

You may, from time to time, unearth a worm with a greyish maggot attached to it. This is likely to be the larva of the cluster-fly (see page 155), which has a very strange life history. The larva spends most of its life inside the body of a worm or else attached to the outside. It absorbs its food from the worm and is thus a parasite. The afflicted worm is completely destroyed in the end.

THE BRITISH EARTHWORMS

Of the 25 species of earthworms found in the British Isles, only ten are at all common in garden soil. They are not evenly distributed, for some species prefer damper or heavier soils than others. There are few earthworms in acidic, sandy soil, and the animals also avoid waterlogged soils, although it is very difficult to drown a worm. The scarcity of worms on acidic soils is partly responsible for the development of peat and coarse vegetation. Without worms to pull the leaves down into the soil, the dead plants do not decay very quickly and accumulate on the surface as peat. Only the coarser plants can penetrate this layer. This is one of the reasons why the finer grasses tend to disappear from a lawn when worm-killers have been applied.

The greatest worm populations are to be found under old grassland and orchards, where the soils have been undisturbed for long periods and where there is plenty of food in the form of dead grass and leaves. Estimates of populations in such places go as high as 3 million worms per acre, but a figure between half a million and one million is probably nearer the mark for most grasslands. Populations in gardens are considerably lower. If you want to get some idea of the worm population in your own garden you can use the following simple procedure. Mark out an area one yard square and make up a solution of potassium permanganate containing about ½ oz crystals to a gallon of water. Pour the solution over the marked area and wait for the worms to come to the surface. This method does not give a very accurate result, because many of the worms fail to react to the solution, but you will probably be surprised by the numbers that do come up. Carry out the experiment in damp weather for best results.

Although they differ in various anatomical details, the common garden earthworms nearly all look alike to the non-specialist. This is why so few of them have common names: you can't give a species a name if you can't distinguish between it and its relatives. To the gardener, they are all simply earthworms.

The largest of our earthworms, and also one of the commonest, is *Lumbricus terrestris*. Bright pink, with a tinge of violet, this worm reaches lengths of about one foot. There can be few gardens without it. *Lumbricus rubellus* is another very common species, known to anglers as the red worm because of its bright colour. It rarely exceeds six inches in length. Another common relative is *Lumbricus castaneus,* only an inch and a half long but recognisable by its bright orange clitellum. The species of *Lumbricus* can be distinguished

Lumbricus (left) and *Allolobophora* can be distinguished by the underside of the snout

from all the other common worms by the structure of the first two segments, although a lens is necessary to detect the difference. The cast-forming species, *Allolobophora longa* and *A. nocturna,* are often mistaken for *Lumbricus terrestris,* but they are somewhat smaller and much browner in colour. The related *A. chlorotica* has a distinctly greenish tinge as a rule. *Octolasium lacteum* is quite easily recognised by its bluish colour and orange or pink clitellum. The related *Octolasium cyaneum* is also greyish blue, and it has a red clitellum and a yellowish tail which discharges a thick milky fluid when disturbed. Both *Octolasium* species occur mainly in the moister soils.

The only other common earthworm of the garden is the brandling, scientifically known as *Eisenia foetida.* It is a small worm, dark red or brown and marked with clear orange bands. It exudes a foul-smelling yellow fluid when disturbed, but this does not impair its value as bait for the angler. The brandling is most likely to be found in the compost heap or in recently manured ground, but it also thrives happily under the bark of fallen or dead trees.

Potworms

While turning the compost heap, or digging the compost into the garden, you will probably notice clusters of small white or greyish worms wriggling vigorously without seeming to get very far. These are the small oligochaete worms known as potworms. They are rarely more than about 10 mm long and they could easily be mistaken for fly maggots (see page 154), but close examination shows that they are much more cylindrical than the latter. Potworms are much less common than earthworms in the soil, but they are abundant in compost heaps and other organic deposits. They

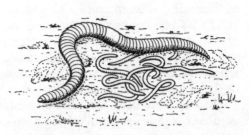

Wriggly, white potworms accompanied
by a brandling worm

The thunderworm (*Mermis*)

congregate in large numbers around the 'juiciest' material and are
almost always found in clusters. They feed on the decaying material
and on the microscopic organisms in it, and their life stories are very
much like those of the earthworms.

Nematodes and eelworms

Summer showers sometimes bring out a most peculiar creature
known as the thunderworm. It may be as much as 20 inches long
and it looks just like a piece of brown cotton. It is most frequently
seen snaking its way over plants that are still wet with rain, but it
doesn't stay out for long and goes back down into the soil as soon as
the sun dries up the moisture. The animal can sometimes be found
resting among the roots when we pull up weeds during the summer.
Thunderworms lay their eggs in the soil, and the young worms bore
their way into beetles and other insects. They remain there, feeding
on the tissues of the insects, until they are grown up and ready to
escape into the soil.

Thunderworms belong to a large group of animals known as
nematodes or roundworms. They are not related to the earthworms
and their bodies are not divided into rings or segments. The
roundworms are probably the most abundant of all the world's
animals and there is virtually nowhere on earth without them. They
live in the soil and in the water, and nearly every other animal and
plant has parasitic nematodes living inside it. It has even been said

69

that if everything except the nematodes could be swept away the abundance of those animals everywhere would ensure that the outlines of the earth and its mountains, rivers, and forests would still be visible. Figures of 20 million roundworms per square metre of soil surface have been quoted for roundworm populations in some places, and it has been estimated that there may be 90,000 worms in one rotting apple. Such numerous creatures must obviously be very small. Most of those that live in the soil are less than 1 mm long, and many are quite invisible without a microscope. The gardener is thus very unlikely to notice the roundworms, but he is certain to notice their effects from time to time. Although many species feed freely on decaying material or on other microscopic organisms, others attack plants and do much damage to the roots. These plant-eating species are usually called eelworms, and one of the most damaging is the potato-root eelworm. Heavy infestations of this little creature severely weaken potato plants and cause

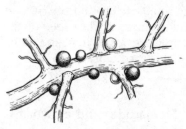

Highly magnified egg-filled cysts of the potato-root eelworm breaking through the root. The cysts will later fall off and the little worms that hatch from them will tunnel into a new crop of potato roots

serious losses. Each female deposits up to 600 eggs in the soil in a tough bag or cyst. Extremely resistant to drought and to severe cold, the eggs can survive unharmed for up to ten years, just waiting for the next potato crop to stimulate them into hatching. Until now, the only effective method of controlling the potato eelworm has been to maintain a long rotation, with several years between potato crops. During such an interval, most of the eelworm eggs hatch spontaneously (without the stimulus of nearby potato roots) and the young worms die from lack of food. Promising new control methods are now becoming available, however, and long rotations may not be necessary in the future.

CHAPTER 4

Snails and Slugs

THE snails and slugs belong to the large group of animals known as the molluscs. This group or phylum is second in size only to the arthropods and, as well as the snails and slugs, it includes the squids and octopuses and all the aquatic bivalves, such as the cockles and mussels. These are all soft-bodied animals without internal skeletons, but the majority of them have some sort of shell which both supports and protects the body. Within the molluscs, the snails and slugs belong to a group called gastropods, a name which means 'belly feet' and which refers to the way in which the animals creep about on their bellies. The slugs have descended from various groups of snails through the reduction or complete loss of the shell, but their modes of life remain very similar.

Snails

The snail's body consists of two main parts – the belly, on which it creeps along, and the visceral hump. The latter contains most of the internal organs and it is always concealed within the shell. The belly

A banded snail showing how the head merges gradually into the foot. The eyes are at the tips of the longer tentacles

is more usually known as the foot, and its lower surface is called the sole. Its front end is called the head, although there is no clear division between the head and the rest and the whole belly region is sometimes called the head-foot. In most of our land snails, the head end bears two pairs of tentacles, although the round-mouthed snail (page 75) has only one pair. When two pairs are present, the eyes are carried at the tips of the larger pair. The eyes are probably unable to pick out shapes, but they are very sensitive to changes in

71

light intensity and the snail will often react strongly if a shadow falls on it. The tentacles are also sensitive to smell and to touch. If a tentacle bumps lightly into something, the eye will be withdrawn by pulling in the tip of the tentacle and the snail may turn slightly to the other side before expanding the tentacle again. A stronger disturbance may cause the whole tentacle or even both tentacles to be withdrawn into the head. Severe disturbance, such as when we pick a snail up, causes the whole body to be withdrawn into the shell for safety. Such action is often accompanied by a copious secretion of froth, which may deter some birds and other animals with designs on the snail. The round-mouthed snail, in common with many aquatic species, has an added protection in the form of a horny door or operculum. This can be seen perched on the tail end of the active animal, but when the foot is withdrawn it fits firmly across the mouth of the shell.

The visceral hump of the snail is coiled like the shell and it is covered by a thick cloak of skin called the mantle. The swollen edge of this cloak can be seen around the opening of the shell when the snail is active. The shell itself is a non-living part of the snail, secreted by the edge of the mantle. The outer layer of the shell, which contributes most of the colour and pattern, consists of a thin, horny material. The rest of the shell consists of layers of calcium carbonate, the innermost of which is smooth and pearly. Additions are made to the shell periodically to keep pace with the growth of the snail's body and the shell usually bears a number of distinct growth lines, showing where growth has stopped and started again. Growth always stops during the winter and snails can often be found in the spring with just a very flimsy layer around the mouth of the shell. This is the newly formed horny layer awaiting the deposition of the harder calcium carbonate inside it. Fully grown shells can usually be distinguished from young ones because the mouth is normally strengthened by a distinct rim at or just inside the lip.

A garden snail shell cut open to reveal the living chamber coiling around the central spire or columella

Sinistral and dextral shells

The snail shells are always spirally coiled, but the shape is very varied: some shells are almost flat, some are conical, and others are almost cylindrical. But, despite this variation, the shells nearly all coil in the same direction. If you hold a shell upright with the opening facing you, the opening will almost always be on the right of the coil. Shells that coil in this direction are said to be dextral. Shells that coil in the opposite direction are said to be sinistral. A few species habitually have sinistral shells, but the real prize for the shell collector is the occasional freak – the occasional sinistral specimen of a species that normally has dextral shells. Many shells have a distinct hollow on the underside. This is called the umbilicus and it passes up between the shell whorls. In many species, however, the lip of the shell grows over the opening and conceals it.

Shells from below: *left* shows an open umbilicus; *right* umbilicus covered over by the growth of the lip

Part of the space between the mantle and the visceral hump forms the snail's lung. The lining of the lung is well supplied with blood vessels, and the cavity opens to the air through a small hole just under the lip of the shell on the right hand side of the animal. The entrance is not permanently open, but you will see it open and close periodically if you watch a snail for a short while.

The movement of the snail is brought about by the muscles of the sole, aided by a thick mucus secreted by glands just under the head. Allow a snail to glide round in a jam jar and you will see numerous light and dark bands moving forward along the sole. These are produced by the rhythmic muscular action which lifts each region of the sole in turn and moves it forward a little before putting it down again. The whole process is continuous, and so the whole foot moves smoothly forward, lubricated by the abundant mucus. The latter soon dries when the snail has passed and it hardens into the familiar silvery trail.

Some snails are carnivorous, but the majority of those in our gardens are vegetarians. They eat both living and dead material and some species certainly make a nuisance of themselves in the garden

by eating tender seedlings and other plants. But it is probably true
to say that the tidy gardener suffers more from the activity of snails
than the untidy one who doesn't bother too much about picking up
all the dead leaves and other rubbish: many snails prefer rotting
material and will attack living plants only if such decaying matter is
unavailable. Only two of our snails – the garden snail and the
strawberry snail – really do much damage in the garden.

Food is sought out by smell and taste, the snail using its tentacles
and the lobes around its mouth to determine the suitability of the
material. The mouth itself is on the underside of the head and it is
provided with a file-like tongue called a radula. Working against a
hard ridge in the roof of the mouth, the tiny teeth on the radula rasp
away at the food very efficiently. The teeth at the front wear away
quite rapidly, but the radula grows continuously from the back and
new sections are always coming into use.

The round-mouthed snail and a few other species have separate
sexes, but most of our land snails are hermaphrodites, meaning that
they have both male and female organs in each individual. The
degree of hermaphroditism varies, however. Many species start
their adult lives as functional males and then, as sperm-production
gives way to egg-production, they become females. The garden
snail and some of the more advanced species are true hermaphrodites, producing eggs and sperm simultaneously. Pairing is always
necessary, however, and the more advanced species have evolved
complex courtship rituals. Some of these involve the firing of a
chalky 'love dart' by each snail into its partner. The eggs which are
like small, round pearls, are laid soon after mating. They are deposited singly or in groups and they are usually buried in the soil. As
long as they keep moist and escape the attentions of ground beetles
and other predators, they hatch in a few weeks as miniature snails.

Snails are attacked and eaten by a wide range of other animals,
including ground beetles (page 187), frogs, hedgehogs, and shrews,
but their most famous enemies are the thrushes. These birds (page
229) can often be seen in the garden hammering snails against paths
and stones until the shells break and the juicy flesh can be extracted.

The soft skins of the snails are not at all waterproof and, although
the animals clothe themselves with several kinds of mucus, they are
always in danger of drying out. This explains why the animals are
rarely found in really dry situations. Our garden species are usually
active at night or after rain, when the air is humid and little moisture
is lost by evaporation through the skin. During the winter, or
during dry spells during the summer, the snails usually hide away
under logs or stones or in some other well protected place and

Hibernating garden snails, their shells closed by epiphragma

retreat right into their shells. Several layers of mucus may be secreted across the mouth of the shell and they harden to form a protective disc called an epiphragm. The snails often congregate in large numbers at such times and their shells become glued together with the mucus.

The distribution of snails is controlled by the soil as well as by moisture. Large species and those with thick shells need plenty of lime in the soil and are often confined to areas of chalk and limestone. Most other species are more common in lime-rich areas. Very sandy areas often have no snails at all, or else just a few species with thin, horny shells.

There are about 80 kinds of land snail in the British Isles, but only about twenty of these occur regularly in gardens. Most of the others live in marshy places or woodlands, where they can find the abundant moisture and the decaying material that they like. The more common garden species are briefly described in the following paragraphs and illustrated on Plate 6.

The **round-mouthed snail** (Plate 6) has an operculum and its eyes are at the base of its single pair of tentacles, showing that it is not closely related to the other land snails. It has a rather thick shell and it is confined to chalk and limestone regions. Its natural homes are the woods and grasslands, but it also extends along the hedgerows and it is sometimes common in newly established gardens on the chalk and limestone. It was the commonest snail in my own garden on the Chilterns, but I noticed a definite decline in its numbers during the four years that I lived there and I suspect that it dislikes disturbance.

The large Roman or edible snail occurs in some gardens in the lime-rich areas of southern England, but the largest snail normally seen in the garden is the one known simply as the common or **garden snail** – a name that testifies to the ubiquity and abundance of the species. The shell (Plate 6) is basically a rather dull brown, but it is decorated with several darker bands which are broken up to a large extent to give it a mottled appearance. Most specimens of the garden snail are rather dirty, and this may be due to their habit of 'roosting' together and crawling over each other. During the daytime, they can often be found clustered together among empty flower pots, and if you mark them you will find that most of them return day after day to the same shelter. Abundant in most gardens, this snail often harms strawberries and other low-growing fruits and vegetables. If you think you have too many specimens in your garden, why not eat some of them! Amusing recipes can be found in many of the older cookery books.

The boldly banded yellow and brown shells that occur in the hedge and other areas of dense vegetation belong to two distinct species of snails – the **brown-lipped** and the **white-lipped**. These names will be obvious if you look at the lips of the adult shells (Plate 6). The animals also differ slightly in the colour of the body, the brown-lipped snail being a leaden grey while the white-lipped snail is a greenish grey with a yellowish tail end. The shells of both species are extremely variable and, although there are typically five brown stripes running round each whorl, any or all of the stripes may be missing or they may all be fused together to make a broad band. Both species are widely distributed, but the brown-lipped snail is absent from northern Scotland. The white-lipped snail is probably the more common in gardens and it is sometimes called the garden snail. Both species normally eat grass and other weeds in the hedge, but they will also attack lettuces and other tender vegetables.

The **Kentish snail** (Plate 6) is a poorly named species because it lives in nearly all the English counties and also ventures across the borders into Wales and Scotland. The shell is basically white, but it has a bluish or lead-coloured tinge on the upper whorls and there is generally a reddish tinge on the lower surface, especially near the aperture. Like the brown-lipped and white-lipped snails, the Kentish snail is very much at home in the dense herbage at the bottom of the hedgerow and it often spreads out into the herbaceous border. It feeds on decaying leaves and large numbers are often seen on roadside verges when the grass has been cut and left to rot.

The **strawberry snail** (Plate 6) is one of the commonest and least desirable snails in the garden. It occurs all over the country except for northern Scotland, and can be found hiding during the day in the compost heap, under rhubarb leaves, or in any other reasonably moist situation from which it can venture out at night to browse on our crops. It is especially fond of strawberries, but it will destroy seedlings of many kinds and few mature crops are entirely safe from its activities. The shell of this species is sometimes white or yellowish, but it is usually reddish brown and it often has a pale band running around the circumference. When young, it is clothed with short hairs, while the adult has a strong white rib just behind the lip of the shell. The animal itself is usually dark grey, but pale grey specimens are not uncommon. The closely related **hairy snail** (Plate 6) occurs in the same sort of damp places as the strawberry snail, but it is less common in the garden. It is quite similar to the strawberry snail, but it is usually a little smaller and it is clothed with fairly obvious short bristles.

The **rounded snail** (Plate 6) lives under stones and logs and among dead leaves and is often found in company with the strawberry snail. Its shell is yellowish brown, studded with darker brown spots, but the easiest way to identify it is to look at the umbilicus. This is very wide and it clearly shows the smaller whorls of the shell. At its widest point, it takes up about one third of the shell's width.

The garden supports several snails with very thin, horny shells. These are known as glass snails. One of the commonest, and also one of the smallest, is the **garlic glass snail** (Plate 6), easily recognised by its shiny brown shell and the strong smell of garlic which it releases when handled. It is often abundant around the compost heap and it can be found under almost any log or large stone. The related **cellar glass snail** (Plate 6) is nearly twice as large and its shell is yellowish brown on top and white around the umbilicus. Its body is paler than that of the garlic glass snail. The cellar glass snail occurs in all kinds of damp places in the garden and often invades cellars and damp out-buildings. It feeds on fungi and various small animals such as worms and insect larvae. **Draparnaud's snail** (Plate 6) is even larger. It lives in the same situations as the previous two species, but it feeds mainly on other animals. The **smooth glass snail** (Plate 6) has a dull and rather waxy reddish brown shell.

The **pellucid glass snail** (Plate 6) is not closely related to the last four species. It has a pale grey body and a very thin greenish shell up to 6 mm across. The shell is rather oval in shape because the last whorl is very broad and the mouth of the shell occupies about half of the total width. The snail feeds on small animals and rotting material and it is commonly found in the compost heap and the hedge bottom. Unlike most of our snails, it breeds in the winter months and adults are rarely seen in the summer.

Gardens with old walls will almost certainly support the skittle-shaped **two-toothed door snail** (Plate 6), one of our few species with sinistral shells. The snail hides in crevices by day and emerges at night to rasp away at the lichens and mosses on the wall. It is not confined to walls, however, and it is just as frequently met with under logs and stones.

Slugs

Asked to select the most troublesome garden pest, most gardeners would probably choose the slug. This is understandable, because slugs are abundant in the garden and several species can be found chewing our plants, but they don't usually do as much damage as we imagine. Most of them prefer to eat decaying leaves and other parts of the plant that are not used for human consumption in any case, so they don't always deprive us of food even if they do nibble our vegetables. Perhaps even more than with the snails, the tidy and fussy gardener suffers more than the untidy one because the neat garden provides fewer dead leaves and drives the slugs to eat the better parts of the plants.

The slugs are really no more and no less than snails which have almost or quite lost their shells. They have also lost their visceral humps, and this means that the digestive systems and other internal organs have to be packed into the head-foot, but the biology of the slugs remains essentially the same as that of snails. The mantle still covers part of the body and, as in the snails, it encloses the lung. A few slugs retain a small shell at the hind end (see page 79), but the shell has been reduced in most species to a very thin plate or just a few chalky granules embedded in the mantle.

With no portable home into which they can withdraw, the slugs are more susceptible to drought and to enemies than the snails, although they protect themselves to some extent with various kinds of mucus. Many species are active all through the year as long as the weather remains kind, but during very dry or very cold weather they tunnel deep down into the soil. Some species live most of their lives in the soil, but most of them are surface feeders and they come out to feed at night or when the air is damp after rain. They dislike rain falling on them, but they often emerge in their thousands as soon as it stops and this is when they are most likely to be seen crawling on paths and vegetation. The lack of a shell does have one advantage, however, and that is that the slugs are able to colonise the sandy soils denied to the lime-requiring snails.

Close examination of slugs will often reveal numerous minute creatures running all over their bodies. These little creatures are **mites** (see page 221) and they tend to be more frequent on the keeled slugs (page 80) than on the other groups. They don't seem to be hindered by the mucus that coats the slugs and they probably feed on it. The slugs are certainly not inconvenienced by their little passengers and don't so much as cough when the mites scuttle in and out of their breathing pores.

Although the slugs have descended from the snails, they have not all descended from one group of snails and they are not all closely related. Our British slugs belong to three very distinct groups: the shelled slugs, the keeled slugs, and the round-backed slugs. They total about 24 British species, and about half of these may be expected to turn up from time to time in the garden.

The shelled slugs are easily recognised by the small mantle and the external shell perched on the hind end of the body. When extended, the body tapers markedly to the front in connection with the mainly subterranean habits of these animals. They are carnivorous creatures and their diet consists mainly of earthworms. The prey is generally caught under the ground, but the slugs often emerge from their burrows on warm, damp nights and attack worms exploring the surface (see page 64). A worm attacked in such a position will immediately withdraw into its burrow, but such is the grip of the slug's radula that the slug is merely drawn in to the burrow after the worm. It can then continue its meal in peace. All three of our shelled slugs occur mainly on cultivated land and all three may turn up in gardens, but the most abundant is *Testacella haliotidea* (Plate 7). It is found all over the British Isles apart from the northern half of Scotland. It is most likely to be seen in the spring.

Great grey slugs mating. They may stay in mid air for two hours or more, gyrating around each other as they exchange sperm. Nuptials completed, the slugs either drop to the ground or climb back up the string and eat it as they go

The keeled slugs all have a keel or ridge on the hind part of the body, and the lung opening is more than half way back along the right hand side of the mantle. The largest member of this group likely to be found in the garden is the **great grey slug** (Plate 7), a species which is always more common around human habitations. It can often be found crawling in cellars and damp out-buildings, and even across the patio on a damp evening. It feeds mainly on fungi. The mating habits of this species are truly remarkable, for the courting pair normally climb up into a bush or tree and then, entwined together, they lower themselves on a rope of very thick mucus. Mating takes place suspended in mid-air. The **yellow slug** (Plate 7) is a somewhat smaller and smoother species than the great grey slug. It is grey, with a distinct greenish or yellowish tinge, and it has a yellow sole. The tentacles are steely blue. This species feeds on fungi and decaying matter and it can often be found crawling on the lower parts of damp walls.

The small fawn and white slug that we so often find in the centres of our lettuces and cabbages is the **netted slug** (Plate 7), our commonest and most damaging slug. It is one of the few slugs to eat green leaves, but it makes up for this by attacking a very wide range of crops. This is one species that the gardener can very well do without.

The three keeled slugs mentioned so far all have only a short keel on the hind end of the body, but the next three have a keel running forward from the tail end right up to the hind edge of the mantle. All are basically subterranean and they are especially common on cultivated land, where they do considerable damage to root crops, including potatoes. **Sowerby's slug** (Plate 7) is dark grey and, compared with other slugs, it is relatively dry-skinned. The sole is

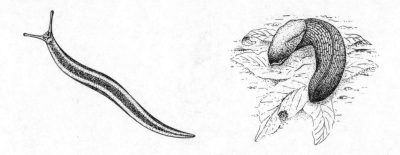

The Budapest slug: the distinctly banded sole (*left*) and the curved resting position (right) distinguish this species from Sowerby's slug

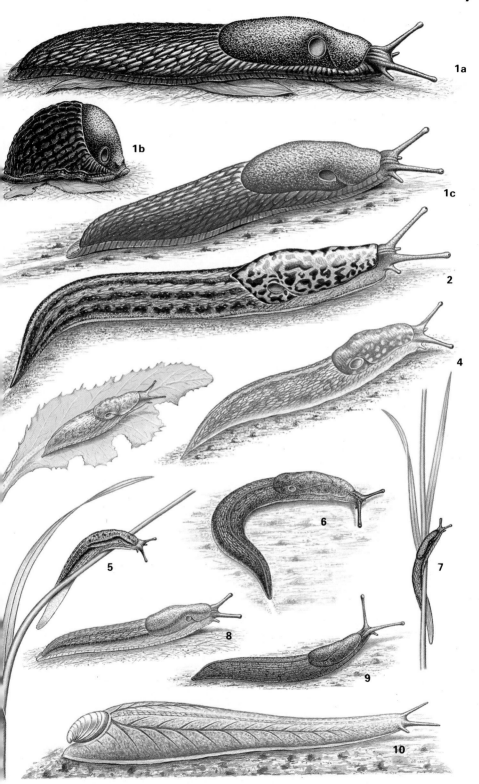

7

1a

1b

1c

2

4

5

6

7

8

9

10

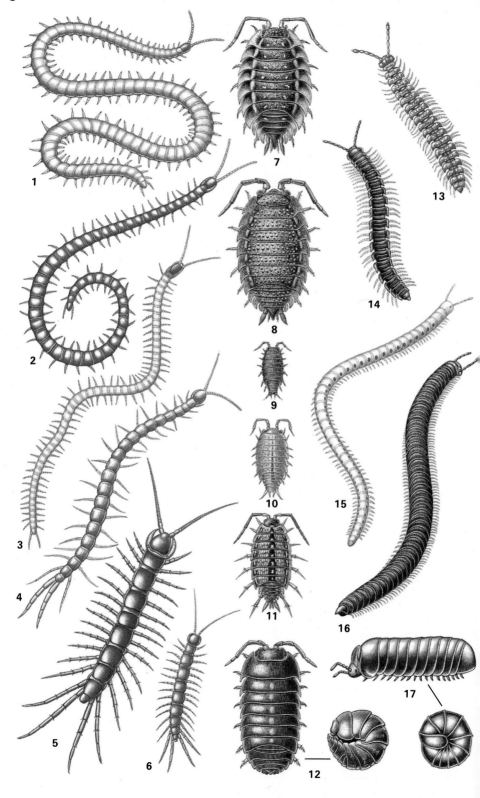

1

2

3

4

5

6

7

8

9

10

11

12

13

14

15

16

17

pale and the keel is also paler than the rest of the body. This latter feature separates Sowerby's slug from the **smooth jet slug** (*Milax gagates*), in which the keel is similar to or darker than the rest of the body. The two species can also be separated by the colour of the mucus: Sowerby's slug produces yellow mucus, whereas that of the smooth jet slug is colourless. Both species are widely distributed up to southern Scotland. The **Budapest slug** (Plate 7) is brown or black, with a longitudinally striped sole and an orange or yellow keel. This species frequently contracts into a character-istic semi-circular shape when disturbed (see figure opposite).

The round-backed slugs have no keel, although they often bear numerous rows of elongated tubercles. The breathing pore is near the front of the right-hand edge of the mantle. The largest member of this group is the **large black slug** (Plate 7). It is found in gardens, hedgerows, verges, and many other places and it feeds on almost anything. It does not do much damage in the garden, however. The mucus secreted by this species is extremely thick and strong and it is quite difficult to pull the slug away from its position. It is even more difficult to remove the mucus from one's hand afterwards. The species also has immense powers of contraction, and it will con-dense itself into a hemisphere if picked up: what is more, the hemisphere will then start to sway about, looking like an animated prune. The rich chestnut coloured slugs that are often seen on the verge or in the garden, differ only slightly from the black ones and the two are regarded as varieties of the same species.

The **garden slug** (Plate 7) is one of the smaller round-backed

Front ends of a keeled slug (*left*) and a round-backed slug showing the different positions of the breathing pore

slugs, but it is certainly the most destructive. It is a dark brownish grey or black, smoother than the large black slug, and with a yellow or orange sole. Seedlings, lettuces, strawberries, and many other low-growing crops are attacked by this species, and it often feeds on potato tubers in company with the *Milax* species. **Bourguignat's** slug (Plate 7) is a similar but much less damaging species which is easily distinguished by its white sole. It prefers to eat fungi and decaying material.

The only other slug that occurs regularly in gardens is the **dusky slug** (Plate 7), a dusky brown species which can be recognised by the lyre-shaped mark on the mantle. It feeds on fungi and dead leaves.

The troublesome slugs can be controlled when necessary with one of the various slug killers available on the market. Alternatively, they can be trapped by placing a few bricks or pieces of wood around the garden. The slugs will use these as daytime retreats and they are then easily destroyed.

CHAPTER 5

Woodlice, Centipedes and Millipedes

THE three groups of animals which we shall look at in this chapter all belong to the immense arthropod phylum (see page 17) and they all agree in having segmented bodies and several or many pairs of jointed legs. Beyond that, they are not closely related, but they all inhabit the same kinds of situations and it is convenient to deal with them together. The gardener will certainly find them together.

WOODLICE

I doubt if there are any gardens, either in the town or in the country, which do not harbour woodlice. These small, oval animals can be found under logs and stones, in bark crevices, and among the dead leaves in the hedge bottom. Even the humblest window box probably has a few woodlice lurking underneath it, and older houses, especially those with damp stone floors, have more than their share

Oniscus asellus, one of our commonest woodlice

of these little creatures. It is not surprising that such abundant and ubiquitous animals have received a wealth of local and often very amusing names. These include bibble-bugs, sow-bugs, cud-worms, tiggy-hogs, shoe-laces, sink-lice, slaters, and coffin-cutters. W. E. Collinge, writing in 1935, was able to list 65 of these local names, but it is probable that many are no longer used.

Woodlice are usually treated harshly by gardener and housewife alike, and they are frequently trodden on as soon as they appear. In many areas it is believed to be unlucky to have a woodlouse in the house. They are harmless creatures, however, and certainly don't deserve to be slaughtered wherever they are found. They may occasionally nibble young seedlings, but they are generally much more interested in dead leaves and other decaying material and their presence in the garden is probably far more beneficial than harmful. Those species that are able to roll up into a ball were once thought to have a medicinal value and they were swallowed alive in attempts to cure digestive ailments. They were also given to cattle, and this is probably why they are called cud-worms in some areas. The practice has stopped now, but we still refer to these woodlice as pill-bugs.

The woodlice belong to the class of arthropods known as the crustaceans, which is a predominantly aquatic group containing the crabs and lobsters. Although they now live on land, the woodlice have not completely shaken off their aquatic habits. Their skins are not completely water-proof, and the animals nearly all dry up very rapidly in dry air. This is why almost all of them are confined to damp places and why they come out to feed only at night, when the air is cooler and damper. Many of the species can breathe only if their bodies are covered with a thin film of moisture, although they soon drown if completely immersed in water.

A woodlouse's body consists of three main regions, although these are far less distinct than the three regions of an insect's body (page 107). The head is small and it is sunk back into the rest of the body to give a smooth, rounded outline. It carries two pairs of antennae or feelers, but only one pair is at all obvious. As in most other arthropods, the antennae are sensory organs which help the animal to feel and smell its way around. The tough jaws and the rest of the feeding apparatus are concealed underneath the head. The central and largest part of the body is called the *pereion* or thorax and it is roofed over with seven broad, overlapping plates. It bears seven pairs of legs on the underside. The hindermost region, which is not always very distinct from the pereion, is called the *pleon* or abdomen. It has six segments, but only four of the dorsal plates or shields are very obvious. The last plate, which is often triangular, is called the *telson*.

The first five pairs of limbs on the pleon are quite unlike normal legs. Each leg consists of two leaf-like flaps lying on top of each other. The inner flap is very thin and well supplied with blood. It acts as a gill, enabling the woodlouse to absorb oxygen from the air, but it will work only when surrounded by a film of water in which the oxygen can dissolve. Woodlice don't just dry up in a dry atmosphere: they suffocate as well. Some species are on the way to solving this problem, however, through the development of minute breathing tubes in the outer flaps of some of the abdominal limbs. A tiny pore on the surface allows air to enter the tubes, which spread through the limb to a greater or lesser extent. The walls of the tubes are always moist, and so oxygen can pass through into the blood very easily. These tubes are called *pseudotracheae* and they show up as little white patches on the underside of the animal. Woodlice possessing them certainly tolerate dry conditions far better than those species without them, but the animals still depend to a large extent on their gills. The pseudotracheae have a long way to go in their evolution before they can match the breathing tubes of the insects and the centipedes and millipedes.

The last pair of limbs on the pleon are much more like legs than the others. They stick out from the hind end and they are called uropods. Each one is forked, with the outer branch usually much stouter than the inner one. The uropods probably act as sensory organs, analagous with the hind legs of some centipedes (page 92), and they also secrete repellent fluids which protect the animals from some of their enemies. Repellent fluids are also secreted from most segments of the body.

Some woodlice, including the pill-bugs, will nibble grass. Many of them will also take an occasional tender seedling, but the bulk of a woodlouse's food consists of dead and decaying plant material. As their name suggests, rotting wood is a favourite item of diet for many species. The animals will also feed on animal dung, including their own. This reliance on decaying material explains why the woodlice are basically useful creatures. They speed up the decay and break down of dead material, and thus speed up the return of useful minerals to the soil where they can be used by new plants. It is only in the greenhouse, where tender young seedling are, or should be, more common than dead leaves and rotting wood that the woodlice really become a nuisance.

Their eating habits also help to explain their distribution. Few will be found in the open vegetable garden, but they are much more numerous in the relatively undisturbed herbaceous border, where there are always some dead leaves around the bases of the plants. The animals are most numerous, however, under the shrubs and along the walls and hedgerows. Here they find both food and shelter.

Although protected to some extent by their repellent fluids, the woodlice are eaten by a wide range of other animals. Shrews, toads, ground beetles, centipedes, and some spiders (see page 213) are

85

among their most numerous predators. The animals also suffer from attack by parasites* of several kinds. Among the commonest of these are several kinds of blow-fly. Stimulated by scent, the female flies seek out the woodlouse haunts and lay their eggs there. The maggots which hatch from the eggs bore their way into the woodlice and remain there, feeding on the tissues of their hosts. There is normally only one maggot in each woodlouse, and by the time that the maggot is fully grown the woodlouse is nothing but an empty skin. If you lift a log or stone and find a woodlouse sitting quite still instead of scurrying for shelter again, the animal may well be carrying one of these unwelcome guests.

During the breeding season, which lasts for most of the summer, the females develop a brood pouch under the pereion. The pouch is formed by a number of overlapping plates which grow in from the sides of the body and form a false floor to the body. The space between the body and this false floor is filled with liquid and the female lays her eggs into it. Laboratory studies indicate that the eggs of *Porcellio scaber* (page 88) take about a month to hatch. The fluid then gradually disappears from the pouch and the little woodlice, about the size of a grain of rice, leave after a few days. They are very pale, and they have only six thoracic segments, but they soon change their skins to reveal seven segments.

A transverse section of a 'pregnant' woodlouse, showing the youngsters in the brood pouch

Tidying up neglected corners of the garden, the gardener may well come across some strange-looking woodlice which are half white and half grey. These are not unusual species, but merely woodlice which have been caught in the act of changing their clothes. In common with all the arthropods, the woodlice have to moult or change their skins several times during their lives. This is because each one is enclosed in a tough outer coat which does not grow and keep pace with the animal itself. Woodlice moult in a

*A parasite may be defined as an organism, plant or animal, that lives in close association with a member of another species, taking food from it and giving nothing in return. The species which is attacked is called the host and the effect of the parasite can vary from mild inconvenience to the death of the host.

rather unusual way, however, shedding the skin in two distinct stages. The half white and half grey woodlice that we sometimes find have just moulted the skin from the white half.

The fact that we often find numerous woodlice huddled together under one log or in one small bark crevice might suggest that the animals actively search for such places in which to rest, but detailed investigations into the behaviour of the woodlice have shown that this is not so. Their lives are governed by instinctive responses to light and humidity, and these automatic responses are such that the animals are bound to end up in moist, dark places. The response to light can be investigated very easily by confining some woodlice in a shallow dish, half of which is covered with a cloth and half of which is exposed to light. The woodlice will very soon congregate in the dark half. If you then place the cover on the other half of the dish, you will see the woodlice streaming across to the dark side again. This instinctive movement away from light ensures that the animals are back in bed before the sun comes up in the morning. Their responses to humidity are more complex and of two main types. They can be seen by putting some woodlice in an evenly-lit dish with dry soil in one part and damp soil in the other. Woodlice put into the drier end will walk quickly and turn rather infrequently, and such activity will eventually bring them into the moister end of the dish. As soon as they encounter the moister conditions, they automatically slow down and begin to turn this way and that, rarely taking more than a few steps in any one direction. If the conditions are sufficiently moist, the woodlice may stop moving altogether. These reactions explain how woodlice find and accumulate in moist places without any conscious effort on their part. The animals also react to the stimulus of touch, slowing down and perhaps stopping as soon as both upper and lower surfaces of the body are in contact with something. This reaction explains why woodlice congregate in narrow crevices and under logs.

The reactions outlined above all help to show why woodlice hide away at day-break, when the sun comes up and the air becomes drier, but they don't tell us why woodlice get up and wander about in the evening. Why don't the woodlice continue to stay in their snug crevices? It may be that they get hungry, but recent researches indicate that moisture – too much of it this time – stimulates their activity. Hidden away in their moist retreats, the animals absorb water from the surroundings, and it is thought that they eventually become over-loaded with water to the extent that they are driven, again by instinct, to move out into less humid conditions where they can lose the excess water by evaporation. On this basis, it can be argued that woodlice do not stay out long on dry, windy nights because they lose the excess water quickly and then, as a result of the reactions we have already seen, they return to their shelters. Conversely, the animals stay out longer on damp nights because it takes them longer to evaporate the excess water. It must be admitted, however, that there are other possible explanations and that biologists still have much to learn about the behaviour of the woodlice.

Garden woodlice

A total of 42 species of woodlice have been recorded from the British Isles, but no more than 29 of these can be regarded as natives of our islands. Some of the others have been imported with plants and have become well established as synanthropes (see page 17), but they have a very restricted distribution. Many of our native species are confined to coastal habitats or to woodlands, and only six species can really be regarded as garden animals. They are all much more abundant on lime-rich soils than in other regions because they need lime to make their shells. The animals can be found at all times of the year, but during the winter and during very dry weather they burrow down into the soil or leaf litter and they are more difficult to find then. Our common garden woodlice are all illustrated on Plate 8.

Oniscus asellus is one of our largest and commonest species and it is abundant in gardens all over the British Isles. It reaches lengths of about 16 mm and it may be 8 mm wide. Somewhat flatter than our other large woodlice, its body is usually brownish black, with paler mottling and very pale edges to the segmental plates. It is usually rather shiny. The species can also be identified by the long, pointed telson. *Oniscus asellus* is particularly fond of rotting wood and it is usually the commonest species under logs and stones in the garden.

Porcellio scaber is as common and widely distributed as *Oniscus asellus,* and it may be even more common in the garden because it can tolerate drier places. Unlike *Oniscus,* it possesses pseudo-tracheae. This species is about the same length as *Oniscus,* but it is a little narrower. The dorsal surface is covered with prominent tubercles and is rarely very shiny. It is usually a rather dark, steely grey colour, but lighter mottled varieties do occur and young specimens are very often mottled with yellow and brown. *Porcellio* can be found under stones and logs and it is the commonest species in greenhouses, but it is even more common in bark crevices and on old walls. If you take a torch to a tree trunk or a wall on a humid night, you will probably be very surprised at the numbers of wood-lice you find, and most of them will be *Porcellio scaber.*

Philoscia muscorum is a brownish or reddish species heavily mottled with lighter patches. These patches are sometimes so numerous that the whole animal appears yellowish. The abdomen or pleon is sharply marked off from the pereion, and there is not the smooth outline that we see in *Oniscus* and *Porcellio*. The animal is very abundant in the countryside, especially in grassland, but it is far less common in gardens than the two preceding species. It can be found there, however, usually under damp logs or in the leaf litter under the hedge. It becomes rare in the north. Unlike *Oniscus* and *Porcellio,* which pull their shells down tightly and sit still when disturbed, *Philoscia* is a very active creature and scuttles away on its relatively long legs. Its body is never more than about 11 mm long.

Androniscus dentiger is a very attractive woodlouse which ranges from white to deep pink. It is about 6 mm long and its surface is covered with prominent tubercles. The species is not particularly common in gardens, but its liking for limestone sometimes attracts it to damp old walls and cellars. Although widely distributed in the southern half of Britain, the species is rare in the north and occurs there only in and around gardens – indicating that it has been taken north by man.

Trichoniscus pusillus is no more than 5 mm long and it rarely comes out from the leaf litter or turf in which it lives. The species is not very often noticed, therefore, but it is often abundant in the compost heap. It is sometimes common in greenhouses as well. The species is usually brown, with paler markings, but purple varieties occur here and there. *Trichoniscus pygmaeus,* with a length of about 2·5 mm, is our smallest woodlouse. It is rarely noticed but, like *T. pusillus,* it is abundant in the turf and in the compost heap. It can also be found under stones in damp places. These two species are so small and their shells are so thin that they die very rapidly if exposed to dry air.

Our only common **pill-bug** is *Armadillidium vulgare,* a large woodlouse, up to 18 mm long and with a much more rounded or domed appearance than the other garden species. The colour varies, but most individuals are slate grey. The shell is much thicker than that of the other woodlice and it is much more water-proof. The animals can thus inhabit drier places than the other species, and they are often abroad during the daytime. Well-developed pseudotracheae enable them to breathe efficiently under such conditions. The thick shell requires plenty of lime, however, and the pill-bugs are restricted to lime-rich areas. Their normal habitats are the dry grasslands of the chalk and limestone in southern England, and they are relatively rare in the north. They are not common garden animals, but they do occur quite frequently around old walls and buildings where crumbling mortar adds lime to the soil.

The pill-bug's ability to roll up into a tight ball, with the tough skeletal plates on the outside, gives it several advantages. Evaporation from the lower surface is drastically reduced when the animals are rolled up, and this helps them to survive short periods of drought. The rolled-up animals are also much more difficult for shrews and other small predators to get at, because the balls are too large for them to get their jaws round. The repellent glands of the uropods are less well developed than in other woodlice because there is less need for them.

The pill-bug is quite likely to be confused with the pill millipede (Plate 8 and page 104) at first, but the two are quite easy to distinguish. The millipede is generally a much blacker and more glossy animal and, when it is active, it can be seen to have far more than the seven pairs of legs of the woodlouse. When the animals are rolled up, the small plates covering the pleon or abdomen of the woodlouse will identify it. The millipede has no such small plates. There is one more woodlouse that is fairly common in gardens, but it will not be seen unless you dig into an ant's nest. It is a little white woodlouse, under 4 mm long and known as *Platyarthrus hoffmannseggi*. The animal lives in the nests of several species of ants and probably feeds on scraps. Its repellent glands protect it from the ants.

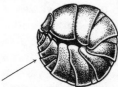

A rolled-up pillbug showing the small segments at the hind end

Transverse sections of the pillbug (*left*) and *Oniscus*, showing the very much higher 'dome' of the pillbug

CENTIPEDES

The centipedes and the millipedes (page 99) are nearly all long and slender animals with many body segments and numerous legs. They were once lumped together into a single group known as the Myriapoda. This name means 'many feet' and it was a very apt one for these animals. It is still quite a useful term, although we now realise that the centipedes and millipedes are not closely related and we put them into two separate classes. The centipedes belong to the class Chilopoda and the millipedes belong to the class Diplopoda. There are many differences in the habits of the two groups, but the most obvious difference is in the arrangement of the legs: centipedes have one pair of legs on each body segment, while the millipedes have two on nearly every segment.

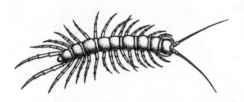

Lithobius forficatus, a very common centipede in the garden and in the shed

Centipedes are all relatively slender animals, several or many times longer than they are broad. The British species range from 5 mm to about 70 mm in length and their colours vary from pale yellow to deep brown. Their bodies are always distinctly flattened. Although, like all arthropods, the centipedes are covered with a tough outer coat, they lack a water-proof layer and they are confined to moist places where there is no danger of drying up. Many live in the soil and leaf litter, while those that hunt freely on the ground are strictly nocturnal and spend the day hiding under logs and stones where they can keep moist. Like the woodlice, they react strongly to touch and they do not normally come to rest unless both upper and lower surfaces are in contact with the surroundings. Such behaviour ensures that the animals end up under stones or bark, where they can be sure of moisture. The centipedes have not been studied nearly as fully as the woodlice have, but it is likely that the two groups react in much the same way to light and humidity (see page 87).

The centipede's head is quite flat and covered with a round or oval shield. It carries a pair of prominent antennae, which are the animal's major sense organs, enabling it to smell and feel its way around. Many of the species are quite blind, but some carry a number of simple eyes on the front of the head shield. Even so, with a few notable exceptions, their eyesight is very poor. The underside of the head bears a pair of stout jaws and two pairs of accessory jaws or maxillae, which hold the food while it is being chewed.

Curving round the sides of the head there is a stout pair of poison claws with which the centipede catches and kills its prey. The poison produced by these claws is very strong and some of the large tropical centipedes can give a man very painful and sometimes dangerous bites. Our British centipedes are quite harmless, however, because they are all small and rarely able to pierce the human skin.

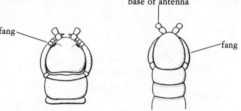

Heads of *Lithobius* (*left*) and *Cryptops*, showing the poison fangs, and the absence of eyes in *Cryptops*

The poison claws are attached to a narrow, collar-like segment just behind the head. This segment is followed by the leg-bearing trunk segments, of which there are between 15 and 101 in the British centipedes. The exact number varies from species to species and often within a species as well, but it is always an odd number.

The upper and lower surfaces of each trunk segment are covered by protective shields, the upper ones of which are called tergites. Many of our centipedes exhibit a striking alternation between long and short tergites along the body, an arrangement which, as we shall see on page 96, is concerned with maintaining the rigidity of the body when running at speed. Many of the trunk segments have a tiny pore or stigma on each side. These pores are the openings of the breathing system. They lead to minute tubes called tracheae, which spread through the body and carry air to all parts.

As a result of the number of trunk segments, centipedes do not have the hundred legs which their name suggests: there are between 30 and 202 legs in a fully equipped adult specimen. The centipede has quite a problem controlling so many legs when moving about, but the problem is eased in many species because each leg is slightly longer than the one in front. With this arrangement, the centipede is less likely to trip over its own feet. The last pair of legs is always rather different from the rest and usually trails behind the body. These legs are well supplied with sensory bristles and they act rather like an extra pair of antennae. This is a very useful feature for animals whose hind quarters are some way from the head and which often need to back out of crevices.

The centipedes are all basically predatory animals, although one of our garden species (page 95) does occasionally take to nibbling plant roots. They use their speed to run down and catch a variety of other creatures, including woodlice, harvestmen, spiders, mites, springtails, beetles, and many other insects. They also eat worms and slugs. This diet sheet illustrates very well the problem of trying to organise garden animals into 'friends' and 'foes'. By eating slugs and leatherjackets (page 163), the centipedes are certainly doing the gardener a good turn, but how much of this good do they undo by eating the useful spiders? Such questions are quite unanswerable when posed under the infinitely variable conditions of a garden, but it is probable that the animals do far more good than harm.

Their speed and their poison claws give centipedes an effective defence against most of their enemies and we know relatively little about the animals that eat them. Birds, including domestic chickens, eat centipedes when they can catch them, and so do shrews and toads. Ground beetles, spiders, and harvestmen probably take appreciable numbers of the small centipede species and their young stages, but the centipedes' most important enemies are other centipedes. Injured specimens are readily eaten in captivity, and their cannibalistic tendencies ensure that one rarely finds more than a single centipede under one log or stone.

We still know relatively little about their reproduction. The females lay their eggs throughout the spring and summer, but the eggs are rarely found. Those of many species are sticky and they are rolled in the soil as soon as they are laid, thus making them almost impossible to find. Other species actually look after their eggs and young for a while. The way in which the young centipedes grow up differs from species to species and more will be said about this later. Several moults or skin changes are necessary, however, and these give the centipede the chance to replace legs that have been lost. One often sees a centipede with one or more legs shorter than the rest. The short legs are being regenerated and they get larger at each moult. If a centipede loses a leg when it is very young, it can regenerate a perfect new one. If, however, the leg is lost later in life, there may not be enough moults remaining for its complete regeneration and the centipede will always have one short leg.

The centipedes are basically a tropical group and only 44 species have been recorded in the British Isles. Even then, not all these are natives of our islands. Several species have been brought in with plants and have succeeded in establishing themselves. These introduced species are usually markedly synanthropic (see page 17), in that they are rarely found away from human activity, but they are generally restricted to small areas around the original points of entry and relatively few gardeners are likely to find them. Only about a dozen species are at all common and widely distributed in gardens. They can be found at all times of the year, but they are most conspicuous during the spring and autumn. Numerous specimens will be unearthed while digging and preparing the soil for sowing in the spring, and again while tidying up in the autumn. During the winter and the drier parts of the summer the animals burrow down into the soil where they are less affected by the cold and drought.

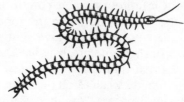

A typical geophilid (soil-dwelling) centipede

Centipedes in the soil

The centipedes most likely to be found living in the soil itself are the relatively long and slender geophilids – a name which literally means 'ground-lovers'. These centipedes have at least 37 pairs of rather short legs and they are often called wireworms, although this name really belongs to the larvae of the click beetles (page 189). The body tapers towards the front and the back, with the widest point being just in front of the middle. The segments in the rear half of the body are a little longer than those in the front half, so the rear legs are a little further apart than those in the front. The plates covering the top and bottom of each trunk segment apart from the first and last are each divided horizontally into two sections. A small amount of movement is possible between each section, and the overall effect is to double the number of joints in the body. The latter thus becomes amazingly flexible, and the animal can fold itself in two with no trouble at all. This flexibility has clearly been evolved in connection with the animals' life in the soil, where the ability to manoeuvre in a confined space is more important than speed. The antennae and the sensitive hind legs are relatively short, again in connection with a subterranean life, for long appendages would get in the way and would soon get broken. The animals have no eyes. Several of the species give out a phosphorescent fluid when they are disturbed. This fluid does not glow very brightly, but it is probably sufficient to frighten off some of the centipedes' enemies. Some of the species also emit a fairly strong almond smell when they are handled.

The geophilid centipedes usually lay their eggs in the spring. The female digs out a small chamber in the soil and lays thirty or forty eggs there. She then coils her body round them and remains there for several weeks, until the eggs have hatched and the young centipedes are able to fend for themselves. If she is removed, the eggs generally go mouldy and die. It is believed that the females lick their eggs from time to time, and in doing so, either remove mould spores or else spread a mould-killing substance over the eggs. There is an interesting parallel here with the earwigs (see page 116). The young centipedes hatch from the eggs with the full complement of legs, although these are little more than short stumps to start with. The babies remain in the brood chamber with their mother for about eight weeks, during which time they change their skins twice. The legs and the poison claws become more fully developed during this period as well, and the animals gradually disperse to fend for themselves. They have to change their skins several times and grow much longer before they are fully mature.

Haplophilus subterraneus (Plate 8) is one of the longest and broadest of our geophilid centipedes. Up to 70 mm long, it may be 1·5 mm wide at its broadest point. The body tapers markedly towards the head, but less so towards the hind end. There are between 77 and 83 pairs of legs (make sure that none has been lost if you are counting them) and the head is slightly broader than it is long. The body is yellow or pale brown, and the head is somewhat darker. *Haplophilus subterraneus* is especially common in grassland soils and in arable fields, but it frequently crops up in gardens throughout the country. Although one of the geophilid species, it is just as often found under stones. It is the only British centipede which is known to cause damage by nibbling plant roots.

Geophilus carpophilus (Plate 8) is a reddish brown centipede, generally about 40 mm long and up to 1·5 mm broad. It has between 45 and 55 pairs of legs. Although essentially a woodland animal, it is common in many gardens. It can be found in the soil and under stones, and it even invades damp sheds. The species is markedly phosphorescent and it is sometimes known as a glow-worm.

The commonest of the garden-dwelling geophilids is *Necrophloeophagus longicornis* (Plate 8). This is a bright yellow centipede with a distinctly darker head. It may reach 45 mm in length, but it is more usually about 30 mm long and 1 mm broad. There are

49 or 51 pairs of legs. The head is noticeably longer than it is broad, and the black poison claws (very easily seen with a lens) project slightly in front of it. The species is very widely distributed and occurs in all kinds of habitats as well as gardens.

Centipedes under stones

The shiny brown centipedes that scuttle away when we turn over stones and logs nearly all belong to the group known as lithobiids or 'stone-dwellers'. They are much broader than the geophilids, their legs are much longer, and they run much faster. The head shield is more or less circular and, unlike that of the geophilids, it bears a number of simple eyes. These are darkly pigmented and, when they are numerous, they form a dark patch on each side of the head. The antennae are relatively long, usually at least one third of the length of the body. The lithobiid centipedes are well adapted for life on the surface and, although they may burrow into the soil during the winter, they are much less common in the soil than the geophilids. Their stouter and less flexible bodies are far less suitable for tunnelling activities.

Adult lithobiids always have 15 trunk segments and 15 pairs of legs, and there is a marked alternation between long and short plates on the upper surface of the body. The plates on the underside are all more or less alike, and so the joints on the upper and lower surfaces are not all in line. This makes for rigidity. When the animals are moving at speed, the thrust and leverage generated by the long legs tend to throw the body into curves, but this tendency is resisted by the staggering of the upper and lower plates. A slight flexing is still noticeable when the centipede runs at speed, but without the staggering of the plates the body would become hopelessly contorted and the legs would become thoroughly tangled.

Female lithobiids can be distinguished from the males fairly easily by their much larger, claw-like gonopods protruding from the body between the hind legs. The female uses her gonopods to hold her eggs while she coats them with mucus and with particles of soil. She then abandons the eggs singly on the ground or among the leaves. Unlike the geophilid babies, young lithobiid centipedes do not have their full complement of legs when they hatch. The newly hatched animal has only seven pairs of legs and seven fully developed trunk segments. More legs and trunk segments appear at the hind end at each moult and after four moults the centipede is fully equipped with its 15 pairs of legs. It has to undergo several more skin changes, however, and the larger species may not reach maturity until they are about two years old. If they escape their enemies, they may live for five or six years.

All but one of our seventeen lithobiids belong to the genus *Lithobius*. They vary a good deal in size, but they are otherwise very much alike and some of them can be distinguished only with the aid of a microscope. Specialists do actually have to count the spines on the legs to separate some of the species. Only two species – *Lithobius forficatus* and *L. duboscqui* – are at all common in gardens.

Lithobius forficatus (Plate 8) is our most abundant and widely distributed species, making itself at home everywhere from woods and moorlands to the sea shore and the town garden. It is a rich chestnut brown animal, between 18 and 30 mm long and up to 4 mm broad. This is the species which usually runs away when you move stones or logs in the garden, and it may also invade the shed and the greenhouse.

Lithobius duboscqui (Plate 8) is a much smaller species, with a maximum length of about 10 mm and a width of about 1 mm. A little paler than *L. forficatus*, it is common in woodlands but especially numerous in the garden. I have found it abundant in compost heaps and it also turns up very frequently under flower pots set out on the path during the summer. The species is widely distributed in England and Wales, but it is said to occur only in and around gardens in Scotland.

One other centipede, not a lithobiid, is sometimes found under stones and logs in the garden. This is *Cryptops hortensis* (Plate 8), a member of the group known as scolopendromorphs. This group includes the largest and most dangerous centipedes, such as *Scolopendra gigantea* from tropical America. This species is a foot long and it eats mice and toads. But, compared with these giants, our little *Cryptops* is an insignificant fellow. Between 20 and 30 mm long and little more than 1 mm broad, it is a pale brown creature with 21 pairs of legs. It has no eyes, although it is a very active animal like the lithobiids. The antennae are no more than about a quarter the length of the body. A single shield or tergite covers the first trunk segment and the segment bearing the poison claws, so that both the claws and the front legs appear to spring from the same segment. The tergites of the trunk segments are all more or less the same size, although there is a very slight trace of the alternation which we have seen in the lithobiids. The legs are relatively short compared with those of the lithobiids and the animal is not quite so fast. The last pair of legs are much stouter than the others and they are probably used as offensive or defensive weapons. *Cryptops hortensis* is widely distributed, although not common, in woodlands, fields and gardens in England and Wales, but it seems to have a particular liking for gardens. The species is also found in the wild in Ireland, but Scottish records suggest that it lives there only in association with man.

As in the geophilid centipedes, the female *Cryptops* looks after her eggs and young for a while. The babies emerge from their eggs with their full quota of legs.

Centipedes in the house

Lithobius forficatus and some of its garden-dwelling relatives occasionally take up residence in the shed or greenhouse and they come into the house from time to time, but none of them can really be called a household animal. The only centipede that can claim that title in the British Isles is the remarkable *Scutigera coleoptrata*. But even this species only just makes it, for it is a native of southern Europe and, although well established in the Channel Isles, it

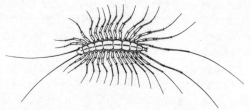

All legs – the amazingly fast *Scutigera*. The head is on the left

occurs only spasmodically in Britain. It probably comes in with tomatoes and other produce from time to time. The animal has 15 pairs of legs, but these are much longer and more slender than those of the lithobiids, especially at the tips. The last pair of legs are so long and slender that they look just like the antennae and, were it not for the prominent eyes, it would be difficult to decide which is the front end of the animal at first sight. *Scutigera* is a *very fast* runner and, although the stout and rounded body has fifteen trunk segments, there are only seven tergites or plates on the upper surface. This arrangement gives the body the necessary rigidity for its high speed running (see page 96). The animal uses its good eyesight and its speed to hunt insects. It frequents the walls of houses and sheds, where it darts after flies, crickets, and other insects with amazing speed. It is an extremely difficult animal to catch.

SYMPHYLANS

When turning the compost heap or working in the greenhouse, you may well come across a pale centipede-like creature about 7 mm long. Although it is often called the garden centipede, this little animal is not really a centipede at all. It belongs to another group of arthropods known as the symphylans. Examination with a lens will reveal that it has twelve pairs of rather short legs and a pair of fairly long antennae. Symphylans are very active creatures, but they are, nevertheless, basically vegetarians. They feed mainly on dead and decaying plant material, but readily attack young seedlings. There are several species in the British Isles, living in various kinds of soil and leaf litter, and the commonest is known as *Scutigerella immaculata*. Its liking for young seedlings makes it a serious greenhouse pest in many places, and it may be necessary to use insecticides or to fumigate the soil to control its numbers.

Although not closely related to the centipedes, the symphylans were once included with them in the old group known as the Myriapoda (see page 90). It is thought that the insects might have evolved long ago from some kind of symphylan ancestor.

Scutigerella

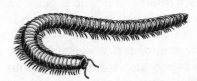

A typical millipede: the legs move in groups and waves appear to travel along the body from back to front

MILLIPEDES

The gardener will most often meet the millipedes in the compost heap or under stones and logs. He may also find them lurking under pots and seed trays in the greenhouse. Most of the millipedes that come to his attention will be the shiny black ones that coil up like watch-springs when disturbed, but there are several more groups of millipedes living in the garden. Some are harmless, but others may be up to no good at all.

With the notable exception of the pill millipedes (page 104), these animals are generally long and slender. The head is short and

99

rounded and it carries a pair of somewhat clubbed antennae. These are sharply angled in the middle and they are constantly tapping the ground for scent signals while the animal is moving about. There may or may not be a number of simple eyes, depending upon the habits of the animal: those species that live permanently under the ground generally have no eyes. There are some simple jaws on the underside of the head but, being vegetarians, the millipedes have no poison claws such as we have seen in the centipedes. Behind the head there is a fairly broad shield-like segment without any legs and this is followed by three segments with only one pair of legs on each. Most of the other body segments have two pairs of legs, but there are a few legless segments at the hind end. The hindermost region of the body is called the telson.

The body segments are basically cylindrical and each is covered by a tough cuticle which is usually impregnated with calcium. The animals are therefore more common in lime-rich soils. The cuticle of each segment is composed of a markedly domed upper shield or tergite, together with two smaller side plates and a sternite on the lower surface. These four plates are often fused together to make a rigid cylinder. The cylindrical nature of each segment is obscured in the flat-backed millipedes (page 104), for here the upper regions of each tergite are drawn out sideways to form prominent 'wings'. Each millipede tergite slightly overlaps the one behind it, and there is a simple ball and socket joint between neighbouring rings. These features give the body considerable flexibility and allow many of the millipedes to coil up. The number of body segments varies between and within the various species, but the British species rarely have more than about 60 segments.

Each sternite carries two pairs of tiny breathing pores which open into the animal's breathing tubes or tracheae. Many millipedes also possess stink glands which open on to the lower surfaces of most of the body segments. The stink glands release pungent fluids containing substances such as chlorine, iodine, and hydrogen cyanide. These fluids repel many of the millipedes' enemies, and they may also exert a disinfectant action to keep the body free from bacteria and fungi. The secretions of our native millipedes are not harmful, but some of the large tropical species are very unpleasant. Some of them actually fire out fluids which can burn the skin and cause blindness if they get into the eyes. Some small millipedes, not normally found in the garden, are clothed with irritating hairs instead of having poison glands.

Millipedes are very much ground-living animals, finding their food in the soil and among the leaf litter, although *Tachypodoiulus niger* (page 103) and a few other species will climb trees to search for food in wet weather. They are usually active at night, when the air is cooler and more humid. Like the other animals that we have looked at in this chapter, they normally come to rest only in moist places. Dry weather causes them to move down through the soil until they reach moister levels. Although each leg is rather small and delicate, the combined thrust of perhaps more than 100 pairs is remarkably powerful and the millipedes have no difficulty in forcing their way through the soil.

Their rather weak jaws indicate that the millipedes feed mainly on soft or decaying tissues. They usually feed on fungi and dead leaves, but they will consume dead animals as well. They are attracted to the decaying matter and they are especially numerous in garden compost heaps and in heavily manured soils. Some of them play a useful role in helping to speed up the break-down of decaying material and the return of minerals to the soil. Several species can be found in ants' nests, where they probably assist the ants by consuming scraps of food and other debris. Some millipedes, notably the spotted snake millipede (page 104), are serious garden pests because they attack the roots and other parts of crops. Such attacks are most frequent during periods of drought, and it is thought that the millipedes attack the crops primarily for the moisture they contain. When once the plants have been damaged, however, the seepage of sap and the inevitable decay of the damaged tissues keep the millipedes in attendance. Potatoes are often found with numerous millipedes inside them, but it is most unlikely that the millipedes attack sound potatoes. They probably invade only those tubers whose skins have been damaged by other pests or by fungal infection.

Although most millipede species secrete repellent fluids, they are not entirely free from predators. They are eaten by certain spiders, by frogs and toads, and by birds and small mammals. Toads and birds seem to be the major enemies, and the starling seems to be particularly fond of millipedes. Investigations in the United States showed that millipedes formed more than 50 per cent of these birds' food during April, although the proportion was much lower later in the year. The millipedes' repellent fluids are obviously not that unpleasant as far as the starlings are concerned. The ability to coil the body up into a tight spiral, or even a complete sphere, gives the animals further protection against some of their smaller enemies because the coiled-up animals are often too large for the predators' jaws. Some of the tropical pill millipedes can roll into balls the size of golf balls.

Our millipedes lay their eggs throughout the summer and, although some species abandon their eggs naked in the soil, the majority give them some form of protection. This protection may be simply a coating of saliva or some other glandular secretion which picks up soil particles and thus camouflages the eggs. Some millipedes coat their eggs with excrement before abandoning them, while many others actually make nests for their eggs. These nests may be constructed in hollows in the soil, under stones or bark, or in rolled-up dead leaves. The female's own excrement is nearly always used in the construction of the nest, moistened with saliva or other fluids so that it can be worked like mortar. Some millipedes exude silken threads which are used in nest building. The female may abandon her nest when once she has laid her eggs and covered them over, but some species, notably among the flat-backed millipedes, remain with their nests for several days. You may well find one of these females coiled around her nest if you lift up damp logs during the summer.

The young millipedes emerge from their eggs in a few weeks, but they do not look much like the adults. They are short, grub-like creatures with only three pairs of legs and only a few body segments. They have to undergo several moults or skin changes before they reach maturity, and they add a number of segments and several pairs of legs at each moult. Moulting is a rather dangerous business for all the arthropods because it leaves the animals in a soft and helpless state for a while, but many young millipedes protect themselves at such times by building little nests, rather like those in which the eggs are laid, and remaining there until the moult is completed. Millipedes may live for anything between a few months and a few years, according to the species. The adults of some species, particularly those living in the cooler regions, exhibit an interesting alternation of fertile and non-fertile stages. The reproductive organs are functional when the animals first mature, but the animals moult again after the breeding season and the reproductive organs become inactive. They remain inactive during the winter, but the animals then moult again and revert to the sexually active stage. Some millipedes have been known to pass through at least four sexually active stages.

Millipedes in the garden

Of the 8,000 or so species of millipedes known to science, less than 50 live in the British Isles, and only about a quarter of these are regularly found in gardens. They belong to several different groups and occupy several different situations or micro-habitats within the garden.

More than half of the British millipedes belong to a group known as the Iuliforma. These animals are much more cylindrical than the other millipedes and they have more than 30 segments. They include the most familiar of the millipedes – the shiny black species up to 50 mm long, which we find under logs and stones and which coil up like springs when they are disturbed. These animals are all basically soil-dwellers, as one might guess from their tough, cylindrical bodies, but several of the species can be found under the bark of fallen trees and branches and some wander freely on the ground and the vegetation at night. Many of the species make earthen moulting chambers and most of them also make nests for their eggs. One of the commonest is *Cylindroiulus londinensis,* a shiny black millipede up to 50 mm long and 4 mm in diameter. The diameter is more or less constant all the way along the body. This helps to distinguish the species from the very similar *Tachypodoiulus niger* (Plate 8), which tapers slightly towards the ends. The two species can also be separated by using a lens to look at the hind end of the body. The telson of *T. niger* has a little pointed 'tail' sticking out at the back, whereas that of *C. londinensis* is quite smooth and rounded or else produced into a blunt process. *Tachypodoiulus niger* is especially common on chalky and limestone soils and it is very active. It is fond of fruit and often climbs raspberry canes and bramble bushes to nibble the succulent fruits. Several other smaller, but otherwise very similar millipedes may be found in the garden from time to time, but their identification is a matter for the specialist.

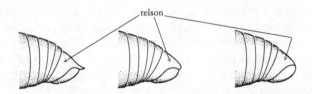

Hind ends of the black millipedes *Tachypodoiulus niger (left)* and two forms of *Cylindroiulus londinensis,* showing the telson which is a useful aid to identification

The length:diameter ratio of the millipedes described above is of the order of 10:1, but there is another group of iuliform millipedes with a length:diameter ratio of about 20:1. The commonest member of this group is the infamous **spotted snake millipede** (*Blaniulus guttulatus*), a creamy white or pale yellow creature whose repellent glands show up as red spots along the sides of the body (Plate 8). The animal is generally about 15 mm long when fully grown, but it is no more than about 0·7 mm in diameter. Its body has about 60 segments. Although it is less often seen than the black millipedes already mentioned, because of its more strictly subterranean habits, the spotted snake millipede is the commonest of all the species in cultivated soils. It causes severe damage to potatoes, sugar beet, cereals, and other crops but, as already pointed out, it needs some other organism to make an initial wound so that it can get in. The spotted snake millipede is more susceptible to drought than some of the other species and it is most frequently found on the heavier soils, where there is less risk of desiccation. Damage by this species usually occurs in distinct outbreaks which are linked to soil fertility and climatic conditions. Heavily manured ground and a damp spring give the animals just the conditions they like for fast breeding, but if there is then a long dry spell the heavy millipede population may turn its attention to crop roots in its search for moisture.

Our common **pill millipede** (*Glomeris marginata*) looks much more like a woodlouse than a millipede at first sight (Plate 8), but it is easily distinguished from the woodlice by having 17–19 pairs of legs. Woodlice have only seven pairs. In addition, the dorsal plates of the pill millipede are a much deeper and shinier black than those of the pill woodlouse and there are no small plates at the hind end. These last two features make it easy to distinguish the pill millipedes from the pill woodlice even when the animals are rolled up. *Glomeris marginata* is up to 20 mm long and 8 mm wide and it has twelve apparent plates along the back. Whereas the iuliform millipedes are distinctly cylindrical, the pill millipedes are more or less semi-circular in cross-section. The sternite and the side plates of each segment are quite small and not fused to the strongly arched tergite. It is this arrangement that allows the animal to roll up into such a tight ball. Pill millipedes live mainly in leaf litter and they play an important part in breaking this material down in some places. In the garden, they are most likely to be found in the hedge bottom or among the debris at the bottom of an old wall, especially where loose mortar has fallen and increased the lime content of the soil. Like the pill woodlice, the pill millipede is rather more tolerant of dry conditions than its relatives. *Glomeris* makes no nest for its eggs, but each egg is enclosed in a little capsule of excrement.

The flat-backed millipedes, such as *Polydesmus angustus* (Plate 8), could be mistaken for centipedes at first because of their relatively long legs and their well separated body segments, but closer examination will reveal two pairs of legs on most of the body segments. These animals have fewer pairs of legs than most other millipede groups, but the greater length of the legs counteracts this and makes up for any lack of thrust. The flattened dorsal surface is formed by wing-like extentions of the tergites and it is usually elaborately sculptured. Flat-backed millipedes generally live in leaf litter or under the bark of fallen trees. In the garden, they are most often seen in and around the compost heap. The females all lay their eggs in tent-like nests made of soil and excrement, and then they stand guard over them for several days.

Polydesmus angustus is the most frequently seen of our flat-backed millipedes. Up to 25 mm long and about 4 mm broad, it is a dark brown animal with heavy mottling and sculpturing on the back. Although normally feeding on dead leaves and other rotting material, it is fond of strawberries and can sometimes be found nestling in little chambers nibbled out of the ripe fruits. The species is also said to like nibbling lupin roots.

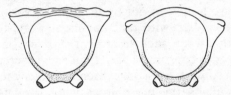

Cross sections of *Polydesmus* (*left*) and *Oxidus*, showing how the flat back is produced by 'wings' extending from the basically cylindrical body

Oxidus gracilis (Plate 8) is another member of the flat-backed group, although its upper surface is slightly domed. It is a tropical species, but it has become firmly established in greenhouses all over the country. Up to 23 mm long and 2·5 mm wide, it has a chestnut to black back and yellowish keels or 'wings' to each segment.

The compost heap and other piles of garden debris may harbour yet another group of millipedes, typified by a little creature called *Microchordeuma scutellare*. This is a pale yellow millipede, only about 7 mm long but with 28 segments. The sides of the body are somewhat compressed and the dorsal surface carries a few bristles. This species is most active in the cooler months of the year and is more common in the northern parts of our islands.

CHAPTER 6

The Insect Hordes

THE insects make up the largest of all the groups of arthropods. In fact, there are more kinds of insects than there are of all the other animals put together. It is generally agreed that there are getting on for a million different kinds of insects in the world, and there are more than 20,000 in the British Isles. Very few insects live in the sea, but they live almost everywhere else, from the seashore to the driest desert and the coldest mountain. Huge numbers make their homes in our gardens and, whether it be June or January, we rarely go into the garden without seeing some of them.

There can be few, if any, plant or animal materials in the homestead that are not attacked and eaten by some kind of insect. Leaves are nibbled by caterpillars and various beetles and pierced by sap-sucking bugs; nectar is sipped by butterflies and many other insects; fruits are hollowed out by maggots of various kinds; and tree trunks are riddled with the tunnels of wood-feeding grubs. Animals do not escape such treatment, for ladybirds and other carnivorous beetles consume a variety of smaller creatures and we ourselves often come in from the garden vigorously scratching arms and legs and cursing the mosquitoes who dared to sample our blood. And it is not only living food that is taken by the insects: fence-posts, furniture, flour, clothes, and carpets may all be destroyed by them. Dung and other decaying materials are also readily consumed by flies and various other insects.

The ability to exist on such a wide range of materials has obviously contributed to the abundance of insects, although each species has a fairly restricted range of foods. Each type of diet requires a particular type of feeding apparatus to deal with it and, during their long existence, the insects have evolved a wide range of mouth-parts, beautifully adapted to deal with all the various kinds of food. There are the tough, biting jaws of the crickets and beetles, adapted for chewing various kinds of solid food; the tubular 'tongues' of the butterflies which act like drinking straws to suck nectar from the flowers; the sharp beaks of the bugs and the blood-sucking flies which pierce the skins of plants or animals and suck out the juices; and the sponge-like 'mops' of the house-flies and bluebottles which soak up liquid food of various kinds.

Most adult insects are fairly easy to recognise as such because most of them have wings. No other invertebrate animal has wings. There are, however, numerous wingless insects in our gardens, including most of the ants (page 179) and many of the aphids (page 119). But these still exhibit the typical insect features of three pairs of legs, one pair of feelers or antennae, and a body which is fairly clearly divided into three regions – head, thorax, and abdomen. You should not, therefore, have any difficulty in deciding whether a given creature is an adult insect or not. It is a different story, however, when we come to look at the young insects. None of them has fully developed wings and, although some have six legs and bear close resemblances to the adults, many of them are entirely different. Some have many more than six legs, and some have none at all, thus losing all similarity with the adult insects. I can well remember the amazed looks on my children's faces when they first discovered that a wriggling maggot really does turn into a bluebottle and that hairy caterpillars really do turn into moths. There is no simple way to recognise all the many forms of young insects, but the key on page 110, together with the illustrations on the following pages, should help you identify many of those that you find in your garden.

Having pointed out the great differences between many adult insects and their young stages, it is worth digressing for a short while to follow the processes by which the youngsters change into adults. Nearly all insects begin their lives as eggs, although the aphids and some other insects may bring forth active young. The newly hatched youngsters then follow one of two paths of development. In one group of insects, which includes the earwigs (page 116), the bush crickets (page 114), and the bugs (page 119), the young insects look quite like the adults except that they are much smaller and have no wings. Young insects of this kind are called nymphs and they generally eat the same kinds of food as the adults. Like all arthropods, they have to change their skins periodically (see page 86), and at each change or moult they get a little bit more like the adult. Wing buds appear after the first or second moult and increase in size at each subsequent moult until they are fully formed. Some insects undergo twenty or thirty skin changes, but the majority of species undergo between three and six moults.

This kind of development, in which the young insects gradually assume the adult form is known as a partial or incomplete metamorphosis.

Bees, beetles, butterflies, and flies, together with several other groups of insects, all follow the second path of development, which is known as complete metamorphosis. The young insects are all quite unlike the adults and they are known as larvae. They very often feed on entirely different materials from the adults. Caterpillars, for example, generally feed on leaves, while the adult butterflies sip nectar from the flowers. There is no gradual change to the adult form as the larva grows: each moult reveals simply a larger larva, and not until the larva is fully grown does it embark on the transformation. The insect's body has to be completely re-built, and this re-building takes place inside the pupa or chrysalis. The fully-grown larva seeks out a suitable place in which to pupate or turn into a pupa and it may spin a silken cocoon around itself for extra protection. It then sheds its skin again and reveals the pupa. The most commonly found pupae in the garden are those of the cabbage white butterflies, which are attached to fences and to the walls of sheds and houses. Each is attached by a silken pad and a girdle which holds it vertically against the support. Pupae of the small tortoiseshell butterfly and the peacock may be found hanging down from window sills or from the leaves of stinging nettles (Plate 14), while the shiny, bullet-shaped pupae of several moths are frequently dug up from the soil. The outlines of the legs and wings of the adult insects are already visible in these pupae, but it may be some time before the insects are ready to emerge. Most moths spend the whole winter in the pupal state. When the adult insect is ready to emerge, the pupal skin splits and the insect drags itself out. Its wings are soft and crumpled at first, but they expand and harden fairly quickly and the insect is able to fly away.

Most other animals possess breathing organs in one part of the body and employ a transport system – the blood stream – to carry the oxygen from these breathing organs to all other parts of the body. The insects, however, possess a system of minute breathing tubes called tracheae. These tubes ramify through the body and open to the air through little pores on the sides of the body. Air is thus conveyed directly to all parts of the body. The breathing pores, called spiracles, are not usually very obvious, but they are clearly visible on the sides of some caterpillars.

None of our insects can claim to be a large animal. The largest that you are likely to find in the garden are the stag beetle (Plate 18) and the privet hawkmoth (page 141). Much larger insects occur in the tropics, but even then they are not particularly bulky. Their bodies are rarely more than about 30 mm thick. At the other end of the scale, there are some extremely small insects. Many are well under a millimetre long and some of them spend their early lives as parasites inside the eggs of other insects. Leaf miners are small insects which live in the spaces between the upper and lower surfaces of leaves. Pale blotches and sinuous streaks on the leaves show where these insects have been feeding on the nutritious inner tissues. Most of the leaf miners are the larvae of beetles, moths, or flies. They attack many kinds of plants, but their mines are especially noticeable on lilac, holly, and blackberry leaves.

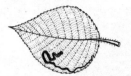 

Two types of leaf mine: *left*, serpentine mine on bramble; *right*, blotch mine on lilac

Identifying insects

Entomologists split the insects up into about 30 major groups called orders, based mainly on the anatomical features of the adults. The wings are often markedly different between the various orders and many of the order names actually describe the appearance of the wings. The butterflies and moths for example, belong to the order Lepidoptera, a name which means 'scale wings' and which refers to the minute scales which cover the wings of these insects.

All but five of the orders can be found in the British Isles and all of our native orders *can* be found in the garden, but the average gardener is not likely to find all of them. Some groups, such as the dragonflies and mayflies, spend their early lives in water and are not likely to be found in gardens far from a pond or stream. Others, such as the lice, live as parasites on other animals and can be found only by searching suitable hosts. The gardener will, nevertheless, come across most of the insect orders at one time or another, although they may not all be resident in the garden. The power of flight allows many insects to visit gardens without actually living there. Most of the bees that visit our flowers and the wasps that arrive to sample the fruit in the summer probably live outside the garden, but they are sufficiently regular visitors to qualify as garden insects. Many of the butterflies qualify on the same basis, but we cannot really accept as a garden creature the grasshopper that occasionally hops in through the fence or the dragonfly that makes a lightning tour of the garden to snap up a few flies before zooming back to the stream.

The following key has been designed to help you to identify the insects which *regularly* occur in the garden and around the house. Use the key in the way explained on page 18, selecting the most appropriate description from each couplet, and you will eventually arrive at the group to which your insect belongs. Young stages are included in the key as well as adult insects.

Key for the Identification of Insects likely to be found in the Garden

Used in the same way as the key on page 18, this key will allow most garden insects to be put into their correct group or order. It cannot be used with certainty when dealing with insects from other habitats. Aquatic insects are not included in the key.

1 Insects with wings   2
  Insects wingless or with vestigial wings*   20

2 Insects with a single pair of membranous wings   Flies (p. 153)
  Insects with two pairs of wings or, if just one pair, these are hard and horny   3

3 All wings membranous   4
  Front wings horny or leathery   15

4 Tiny insects, usually black, with minute feathery wings: often found in flowers   Thrips (p. 128)
  Insects not like this   5

5 Small moth-like insects with powdery, white wings (no more than 5mm across wings)   Whiteflies (p. 124)
  Insects not like this   6

6 Head extending downwards into an orange-coloured beak: abdomen often turned up like a scorpion   Scorpionflies (p. 131)
  No such beak   7

7 Wings covered with dust-like scales: usually a coiled 'tongue' under the head   Butterflies & Moths (p. 132)
  Wings transparent, although they may be hairy   8

8 Very small insects with two 'horns' at hind end and with a needle-like beak under the head   Aphids (p. 119)
  Insects not like this   9

* Many bugs and beetles appear wingless at first because their front wings form tough covers over the body and hind wings. These are treated as winged insects.

9 Slender-bodied insects with lots
of cross veins forming a delicate
network on the wings. Body and
wings green or brown *[handwritten: long-bodied was]* Lacewing flies (p. 130)
Wings with few cross veins **10**
[handwritten: antennae 0 short, dragonflies / insects with a … head]

10 Tiny insects with wings held
roofwise over the body at rest Barklice (p. 128)
Usually larger insects, with wings
held flat over body at rest:
often buzzing in flight *[handwritten: Hymenoptera]* **11**

11 Insects with a distinct 'waist' **12**
Insects without a 'waist' Sawflies (p. 183)

12 Wings flimsy: insects with a definite lobe on the waist:
usually seen emerging from soil in summer Ants (p. 179)
No lobe on waist: wings usually sturdier **13**

13 Slender insects with a dark mark (stigma) near tip of
front wing: females often with spear-like projection
from hind end: antennae with at least 16 segments
Ichneumon flies (p. 183)
Stouter insects frequently without obvious stigma:
antennae with less than 16 segments **14**

14 Insects often very hairy, especially on abdomen: hind
leg often noticeably broad Bees (p. 166)
Insects not very hairy on abdomen: black or black and
yellow bodies Wasps (p. 174)

15 Hind legs long and used for
jumping Crickets and
Bush Crickets (p. 114–6)

Insects not like this **16**

16 Slender needle-like beak under head *[handwritten: Hemiptera]* **17**
No such beak **18**

17 Jumping insects with wings
held roofwise over body at
rest: very short, bristle-like
antennae ← beak
Leafhoppers and Froghoppers
(including psyllids) (p. 125–6)
Wings held flat over body at
rest and usually overlapping Bugs (p. 127)

111

18 Front wings overlapping at rest
   and with obvious veins: long,
   spiky legs: usually indoors
                                      Cockroaches (p. 118)
   Front wings meet in mid-line:
   often shiny and without
   obvious veins   19

19 Body ending in two stout pincers
   or prongs: front wings short and
   covering only part of body   Earwigs (p. 116)
   No pincers at end of body: wings
   usually, but not always cover
   abdomen   Beetles (p. 186)

20 Jumping insects with long back legs   21
   Insects not like this   22

21 Very small brown insects, usually
   associated with domestic animals
   or with birds' nests   Fleas (p. 164)
   Larger insects with long
   antennae: on plants   Bushcrickets (p. 114)

22 Needle-like beak under the head   23
   No such beak   24

23 Very small insects with pear-
   shaped bodies and two 'horns'
   at the hind end   Aphids (p. 119)
   No such 'horns': body more
   flattened and often with small
   wing flaps (developing wings)   Bugs (p. 127)

24 Vestigial wings on thorax   25
   No trace of wings   26

25 Flat, greasy insects with long, spiky legs: usually indoors   Cockroaches (p. 118)
   Insects less flattened: body covered with dust-like scales
                             Moths (some females) (p. 150)

26 Carrot-shaped body with slender 'tails' at hind end   27
   Body not like this   28

27 Insects with two 'tails': in soil
   or compost   Two-pronged
                              bristle-tails (p. 114)
   Insects with three 'tails': usually
   indoors   Three-pronged
                              bristle-tails (p. 113)

28 Tiny jumping insects in soil and
   compost   Springtails (p. 114)
   Crawling, often worm-shaped
   insects, with or without legs   29

29 Insects legless   Fly larvae (p. 153)†
   Insects with legs   30

30 Insects with three pairs of legs only   31
   Insects with three pairs of true legs at the front end
   and a number of stumpy legs further back   32

31 Spiky, shuttle-shaped insects,
   with sickle-shaped jaws:
   often covered with
   debris on leaves   Lacewing fly larvae (p. 130)
   Insects of various shapes, often
   bristly, but without
   sickle-shaped jaws   Beetle larvae (p. 187)

32 Insects with no more than 5   Caterpillars
   pairs of stumpy legs at the   of butterflies
   hind end   and moths (p. 133)
   Insects with more than 5 pairs
   of stumpy legs on hind   Larvae of
   part of body   sawflies (p. 184)

† The larvae or grubs of bees, wasps, and ants are legless, but these are usually found in nests and their nature will be clear. Weevil grubs are also legless, but these are normally enclosed in plants and not often seen.

THE SILVERFISH AND ITS ALLIES

Most people are familiar with the slippery little silverfish, a wingless insect that frequently makes its home in the kitchen cupboard. The gardener is also likely to find it in undisturbed corners of the garden shed, especially if there are old cartons or papers stacked away there. The animal feeds on starchy materials, including the glue of cartons, and on scraps of paper. It will also nibble away at stored bulbs if it gets the chance. The silverfish, which gets its name from its coating of silvery scales, belongs to a very primitive group of insects called bristletails. These insects never have any sign of wings, and it is believed that they have never had any throughout their long history.

The compost heap is the home of several more primitive insects

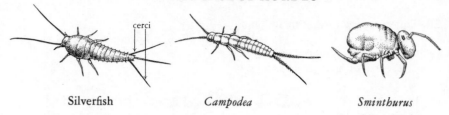

Silverfish   *Campodea*   *Sminthurus*

and you will undoubtedly see some of these while turning the heap or spreading the compost on the garden. A small white creature looking rather like an under-nourished silverfish may catch your eye from time to time. This will be *Campodea*. Although superficially like a silverfish, it is not closely related and closer inspection will show that it has only two 'tails' instead of three. *Campodea* feeds on decaying material.

The most abundant of the primitive, wingless insects are the springtails. Large numbers of these little creatures can be seen jumping about when any pile of reasonably damp debris is disturbed. They have cylindrical or globular bodies, rarely more than about 5 mm long, and they are generally brown or grey. Some are yellowish with darker markings. The springtails can scuttle about among the leaf litter and other debris, but they usually jump when they are disturbed. They are able to do this because they possess a little 'spring' under the hind end of the body. It looks rather like a minute tuning fork, hinged to the body at the back and clipped up under the body when not in use. When the animal is disturbed, however, the spring is released and it flicks sharply down on to the ground, thus shooting the animal up into the air.

Springtails feed mainly on dead and decaying vegetation, together with the minute algae and fungi that live in the soil. A few species attack crop plants and *Sminthurus viridis*, commonly known as the lucerne flea, sometimes causes severe damage to clovers and other pasture plants. Together with some other springtails, it may attack peas. It nibbles the stems and leaves, but rarely does much damage to the pea crop.

BUSHCRICKETS

Although the grasshoppers are not garden insects, because they prefer extensive stretches of fairly long grass, some of the closely related bushcrickets are regular inhabitants of gardens in the southern parts of England. Bushcrickets have the same general body shape as grasshoppers, but they are readily distinguished because their antennae are very thin and at least as long as the body. A

114

female bushcricket can also be distinguished by her blade-like ovipositor, which sticks out from the hind end and which she uses to lay her eggs in the soil or in bark crevices and similar places. Although endowed with long back legs like the grasshoppers, the bushcrickets do not jump so readily. Most of them merely crawl about on the bushes and other plants among which they live. Some can fly fairly well, but several of our species have no wings. Bushcrickets are mainly carnivorous creatures, eating aphids and other small insects. They may nibble a few leaves and flower buds, but they certainly do no harm. Young bushcrickets can be found from April onwards, but the adults are rarely seen before July.

People with gardens near the south coast will probably have heard the great green bushcricket even if they have not seen it. The male of this species has a very loud and strident 'song', which sounds rather like a knife-grinding machine and which goes on for hours during the late summer evenings. The insect produces this sound, which is designed to attract the female, by raising his wings slightly and rubbing their bases together. Although he advertises his presence in this way, he is still very hard to find as he sits in the hedge or the herbaceous border. He is bright green, with a brown stripe along the back, and he is very well camouflaged, but when you do find him you will wonder how you ever missed him in the first place, for he is nearly 50 mm long – one of our largest insects. The female is less often seen because she hides herself away even more and she does not 'sing'.

At apple-picking time I always manage to disturb a number of **oak bushcrickets** (Plate 9), beautiful pale green creatures which, despite their name, frequent a wide variety of trees in late summer and autumn. They are rarely about before nightfall and they usually spend the daylight hours hiding under leaves. It is from these hideouts that I flush them while apple-picking and they frequently hop on to my clothes while I am up in the trees. The oak bushcricket is probably the most commonly seen of our bushcrickets because it flies quite well and it is attracted to lighted windows. Large numbers can also be found around street lights in suburban streets lined with lime trees. The species does not 'sing', but the males make a quiet drumming sound by tapping one hind foot on whatever surface they are resting on.

The **speckled bushcricket** (Plate 9) is another common species, but it is rarely seen because its speckled green body blends in so well with the shrubs on which it lives. The male has a pair of small brown wings perching saddle-like on its back, but the female is almost wingless. The male produces a very faint chirp, but few people ever hear it. Speckled bushcrickets inhabit nettle beds, bramble thickets, and hedgerows. In the garden, they can be found in the shrubbery and among the soft fruit bushes, as well as in the herbaceous border. They are also quite common among the ivy leaves covering old walls. The **dark bushcricket** (Plate 9) can also be found in similar situations, especially in country districts where it spills over from the hedgerows. The male is dark brown, with a pair of small wings, while the female is virtually wingless and tends to be lighter in colour. Both sexes like to sun themselves on the leaves of brambles and other plants. The males utter short and fairly shrill chirps at any time of day, but they are at their noisiest during the evening.

CRICKETS

The only common cricket in this country is the introduced house cricket (Plate 9), which arrived here about 400 years ago from North Africa or south west Asia. It is now well established in most parts of these islands, although it is a distinctly synanthropic species (see page 17), hardly ever found away from human habitation. It is commonly found on rubbish dumps, where the warmth from the fermenting refuse provides it with suitable conditions all the year round, but it otherwise lives under cover – in warehouses, factories, and other premises where there is constant warmth. The gardener is most likely to find the house cricket in the conservatory or greenhouse, or possibly in a lean-to shed. The insect feeds on anything animal or vegetable and it will be quite happy to chew up old papers or sacks in the corner before turning its attention to the stored apples or potatoes. House crickets are most active at night, and the first indication of their presence will probably be the shrill and quite musical chirp of the male. Both sexes can fly well.

EARWIGS

Most gardeners recognise the earwig when they see it, but very few ever stop to give a second look to this fascinating and much maligned little creature. There are several species in this country, but the only one which is commonly noticed is the **common earwig** (Plate 9). The pincers of the male are much more strongly curved than those of the female, but the sexes are otherwise very much alike. Earwigs use their pincers mainly for defence, as you will find out if you press a fingertip gently on to the front end of one of these insects: the tail end is arched forward over the body and the

116

The common earwig, showing the strongly curved forceps of the male

pincers start to snap, although they are not strong enough to hurt your finger.

The common earwig rarely flies but, to many people's surprise, it does have wings. The front wings are short, square, and leathery and they cover only a small part of the insect's upper surface. Elaborately folded underneath them and poking out slightly from the hind edge are the very thin, more or less semi-circular hind wings which keep the insect aloft when it does decide to fly. So much folding is necessary to get these wings stowed away that it has even been suggested that the earwig rarely flies because it is too much bother to get its wings out and put them away again. Some earwig species do fly quite regularly, but many others have dispensed with their wings altogether.

The earwigs are omnivorous creatures and they eat almost anything they find, whether it be animal or vegetable, living or dead. They sometimes chew the petals of flowers – always the best ones, of course – and incur the wrath of the dahlia or chrysanthemum grower, but they are generally quite harmless creatures. They are active mainly at night and they like to spend the daytime in narrow nooks and crevices where they can feel both upper and lower surfaces in contact with something. It is this need for contact more than a liking for petals that causes them to end up in the florets of the dahlias and chrysanthemums. Fussy gardeners trap them in inverted flower pots lightly stuffed with straw or crumpled newspaper. These traps provide ideal resting sites for the insects. Earwigs can also be found with great regularity nestling in the hollows around the stalks of ripening apples, especially when two or three apples are growing in a bunch, and you can always be sure of finding some hiding in the ripe seed capsules of columbines. A cloth draped over an apple branch in my garden some years ago and then forgotten was found to be sheltering numerous earwigs when it was eventually moved. Being fond of these little insects, I left the cloth on the branch and it remained home for them and their offspring for several years, both summer and winter, until it finally disintegrated.

Earwigs live for at least eighteen months and probably considerably longer in many instances, passing the winter in the soil or in some other sheltered place in or out of doors – the folded cloth on my apple tree obviously gave sufficient protection. The adults pair up in late summer and the female lays her eggs when she goes into her winter retreat, often accompanied by the male and frequently by several other earwigs as well. She is a very good mother compared with most insects and she looks after her eggs very carefully. She licks them from time to time, an action which is thought to keep them free of mould or bacterial infection (see also page 95), and she will also collect them up into a group again if they should be scattered – usually by an inquisitive biologist! She also licks the youngsters when they hatch out and she feeds them for the first week or two. Mother and offspring venture outside in the spring, and they stay together for most of the summer until the young ones are fully grown. The youngsters are paler than the adults and their pincers are much more slender.

The **small earwig** (Plate 9) is no more than about 7 mm long and it is much paler than the common earwig. Although both are widely distributed and common, the small earwig is much less frequently seen. It is most likely to be seen around the compost heap, although it flies readily and sometimes comes into houses. The only other native earwigs in this country are *Apterygida albipennis* (Plate 9) and *Forficula lesnei,* both of which seem to be confined to the southern half of England. They inhabit the same sort of places as the common earwig. *Apterygida* can easily be distinguished by its pincers and by the complete lack of hind wings. *Forficula lesnei* is more like the common earwig, but it is no more than about 8 mm long and its hind wings do not project from below the front ones.

COCKROACHES

Although we have three small native species in this country, the cockroaches that one normally hears about are alien species accidentally imported from warmer countries. Several of these foreign species have become established in Britain, although they are normally found only indoors – in buildings such as warehouses and large kitchens where there is constant warmth and abundant food. Virtually any plant or animal material is food for a cockroach, and the insects destroy large amounts of human food. What they don't actually eat they usually contaminate with their oily secretions and foul odours. Colonies occasionally develop on rubbish dumps and thrive there in the same way as the house cricket (page 116).

The only cockroaches that normally invade domestic premises

are the **common cockroach** (Plate 9) and the **German cockroach,** and the gardener may occasionally find these in his shed or greenhouse. The common cockroach, also known as the black beetle, probably arrived here from North Africa or southern Asia during the 16th century and it is now found in nearly every county of Britain. It averages about 22 mm in length and it is very dark brown in colour, the male having a distinct reddish tinge. The wings of the male are fairly short, leaving the tip of the body exposed, while those of the female are just tiny flaps. Neither sex can fly but, like all cockroaches, they have long, spiky legs and can run very rapidly. They are active mainly at night. The eggs, like those of all cockroaches, are laid in purse-like cases called oothecae and the females carry these cases around protruding from their abdomens for a few days before depositing them in the soil or on the ground.

The German cockroach, also known as the steam fly or shiner, probably came from North Africa. It is a pale brown insect about 12 mm long and it is fully winged, although it does not fly a great deal. The female carries her egg purse right up until the time when the eggs are due to hatch.

APHIDS AND OTHER BUGS

The aphids and their relatives belong to a very large group of insects known as the bugs. Their mouths are all in the form of minute hypodermic needles, with which they pierce plants and other animals and suck up their juices. Many of them are serious pests on the farm and in the garden. Entomologists recognise two distinct sections within the group – the Homoptera and the Heteroptera. These differ primarily in the form of the front wing: that of the homopteran may be either membranous or horny, but it is always of uniform texture throughout, while that of the heteropteran bug has a horny base and a membranous tip. In addition, the homopteran bugs hold their wings roofwise over the body when at rest, whereas the heteropterans fold their wings flat. There are, however, many wingless species of heteropterans, and many of the homopterans, notably the aphids, also produce wingless generations. Winged or wingless, however, they can all be recognised as bugs very easily by the slender beak under the head.

The HOMOPTERAN BUGS are all plant feeders and the majority are very small. The only ones which regularly force themselves upon the gardener's attention are the aphids, which include the greenfly and blackfly and many other species. These little insects breed very rapidly during the summer months and often form

119

dense clusters on the leaves and tender shoots of our plants. Rarely more than about 3 mm long, the aphids have relatively plump, pear-shaped bodies and long antennae. The wings, when present, are usually very thin and transparent and they extend far beyond the hind end of the body when at rest. Most aphid species produce both winged and wingless forms. The hind end of the body usually bears a pair of prominent 'horns' called cornicles or siphuncles.

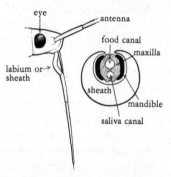

The needle-like mouth-parts of a bug are almost completely enclosed in a sheath, which is pulled back to allow the sharp points to penetrate the food source. The needles enclose two canals – one for the liquid food, and one through which saliva goes down into the wound

These exude waxy fluids which help to protect the aphids against some of their smaller enemies– possibly against some of the minute parasites which attack them. Luckily for the gardener, and for mankind in general, the secretions have little effect on ladybirds and lacewings. These insects, together with some of the hover-fly larvae (page 157), habitually feed on aphids and play an important role in controlling their numbers.

Aphids cause mechanical damage to plants by jabbing their beaks in all over them and blocking the sap-carrying channels, and they also weaken the plants by removing much of the food-laden sap. But the most serious damage is caused by the numerous virus diseases which the aphids carry from plant to plant. The virus particles are extremely small and they are sucked up with the sap from infected plants. Some of them go back into the plants with the saliva when the aphids feed again, and so the diseases spread very easily from plant to plant as the aphids move about. The viruses multiply rapidly inside the plants and interfere with the growth and development of the cells. The leaves often become blotched or streaked with yellow, or they may simply curl up. The viruses have no ill-effect on the aphids, and feeding on infected plants may actually be beneficial to the aphids because infected plants seem to have a more nutritious sap than healthy ones (see page 123).

Important virus diseases include sugar beet yellows and sugar beet mosaic, but the gardener will probably be most familiar with potato mosaic and potato leaf roll. The latter disease, which is spread mainly by an aphid called *Myzus persicae* (see page 122), causes the potato leaves to roll up. Food production in the leaves is thus reduced, and a severe infestation may reduce the potato yield by more than half. British potato growers usually get their 'seed potatoes' – the tubers for planting – from Scotland or Ireland because the climate in these regions is not suitable for the aphid and the tubers are usually free from the virus. The plants may pick up the disease later in more southerly districts, but infection then may be too late to have much effect on the potato yield.

Many aphids have complex life histories which involve feeding on two distinct kinds of plant. The **black bean aphid** (Plate 10) which attacks our broad and runner beans is a typical example. The eggs of this species are usually laid on the spindle tree in the autumn, although the syringa *(Philadelphus)* and the various species of *Viburnum* are also acceptable hosts. Those eggs that evade the attention of blue tits and other birds hatch in the spring and produce wingless females known as stem-mothers. These are able to reproduce without mating and, like most of the summer aphids, they bring forth active young instead of laying eggs. Some give birth to several youngsters in a single day, and so the population increases rapidly. The youngsters are wingless like their mothers and they continue to feed on the trees. Within about 14 days, they are bringing forth young themselves, but this new generation of aphids is winged and the insects fly off in search of their summer hosts. As well as beans, the aphids will attack thistles, docks, spinach, sugar beet, and many other herbaceous plants. They are vectors of several serious sugar beet viruses. Having settled on a suitable plant, the aphids continue to reproduce rapidly and soon give rise to the dense masses of blackfly or 'blight' which clothe the younger shoots of the plants. Some of these summer aphids are wingless, while others are fully winged and able to fly to neighbouring plants where they start further infestations. All of the aphids involved in the story so far have been females, for the males are not born until the autumn. They are winged and they fly back to the spindle or other winter host accompanied by winged females. The latter give birth to a further generation of wingless females, and then the males have their moment: they mate with the wingless females, and these then lay the over-wintering eggs.

It is obviously not wise to try to grow beans or other susceptible crops near to the winter host trees, but removal of the latter will not necessarily clear your garden of blackfly because the winged insects can fly in from far afield. In mild regions, the aphids can abandon egg-laying altogether and pass the winter quite happily on shepherd's purse and other weeds, from which it is an easy step to our crops again in the spring.

The **peach-potato aphid** (*Myzus persicae*) has a very similar life history to that of the black bean aphid. It normally lays its eggs on peach trees and infests potatoes and other herbaceous plants in the summer. Like the black bean aphid, it can pass the winter in an active state on various low-growing plants if the weather is not too cold. It also lives throughout the year in greenhouses.

Gardeners with apple trees may well have noticed little patches of white fluff clustering around young shoots or poking out from cracks in the bark. The fluff is actually a mass of waxy strands and it is produced by the **woolly aphid** (Plate 10) as a protection against parasites and predators. Removal of some of the strands from the tree will reveal a mass of purple bodies nestling against the bark. Like the previous two species, the woolly aphid has a complex life history involving two different host plants. The eggs are usually laid on elm bark, and two generations of wingless aphids generally feed on the elm buds and leaves. Winged individuals are then produced and they migrate to the apple, where they congregate around wounds in the bark or around the young water shoots*. A generation of wingless aphids is produced, and these are the ones which produce the fluff on the twigs and branches.

Winged individuals appear later and fly back to the elm trees to give birth to wingless males and females – the parents of the over-wintering eggs. There is, however, another complication, in that some of the wingless aphids born on the apple move down to the roots and produce several generations there. They cause such severe deformities on the roots that small trees are often killed.

The fat, green aphid or **greenfly** that infests our roses during the summer belongs to the one-host species known as *Macrosiphum rosae* (Plate 10). The eggs of this species are laid on the roses in the autumn and they hatch there in the spring. Several generations of aphids are produced during the summer, with some winged and some wingless individuals in each. Although the winged individuals may fly from plant to plant, they confine themselves to roses. As in

*Water shoots are slender shoots which spring out from the upper surfaces of branches which have been severely cut back or damaged in some other way. Diseased trees often produce them as well.

the black bean aphid, males and egg-laying females occur only in the autumn: the summer generations all consist of parthenogenetic females which bring forth active young without mating.

Cabbages, swedes, and other brassica crops are often attacked by the infamous **cabbage aphid** (Plate 10), which forms dense grey patches on the leaves in summer and autumn. Although it attacks a variety of species in the cabbage family, the aphid is not a migratory species because it does not show a regular movement from one host to another. The eggs are laid on the brassica stalks in the autumn and they hatch in the spring to produce wingless stem-mothers which soon become covered with the characteristic powdery wax. A further generation or two of wingless aphids may be produced and then winged individuals start to appear. They lack the powdery coating and they fly to other cruciferous plants, including the summer cabbage and swedes, where they multiply rapidly. Each individual produces a little cluster of mealy, wingless offspring, and each little cluster soon becomes a big cluster if left alone. Before long, the whole plant is covered with the mealy aphids, and the leaves are turning yellow and wilting. Spraying the plants with pyrethrum or some other insecticide may kill the aphids, but it is usually too late to save the plant when the infestation reaches this stage. The aphids must be removed as soon as the small patches are seen on the leaves. It is sometimes tempting to leave the broccoli and sprouts in the garden until late in the spring in order to get the last little bit of green from them, but this is false economy if the cabbage aphid is about, for it puts the following summer crop in jeopardy. The wise gardener removes the old brassica stumps early, before they can act as distribution centres for the aphid.

Plant sap contains a very large amount of sugar but, except when the plants are infected with virus diseases, it has a very low protein content. The aphids therefore have to ingest large amounts of sap to get sufficient protein for their needs, and this means that they take in a large excess of sugar. They solve the problem very neatly by passing the sugar out through the back end in the form of honeydew – little drops of concentrated sugar solution. Ants very often visit aphids to lick up the honey-dew (see page 182), but the drops usually just fall to the ground. The lower leaves of oaks, limes, and various other large trees are often quite sticky and shiny with honey-dew which has fallen from above, and plants growing under these trees become sticky too. Later in the summer these leaves all turn black because a black mould grows on the dried sugar. The waxy coatings of the aphids prevent the insects themselves from getting sticky.

The undersides of cabbage leaves sometimes bear clusters of tiny moth-like insects with white wings. These are **cabbage whiteflies** (Plate 10) and, like the aphids, they belong to the Homoptera. The females lay their eggs on the leaves and the youngsters hatch in about ten days. They have legs at first, but these degenerate after a day or two and the nymphs spend the next fortnight sitting motionless on the leaves and imbibing the sap. Honey-dew is exuded as in the aphids, and each drop is wrapped up in a waxy coat which prevents the insects from becoming sticky. The adult insects can fly from plant to plant, but they spend most of their time feeding, and heavy infestations can do serious damage to cabbage and other brassicas. The species is common only in the southern half of the country, where it is able to breed throughout the year. The only other whitefly which regularly comes to notice is the greenhouse whitefly, an introduced species which has become a real pest in greenhouses and on various house plants. We do have a few other native species, but the whiteflies are mainly tropical insects.

Fruit trees, grape vines, and various other woody plants sometimes bear little brown domes on their twigs. The domes fit tightly against the bark in the manner of limpet shells and they look like small warts or outgrowths from the plant, but they are actually **scale insects** belonging to the species known as *Parthenolecanium corni* (Plate 10). If you pull off one of the domes in the summer you will find the legless and rather shapeless insect underneath it. This creature bears little resemblance to any other kind of insect, but a sharp 'beak', permanently sunk into the plant tissues, shows that it is clearly some kind of bug. The insect produces a mass of eggs in the summer and its body gradually shrivels away. The eggs remain under the scales during the winter and the little nymphs or crawlers emerge in the spring. They crawl along the stems and then settle down to feed. Although they have legs and antennae at first, these are soon lost and the insects embark on a completely sedentary life. The horny scales begin to develop as soon as the insects settle down. The insect described so far is the female of the species, and this is the sex that is normally seen. Young males lead sedentary lives just like the females, although their scales tend to be smaller, but then they develop wings and fly about like small midges. They are rather rare, however, and most of the females lay fertile eggs without mating. This scale insect is not usually abundant enough to do any harm to trees in this country.

A great many other scale insects live in the British Isles, but relatively few occur in gardens. One of the commonest scale insects in the garden is the mussel scale, although its small size and drab

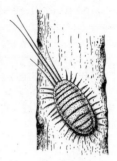

Mussel scales highly magnified. Their
actual length is about a millimetre

A mealy bug

colour make it very inconspicuous on the bark of apple and other
trees. A close inspection is necessary to detect even a very heavy
infestation of these elongated scales, but their presence may be
suspected if branches begin to die back for no obvious reason. The
life history of the mussel scale is much the same as that of *P. corni*,
although the male scales are often produced on the leaves and they
are rather more common than the males of *P. corni*.

The **rose scale** (Plate 10) occurs on both wild and cultivated
roses, particularly on standard roses in the garden. It used to be
so abundant that affected stems looked as if they had been
whitewashed, but the regular spraying to which most cultivated
roses are now subjected has made the pest much less common than
it was at the beginning of the century. The life history of the rose
scale is much the same as that of the previous two species.

A number of foreign scale insects have established themselves in
our greenhouses and they make a nuisance of themselves on a wide
variety of plants. Many of them belong to a group of scale insects
called mealy bugs. These are less specialised than most other scale
insects, and the females retain their legs and a certain degree of
mobility. Fringed by a number of bristly outgrowths, they look
not unlike small, pale woodlice. The commonest species is the
citrus mealy bug *(Planococcus citri)*, which is a serious pest in the
Californian orange groves as well as in our greenhouses.

The largest homopteran bug likely to be encountered in the
garden is the **common froghopper** (Plate 10), which is responsible
for the 'cuckoo spit' which occurs on so many herbaceous plants
during the summer. The insect, which leaps well and has a distinctly
frog-like appearance, is also known as a spittle-bug. Eggs are laid on
the plants in the autumn and they hatch in late spring. The young
nymphs then climb up to the tender shoots and begin to feed on the

sap. At the same time, they exude a fluid from the anus and force air into it. This produces the familiar froth, which surrounds the little insects and protects them from desiccation and from some of their enemies. Adult froghoppers emerge from the spittle later in the summer, but they are rarely common enough to do any harm to our garden plants. The adults are very variable in their wing patterns, although all are basically brown with darker markings.

Cuckoo-spit

Numerous smaller hoppers occur in the garden, but they are not closely related to the froghopper and their nymphs do not produce spittle. Most of them are green or brown and they blend in well with the plants on which they live. Although these **leaf hoppers** are extremely serious pests in the warmer parts of the world, very few of them do any serious damage in the temperate regions. The **potato leaf hopper** (Plate 10) and a bright green relative called *Chlorita viridula* are the only ones likely to be found in the garden in any numbers: clouds of these little insects may spring into the air if you walk through the potato patch, and they will fall back on to the plants just as suddenly. The saliva of these hoppers is poisonous to the potato leaves and small white dots indicate where the insects have been plunging their beaks in to feed, but the potato plants do not suffer much unless the insects are so numerous that their feeding sites join up and destroy large areas of leaf surface. The potato leaf hopper is also commonly found on stinging nettles, and it is likely that it passes the winter on this and other weeds. The **apple leaf hopper** is one of several species which feed on apple

The apple psyllid a bright green insect abundant on apple leaves in the summer

126

leaves, but it should not be confused with the apple psyllid shown here, which belongs to a quite different family of Homoptera.

The HETEROPTERAN BUGS include both plant-feeding and animal-feeding species, although the majority of them are vegetarians. They are, in general, somewhat larger than the homopterans and they do not usually form dense aggregations such as we find among the aphids and scale insects. The heteropterans start life as eggs, which are often extremely attractive when seen under a lens, and the nymphs then gradually develop into adults. Many species pass the winter in the egg stage, but others hibernate as nymphs or adults. There is often a marked difference in the colours of the adults before and after hibernation.

The **forest bug** (Plate 10) is one of the largest bugs to be found in the garden. It belongs to a group which, because of their shape, are known as shieldbugs. They are also called stink bugs because many of the species release pungent odours when handled. The forest bug feeds on a wide variety of trees and is commonly found on apples and cherries in the garden. It matures at about cherry-picking time and the adults sometimes attack the fruit. Younger bugs suck sap from the leaves and probably attack smaller insects as well. The only other shieldbug likely to be seen in the garden is the **pied shieldbug** (Plate 10), which is found on and around the white deadnettle at most times of the year.

The **common flower bug** (Plate 10) is one of our commonest bugs and the gardener will often find it walking over his or her arms after a session of weeding or fruit-picking. The adults hibernate for the winter and lay their eggs in the spring. A new generation of adults appears in June and the bugs are then abundant until the autumn. I always find large numbers on the raspberries at picking time, but it is not the raspberries themselves that the bugs are after, for they are predatory insects and they feed on the aphids and other pests, including the notorious red spider mite. The **hot-bed bug** (Plate 10) is closely related to the common flower bug, but it is rarely seen on the plants. It favours the rubbish heap, where the warmth from the fermenting plants allows it to remain active throughout the year. It feeds on mites and other small creatures.

Several rather slender or oval green bugs occur in the garden, and these all belong to a large group known as mirids or capsids. Most of them are plant-feeders, but the **black-kneed capsid** (Plate 10) is omnivorous and it is an important ally of the gardener because it attacks the red spider mite (see page 222). It is most often seen on apple trees. The **common green capsid** (Plate 10) is also found on

127

apple trees, but the two bugs are easily distinguished by their shapes and by the black 'knees' of the first species, although the black markings are more readily seen in the nymphs. The common green capsid damages fruit trees and bushes of various kinds and is responsible for many of the brown scabs on apples. It also lives on potatoes and other herbaceous plants. It passes the winter in the egg stage on the bark of trees. The **tarnished plant bug** (Plate 10) is another common capsid, particularly abundant in the autumn. It feeds on a wide variety of plants and is sometimes a nuisance on potatoes and raspberries. It is also a pest of chrysanthemums in greenhouses, where it can remain all winter instead of hibernating in piles of rubbish.

Many other bugs will be seen in the garden, of course, but none of them is likely to be doing any harm. Our final example, the **flybug** (Plate 10), is more likely to be seen in the stable or potting shed than in the garden itself, and it often flies to lighted windows on summer evenings. It is a predatory species and it feeds on small flies, silverfish, and other small creatures which lurk in neglected corners and in piles of debris. The bug is found only in the southern half of England.

BARKLICE OR PSOCIDS

These little insects, which include both winged and wingless species, are extremely common everywhere, but they are not commonly noticed in the garden because of their small size. They are mostly about the same size as aphids. The winged individuals hold their wings roofwise over their bodies when at rest and, with their often mottled bodies, they have a very characteristic appearance. They are most likely to be seen during hedge-cutting or apple-picking, when they often fly on to hands and arms. The insects do no harm to the plants, for they feed mainly on pollen grains and the minute algae that grow on tree trunks and branches. The wingless species are more likely to be seen indoors or in the shed, where they live among piles of paper and on dusty shelves. They are often called booklice and they feed on traces of mould in such places.

Winged and wingless barklice

PLATE 9: **Miscellaneous insects.** 1 Common earwig 116; 2 Small earwig 118; 3 *Apterygida albipennis* 118; 4 Green lacewing adult, larva and eggs 130; 5 Brown lacewing 131; 6 Scorpion fly 131; 7 Speckled bush cricket 115; 8 Oak bush cricket 115; 9 Dark bush cricket 116; 10 House cricket 116; 11 Common cockroach 119; 12 Gooseberry sawfly 184; 13 *Coccygomimus instigator* 183; 14 *Netelia testacea* 183; 15 Horntail 185; 16 *Tenthredo atra* 185; 17 Hawthorn sawfly 185, a adult, b emerging from cocoon, c larva; 18 Ruby-tailed wasp 179.

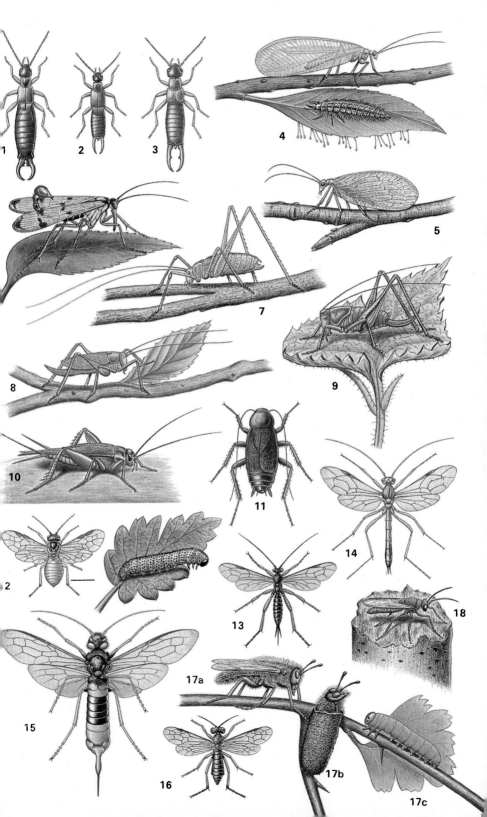

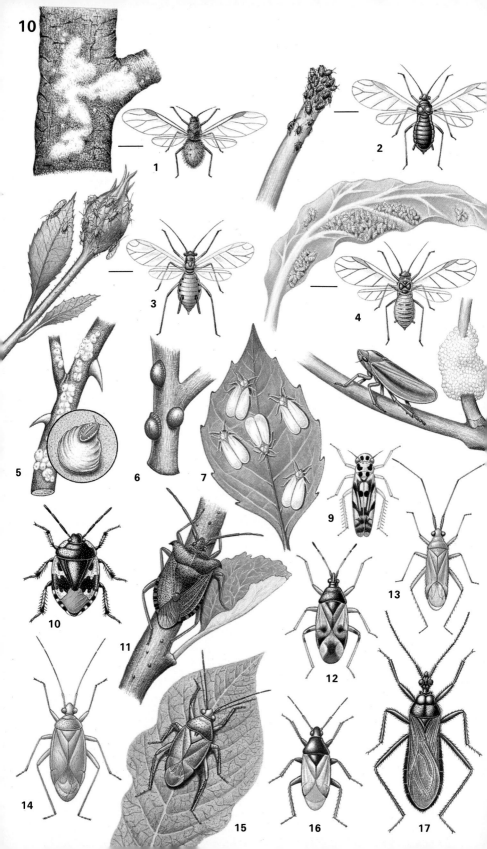

THRIPS

Look carefully into almost any flower during the summer and you will probably find a number of very slender black insects crawling about among the petals and stamens. These are thrips, also known as thunder flies or thunder bugs in some parts of the country. The majority of them are only two or three millimetres long and they all appear to be wingless at first sight, although many of them possess two pairs of narrow, feathery wings. Many thrips live in leaf litter and under loose bark, feeding on fungi and decaying material. Some suck the juices of other insects, but the majority of species pierce plant cells and suck out the sap. This is probably what most of the thrips are doing in your flowers. When, as often happens, there are large numbers of thrips, they can do considerable damage to

A thrips (highly magnified), showing
the feathery wings

crops. Too many thrips in an apple flower, for instance, may well prevent the formation of the fruit. The pea thrips is another very common garden species in June and July. Adults and young live in the flowers and on the developing pods and, by puncturing the outer cells of the pods, cause the familiar silvery mottling. Heavy infestations of these thrips cause severe distortion and stunting of the pods.

During sultry weather, many of the winged thrips take to the air and this is how they get their alternative names of thunder flies or thunder bugs. There are certain days in the summer when I sometimes wish I didn't live next to a cornfield: millions of thrips take off from the cereals and drift through the air to land on hair, face, and arms and one is driven into a frenzy of combing and scratching to alleviate the intense tickling. One is not even safe indoors, for these tiny creatures crawl through the smallest cracks around doors and windows and then swarm on the window panes in an attempt to get out again. Many of our 160 or so kinds of thrips actually hibernate indoors – under loose wallpaper, behind picture frames (or inside them if they can find a way in), or in the roof – and then attempt to fly out again in the spring ready to lay their eggs on the plants.

◀ PLATE 10: **Aphids, Leafhoppers and other bugs.** 1 Woolly aphid 122; 2 Bean aphid or blackfly 121; 3 Rose aphid or greenfly 122; 4 Cabbage aphid 123, with nymphs massing on cabbage leaf; 5 Rose scale insect with one scale much enlarged, 125; 6 *Parthenolecanium corni* 124; 7 Whiteflies 124; 8 Common froghopper 125, and 'cuckoo-spit'; 9 Potato leafhopper 126; 10 Pied shield bug 127; 11 Forest bug 127; 12 Common flower bug 127; 13 Black-kneed capsid bug 127; 14 Common green capsid bug 127; 15 Tarnished plant bug 128; 16 Hot-bed bug 127; 17 Flybug 128.

We very often disturb the pale green lacewings or lacewing flies while working in the garden and send them fluttering gently away to find another refuge. These insects more often come to our notice at night, however, when they come to lighted windows and frequently enter the house. They are among the most beautiful and delicate of our insects, with pale green bodies and thin wings covered with a network of very fine green veins (Plate 9). The delicate appearance of the lacewings is not matched by their habits, however, for they are ruthless destroyers of aphids and other small insects. Put a lacewing on a twig covered with aphids and, assuming that it is hungry, it will systematically work through the colony, devouring one aphid after another with its biting jaws. The lacewings are thus definitely on the gardener's side.

A lacewing at rest

The insects that we have looked at so far in our entomological tour of the garden have all belonged to the group which undergo partial metamorphoses during their life histories (see page 107), but, with the lacewings, we move on to the other major group of insects– those which undergo complete metamorphoses and which have young stages very different from the adults. What then are these young lacewings like? They are obviously quite common, but they are far less often seen than the adults. They start life as eggs, each one of which is carried at the end of a slender stalk. The egg-laying female produces these stalks by drawing sticky threads out from her abdomen, and she then fixes an egg to the end of each one. Some species deposit their stalked eggs in bunches, but others plant them singly on the vegetation. It is not difficult to find these eggs in the garden by turning up the leaves of the taller plants, such as currant bushes, roses, and michaelmas daisies. They are usually attached to the undersides of the leaves or else to the smaller stems. The larvae which hatch from the eggs are rather pale, shuttle-like creatures covered with bristles and hairs, but many of them soon disguise themselves with the skins of their victims, for, like the adults, these larvae are voracious destroyers of aphids. Their methods of feeding differ, however, for the larvae have slender jaws which pierce their prey and then act like drinking straws to suck out the juices. The jaws are then used to flick the empty skins on to the back, where they are held in place by the bristles and where they help to camouflage the larvae. A moving pile of rubbish on your rose bush is most likely to be one of these most useful creatures. A single lacewing larva is capable of destroying more than 200 aphids during its few weeks of life, and then it will eat many more as an adult. The larvae make silken cocoons in which to turn into adults.

Most of our lacewings have two or three generations in a year and both adults and young can be found from April to October. Most of the species pass the winter as mature larvae in their cocoons, but some of them hibernate as adults. The very common *Chrysopa carnea* hibernates in our sheds and houses, but it loses its bright green colour for the winter and is generally a rather dirty pink.

As well as our twelve species of green lacewings, we have numerous brown lacewings in this country. Several live in the garden and come to lighted windows like their green cousins. They are generally somewhat smaller than the green lacewings and their wings are more densely veined (Plate 9). Their larvae feed in the same way as those of the green species, but they are generally much less bristly and they do not adorn themselves with the skins of their victims. The eggs are not stalked.

SCORPION FLIES

Shady gardens with overgrown hedges or with plenty of gooseberry bushes or other shrubs will almost certainly support a number of scorpion flies. Easily recognised by their heavily mottled wings, these insects get their name because the tail end of the male is turned up rather like that of a scorpion (Plate 9). The resemblance ends there, however, because the scorpion fly has no sting and it is quite harmless. The female does not have a turned-up abdomen. Close examination of a scorpion fly will reveal that the head is prolonged downwards to form a stout 'beak' with the jaws at the lower end.

Scorpion flies can be found throughout the summer. They spend most of their time crawling over the vegetation and, although their wings are fully developed, they fly reluctantly and weakly. When disturbed, they generally scuttle round to the other side of the leaf or else run up or down the stem. They are scavenging creatures and their food includes dead and injured insects, over-ripe fruit, and other detritus. They have been known to nibble bird droppings, and they may even be attracted to the gardener's beads of perspiration. They lay their eggs in the soil and the larvae, which look rather like caterpillars, live there as scavengers.

BUTTERFLIES AND MOTHS

The butterflies and moths need little introduction, although some people do have difficulty in deciding whether a given specimen is a butterfly or a moth. The distinction is actually quite simple as far as our garden species are concerned, for the antennae of the butterflies end in small knobs and those of the moths do not. In addition, the butterflies all fly in the daytime and most of the moths are active at night. These distinctions do not hold true, however, when we consider all of the 100,000 or so species of butterflies and moths in the world.

With the exception of a few female moths (see page 150), the butterflies and moths all have two pairs of wings covered with minute scales. These scales give the colours and patterns to the

proboscis
in use

A butterfly with its proboscis extended to suck nectar from a flower. The small drawing shows how the proboscis rolls up under the head when not in use

wings, but they rub off quite easily and insects flying about at the end of the season often have bald patches on their wings. The adult insects feed mainly on nectar, which they suck from the flowers with their long, tubular 'tongues'. When not in use, the tongue, technically known as a proboscis, is coiled up underneath the head. Many adult moths, however, have no proboscis and they do not feed.

Butterflies and moths rely on sight and/or scent to find their mates. If two butterflies are flying fairly near to each other in the garden, they will often fly to each other and then circle round each other as they rise into the air. The initial attraction is visual, but scent then comes into play as the butterflies circle around each other. The males of most butterflies possess scent glands on their wings, but only unmated females of the same species respond to the scent. If the two circling butterflies are of different species or of the same sex, or if one is a mated female, they will soon lose interest in each other and separate. If, however, they are a legitimate pair – a male and an unmated female of the same species – the female will respond in such a way that they stay together and eventually land somewhere to mate. Many moths rely entirely on scent to find their mates, and here it is generally the female who emits the scent. She sits on the vegetation and waits for suitors to arrive. The males generally have larger and more feathery antennae than the females and they are remarkably efficient at picking up the scent.

After mating, the females generally lay their eggs singly or in small batches on the appropriate food plant. The larvae that emerge from the eggs are the familiar caterpillars – relatively slender and soft-bodied creatures with three pairs of true legs at the front and up to five pairs of stumpy prolegs further back. The prolegs are provided with numerous small, but very powerful hooks and they hold the caterpillars very firmly on to the leaves and twigs. All caterpillars have biting jaws and the majority of them feed freely on leaves. Some of the smaller ones are leaf miners (see page 108), while several species tunnel in stems and some, such as the codlin moth caterpillars (page 153), live in fruit. The larvae of the swift moths live in the soil and feed on roots.

The fully grown caterpillars turn into pupae or chrysalises, and they may do this either in or on the food plant or else they may seek a suitable site elsewhere. The caterpillars that one often sees walking across the road or path in a rather determined fashion are usually looking for such a site. Many moth caterpillars spin silky cocoons around themselves before pupating, and they may protect themselves even more by attaching bits of debris to the outisde of the cocoon to camouflage it. Many other species pupate in the soil, the caterpillar excavating a little chamber and possibly lining it with a few silk strands before turning into a pupa. The gardener digs up many of these subterranean pupae, especially during the autumn. Most of them are a shiny chestnut colour and they nearly all belong to moths in the noctuid group (see page 145).

The pupae of most butterflies, including all those normally found in the garden, are without any form of cocoon. Many of them hang freely from little silken pads which the caterpillars make on the food plant or some other convenient support, but others are attached in an upright position, with a single strand of silk around the middle for support. The majority of our butterflies and moths are active during the summer months and they nearly all spend the winter in the pupal stage. Most of the others overwinter as eggs or as hibernating caterpillars, but a few hibernate as adults and some, such as the winter moth (page 150), are actually on the wing during the colder months.

GARDEN BUTTERFLIES

Less than sixty kinds of butterfly are resident in the British Isles and, although most of these can and probably do visit gardens from time to time, only fifteen of them are at all frequent in the garden. Probably only three – the notorious cabbage whites – live in the average garden in the caterpillar state, although the nettle-feeding small tortoiseshell may well breed in the wilder and more untidy gardens.

The **small tortoiseshell** (Plate 11) is one of those butterflies which hibernate as adults and it is one of the earliest to brighten our gardens in the spring. A warm and sunny spell will bring it out of hiding before the end of January in some years, but it will usually go back to sleep again until there are some flowers on which it can feed. It normally hibernates in hollow trees, sheds, and other dark places where its sombre underside conceals it well. The spring butterflies spend a lot of their time sitting on paths and walls and soaking up the sun's warmth, and then pair up and the females go off to lay their pale green eggs on the young shoots of the stinging nettle. Egg-laying usually takes place in April or May and the rather bristly black and green caterpillars (Plate 14) spend their first two or three weeks in silken tents which they spin on the nettles. The caterpillars leave the communal home when they are nearly fully grown and, after a further fattening-up on the nettle leaves, they are ready to pupate. Some of the gold-spangled chrysalises may be found on the nettles, but most of the caterpillars move away to neighbouring shrubs or fences before hanging themselves up to pupate. Pupae can also be found hanging from window-sills when there are nettle beds nearby.

The new generation of small tortoiseshells appears in July and the butterflies are often abundant at lavender and buddleia flowers. A second crop of caterpillars can be found on the nettles in late July and August, and these give rise to more adults in late August and

September. These butterflies drink nectar freely from the autumn flowers and they are especially fond of michaelmas daisies and the large, pink-flowered stone-crop known as the ice-plant (page 259). In a warm autumn, the small tortoiseshells may continue flying until well into October, but then they gradually find snug retreats and begin their winter rest. The small tortoiseshell is particularly common around human settlements because this is where the stinging nettle is most abundant (see page 37).

The **peacock** (Plate 11) is another species which hibernates as an adult and emerges early in the spring, although it never seems to be as common in the spring as the small tortoiseshell. The habits of these two species are very similar, both as adults and larvae, but the peacock normally has only one generation in a year. The butterflies mate and lay their eggs on the nettles in April or May, but the velvety black caterpillars (Plate 14) take longer to grow up than the small tortoiseshell and the summer generation of adults does not appear until late July at the earliest. These butterflies then enjoy themselves for a couple of months, starting with the buddleia and then moving on to all the other flowers of late summer and autumn. They often rest on the flowers with their wings closed, but they open them suddenly and flash the large 'eyes' if they are disturbed. It is not difficult to imagine the shock that such an action might give a small bird that gets too close to the butterfly (see also page 142). By the time the peacocks finally settle down to hibernation, many of them are very tattered and worn. This might explain why relatively few of them seem to appear again in the spring. The peacock is found throughout England, Wales, and Ireland, but it does not appear to be common in Scotland.

The only other butterfly which is common in our garden early in the spring is the **brimstone** (Plate 11), which hibernates in evergreen shrubs or among the ivy leaves on an old wall and which emerges at about the same time as the small tortoiseshell. Although the male has a brilliant yellow upper side, the female is very pale green – almost white when seen from a distance and easily confused with the cabbage whites. Both sexes, however, have greenish undersides with prominent veins and they are thus well camouflaged when they are hibernating among the evergreens. Although it visits the aubretia and other spring flowers, the brimstone is less closely connected with human activity than the previous two species and it is common in many open woodlands. The butterflies that visit our gardens probably breed in the hedgerows.

The slender green caterpillars feed on buckthorn bushes in June and a new generation of butterflies emerges at about the end of

July. These butterflies can be seen in our gardens until well into the autumn, when they seek winter quarters. The brimstone is very common in southern England and in parts of Wales and Ireland, but it is absent from Scotland.

Many people look out for a favourite sign each year to tell them that summer is really on its way. It may be the return of the swallows, or the bursting of the apple blossom, but for me it is the sight of the **orange-tip** butterfly flitting through my garden – usually during the last few days of April. Only the male of this attractive species has orange tips to his wings (Plate 11), and the female can easily be mistaken for a small white (page 137) until she settles and shows her mottled underside. She may visit the honesty flowers, and she may even lay some eggs on them, but neither sex of this species seems keen to settle for long. They spend most of their time flitting up and down the gardens and hedgerows. The orange-tip caterpillars normally feed on lady's smock or cuckoo flower, jack-by-the-hedge, and other cruciferous plants. The butterflies are thus found mainly in country gardens with plenty of hedgerows and meadows within easy reach. The species can be found in most parts of the British Isles, but it is rare in Scotland.

The damaging **cabbage whites** first appear at about the end of April, having passed the winter in the chrysalis stage. There are actually three species – the large white, the small white, and the green-veined white – all of which are illustrated on Plate 11. All are widely distributed and common in the British Isles.

The sexes of the **large white** are easily distinguished because the female has two black spots and a stripe on the upper side of each front wing, while the male is unmarked except for the black tips and leading edges of the wings. The female lays batches of conical, yellow eggs on the leaves of cabbages and other plants in the same family. She will also lay on nasturtium leaves, which contain the same rather pungent oils as those of the cabbage family. The eggs are usually laid during May, and the caterpillars feed up in June. They are basically a yellowish green, but they are heavily peppered with black (Plate 14). Although they are voracious feeders, this first generation of caterpillars is not usually numerous enough to do a great deal of damage. When fully grown, the caterpillars seek a fence or a wall on which to pupate. Many enter the garden shed for this purpose. The pupae or chrysalises are yellowish with black spots and they are usually fixed vertically to the wall, held in place by a silken girdle or safety belt. Adult butterflies emerge in August and their numbers are multiplied many times over by the swarms of immigrants which arrive from the Continent at about this time.

These butterflies feast upon the buddleia and the other summer flowers and then they turn their attentions to the cabbage patch. Eggs are laid and the young caterpillars soon get to work unless we systematically search out the batches of eggs and squash them. Heavy infestations of caterpillars soon reduce the cabbage leaves to skeletons and they fill the air around them with a rather unpleasant odour, well known to anyone who has squashed any of these creatures. The fully grown caterpillars seek walls and fences on which to pupate, but only a small proportion ever complete the transformation. Many of the caterpillars will have been visited by a little ichneumon fly (see page 183) called *Apanteles glomeratus* which will have laid its eggs inside the caterpillars and condemned them to death. Each affected caterpillar may contain more than 100 *Apanteles* grubs feeding inside it. But the grubs are careful not to touch any of the caterpillar's vital organs until they themselves are nearly fully grown. This happens at about the time when the caterpillar would normally pupate. The grubs then emerge from the

A parasitised large white caterpillar surrounded by the yellow cocoons of the *Apanteles* parasite

caterpillar's body and leave just an empty skin clinging to the wall. They spin little yellow cocoons around it and they then pupate themselves. Don't be tempted to remove these yellow clusters on the grounds of tidiness, for they shelter our most powerful allies in the fight against the large white. *Apanteles* destroys so many of the caterpillars that it is doubtful if the large white would survive in Britain if it were not for the massive immigration each summer. But *Apanteles* is not the large white's only enemy. Those caterpillars that escape *Apanteles* and do manage to pupate are at risk from another very small insect called a chalcid. This insect lays its eggs in the chrysalis and its grubs feed there during the autumn and winter. If you don't clear away the chrysalises from the shed walls during the winter, you might well see some of them covered with freshly emerged chalcids during the spring.

The **small white** butterfly is usually more numerous than the large white, especially in the spring. Its wing pattern is similar to that of the large white, although the male often has a single black spot on the upper side of each front wing. As in the large white, the pattern is much blacker in the summer generation than in the spring insects. The eggs are laid singly instead of in batches and they are much more difficult to find than those of the large white. The caterpillars are also more difficult to see because they are green and they lie along the mid-ribs of the cabbage leaves where they are very well camouflaged (Plate 14). They pupate in the same way as the larvae of the large white and the summer generation is on the wing in July and August, usually augmented by immigrants from the Continent. A further generation usually appears in September in the southern parts of the country, but these butterflies are often much smaller than the earlier ones. Caterpillars from this autumn generation can be found on the cabbages until well into October. They suffer from the same parasites as the large white, but not to the same extent.

The **green-veined white**, easily identified by the green lines on its underside (Plate 11), is much less of a pest than the other two whites and it prefers various cruciferous weeds to the cultivated cabbages. It is, therefore, much less restricted to human habitations than the other two species. The butterfly is on the wing in May and again in August and September. The caterpillar is very similar to that of the small white.

The caterpillars of our satyrid butterflies, usually known as the browns, all feed on grasses and the adults are found mainly in open country. A few of them come to gardens, however, the most frequent visitor being the **wall brown** (Plate 11). This butterfly is on the wing in May and June, and a second generation appears in August and September. It likes to bask on walls and stones that are warmed by the sun, although it is a rather restless butterfly and it rarely settles in one place for very long. It is common in most parts of England, Wales, and Ireland, but it only just creeps into Scotland. Country gardens with plenty of grassy lanes and hedgerows nearby will also be visited by the **ringlet** and the gatekeeper or **hedge brown,** both illustrated on Plate 11. These butterflies are on the wing in July and August and both love to drink from bramble blossoms. They are common in southern England, but rare in the north. The gatekeeper is absent from Scotland.

Our blue butterflies are nearly all insects of the open grasslands, but the **holly blue** (Plate 11) is a notable exception. It is basically a woodland butterfly, but its range extends to parks and gardens. Even town gardeners are likely to meet this attractive insect.

The male has a clear violet-blue upperside, while the female is heavily edged with black. The undersides of both sexes are pale blue with black dots. Holly blues pass the winter in the chrysalis stage and they are on the wing in April and May. A further generation flies in August. The butterflies can usually be seen flitting around trees and shrubs and they are especially noticeable around holly trees and ivy-covered walls, for holly and ivy are the main food plants of the caterpillars. Eggs are laid in the flower buds and the caterpillars feed on the flowers and the developing fruits. Although recorded from Northern Ireland, the holly blue is rare in northern Britain and absent from Scotland.

The **small copper** (Plate 11) is related to the blues and, like them, it is basically an insect of open country. It is very often seen on commons and waste land, although you will rarely see more than one at a time. Each butterfly seems to have its own territory, such as a clump of thistles or other flowers, and it chases other individuals away. The butterfly appears in May and produces two further broods during the summer and autumn. These broods overlap each other and adults can be seen at any time from May to October or even November. The butterflies often enter the garden in late summer and establish their territories on the michaelmas daisies. The caterpillars feed on docks and sorrels, those hatching in the autumn going into hibernation before completing their growth in the spring.

Our gardens are often visited in the autumn by three more members of the tortoiseshell family: the red admiral, the painted lady, and the comma. The **red admiral** (Plate 11) usually appears in the garden at about the beginning of August, and remains for two or three months, feeding on the buddleia and other flowers and then turning its attention to ripe plums and other fallen fruit. At the approach of winter, some of the butterflies may hide away in sheds and other buildings, but they do not normally survive the cold

A red admiral butterfly feeding on a fallen apple

weather. Our red admiral population is renewed every year by immigration from southern Europe. The insects arrive in May and settle down to breed on the nettles. It is mainly the children of these immigrants that come to our gardens. They don't all perish in the autumn, however, for large numbers can be seen flying south and many probably reach the warmth of the Mediterranean.

The **painted lady** (Plate 11) is another well known migrant that reaches us each year from North Africa and sometimes comes over in enormous numbers. The insects normally arrive in May, although February immigrations have been recorded, and they lay their eggs on various thistles. A new generation of adults appears in August and, augmented by further immigrants, they spend some time on our wild and cultivated flowers before beginning the long journey south. Most of the butterflies perish, but some undoubtedly make it to the winter breeding grounds on the edges of the Sahara.

The **comma** (Plate 11), named for the white, comma-shaped mark on the underside of the hind wing, is a resident species found all over Wales and the southern half of England. It hibernates as an adult, choosing to sleep on tree trunks and dead herbage where its ragged wings make it look just like a dead leaf. The butterfly usually wakes up in March, but it it not often seen in gardens in the spring. It prefers to visit sallow catkins along the edges of the woodlands at this time. Eggs are laid on stinging nettle and elm, and also on hops. The fully grown caterpillar is rather spiky, with five broad white patches on its black back. The pupa or chrysalis looks just like a shrivelled brown leaf clinging to a stem. A new generation of butterflies is on the wing in July and a further generation appears in September. These autumn butterflies frequent the usual flowers in the garden and also enjoy feeding at fallen fruit before hibernating.

MOTHS IN THE GARDEN

There are more than 2,000 species of moths in the British Isles and many of them are permanent residents in the garden. It is not possible here to do more than mention some of the commoner and more obvious species and groups that the gardener will find. Most adult moths are nocturnal and the average gardener will rarely see them going about their business. He will see them resting on walls and fences, however, and he will disturb them quite often while weeding or hedge-trimming. He will also see them on the windows at night, for many of the moths are attracted to light and regularly come to lighted windows. The easiest way to learn just how many moths are flying around your garden at night is to leave a window open on a warm evening and let them come in. The trouble with this method, however, is that you also get your walls and ceilings covered with little flies (see page 160).

With the exception of the cabbage white butterfly caterpillars (Plate 14), almost all the caterpillars that you find in the garden will be the caterpillars of moths. Many are very attractive, but the more sombre ones are not always easy to identify. The shiny pupae that you dig up will also yield moths in due course if you put them on some sand or peat in an old shoe box and keep them in a cool place. A jam jar is too small for most pupae because it does not give the emerging moths room to spread their wings.

Our largest moths belong to a group known as HAWKMOTHS, although not all hawkmoths are particularly large. They are stout-bodied insects with narrow front wings and very fast flight. The largest species normally found in the garden is the **privet hawk-moth**, whose blackish brown front wings span up to 12 cm. The body and the hind wings are striped with a delicate pink. The moth can sometimes be seen resting on garden fences and on tree trunks during June and July, but the fully grown caterpillar (Plate 14) comes to one's attention more frequently. It feeds on privet, lilac, and ash during July and August and reaches a length of about 10 cm. Like most hawkmoth caterpillars, it has a curved horn at the tail end. Although the purple and white stripes on the bright green background afford the caterpillar some excellent camouflage when it is among the leaves, the animal eats so much that, by the time it is fully grown, it finds itself sitting on bare twigs and easily seen. The whole body becomes pinkish when it is ready to pupate. Privet hawkmoths are quite common in the southern half of Great Britain, but rarely seen north of the Humber.

A privet hawkmoth at rest, with the dark front wings covering the pink-banded body and hind wings

The **poplar hawkmoth** (Plate 12) is the commonest of our hawkmoths and it can often be found resting in gardens with poplar trees nearby. It holds its wings and body in such a way that it looks very much like a bunch of leaves. The caterpillar, which is green with yellow stripes and a heavy dose of yellow spots, feeds on poplar and willow leaves. The moth is found all over the British Isles and it is usually on the wing in May and June. The caterpillars feed up in June and July and, in southern districts, some of them may produce a second generation of moths in August. A second crop of caterpillars can then be expected in September.

The **eyed hawkmoth** (Plate 12) is another frequent garden resident, especially where apple trees are grown. Its pinkish brown front wings give it a passable resemblance to bark when it is at rest, but the moth has a very striking second line of defence in case it is disturbed. When the gardener or an inquisitive bird gets too close, the moth raises its front wings and exposes the two large eye-spots on the hind wings. It begins to sway backwards and forwards and it gives a very convincing imitation of a much larger and fiercer creature. It gives a shock to the bird and often to the gardener as well. The caterpillars are green with pale stripes and they look like rolled-up leaves as they cling upside down to the twigs of apple and willow trees. The moth is usually on the wing in June, and there is sometimes a second generation in August and September. It is widely distributed over England, Wales and Ireland.

The only other hawkmoth regularly seen in gardens is the **hummingbird hawkmoth** (Plate 12), but it is common only around the south coast. It is a migrant species which arrives here from the Continent during the summer. Unlike most hawkmoths, it flies by day and it is usually seen as a brown blur hovering in front of petunias and other tubular flowers and plunging its long tongue into them to reach the nectar. It is often very numerous in the sea-front gardens of our south coast resorts. In a good year the moths spread out over the country and they often produce a second generation in late summer. The caterpillars are pale green and they feed on various kinds of bedstraw. Humming-bird hawkmoths often enter sheds and houses to spend the night in secluded corners. They may occasionally survive the winter in such places, but most of our specimens perish in the autumn or else fly back to the Continent.

The yellow and black caterpillars of the **buff-tip** (Plate 14) are very common and conspicuous on trees and hedgerows during August and September. Oak, birch, and sallow are among the favourite food plants of this species, but it will eat the leaves of almost any tree or shrub and it is quite happy with plum or apple in the garden. The caterpillars spend most of their lives feeding in colonies and often strip every leaf from a branch. They separate when almost fully grown and turn into dark, glossy pupae in the soil. The adult moths (Plate 12) emerge the following June, but they are rarely seen except when they come to light. The wings are wrapped around the body when at rest and their buff tips, together with the buff hairs on the thorax, give them the appearance of broken twigs. The buff-tip is found all over the country, but it is especially common in the south.

Many kinds of caterpillars spin silken 'tents' on their food plants and feed there in colonies for the early part of their lives. We have already met this habit in the small tortoiseshell and peacock butterflies, but it is even more widespread among the moths. The majority of the garden 'tents' in Wales and the southern half of England belong to caterpillars of the **lackey moth,** although the tents of the ermel caterpillars (page 152) are also very common. Most of the lackey tents are spun up on hawthorn hedges, but the caterpillars are not at all fussy about their food and they will attack a wide variety of trees. They often cause serious defoliation of apples and plums. The lackey passes the winter in the egg stage and the eggs hatch in April. The young caterpillars then cover the twig with silk and feed in the shelter so formed, but they can often be seen sunning themselves on the outside of the shelter. The latter is extended to cover more and more of the branch as the caterpillars grow and need new food supplies. The older part of the web is vacated and it becomes merely a respository for the caterpillars' droppings and old skins. The caterpillars separate when they are nearly fully grown (Plate 14) and they spin yellowish cocoons on the leaves. Adult moths (Plate 12) appear in July and often come to lights. They fly very swiftly and are difficult to catch. They lay their eggs in bands around the twigs of the food plants and leave them to survive the rigours of winter.

Large numbers of our caterpillars are clothed with long and often brightly coloured hairs. These hairs very often have irritating properties and can cause skin rashes if they are handled. Although not all people are susceptible to the irritation, it is a wise plan to handle these caterpillars with caution and avoid touching one's eyes after handling them. One of the hairiest, and also one of the commonest of these hairy caterpillars in the garden is the 'woolly bear' – the caterpillar of the garden tiger moth (Plate 14). The young caterpillars can be found occasionally in the autumn, but they are very small and they go into hibernation fairly early. They are much more easily discovered in the spring, when their favourite haunts are the docks and deadnettles and other low-growing plants under a sunny wall or hedge. They grow rapidly in April and May and they pupate in loose cocoons among the herbage in June. The brightly coloured adult moths (Plate 12) are on the wing in July and they are often flushed from their hiding places among the vegetation. Their bold colours warn of their distasteful qualities and so protect them from birds (see page 165).

The caterpillar of the **white ermine moth** (Plate 14) is quite similar to that of the garden tiger, although slightly smaller. It can be recognised by its long brown hairs and the distinct reddish stripe along the back. It feeds in July and August and can usually be found among the docks and dandelions. The winter is passed as a pupa in a flimsy cocoon and the adult moth, whose wings are usually pure white with numerous black dots, emerges in June. The closely related **buff ermine** (Plate 12) has a very similar life history, but its caterpillars are a lighter brown than those of the white ermine and they lack the distinct red stripe on the back. Both species are found all over the British Isles, although the buff ermine is less common in Scotland. The muslin moth is another close relative whose female has very silky, lightly spotted wings. The male is brown. The species flies in May.

English and Welsh gardens with hawthorn hedges around them will almost certainly support the **goldtail moth** (Plate 12), which gets its name from the tuft of golden hairs at the tip of the abdomen. The moth is on the wing in June and July and very often comes to rest on the windows. The female lays her eggs on the leaves of hawthorn and various other trees, including apples and pears in the garden, and covers them with the hairs from the tip of her body. The caterpillars hibernate soon after hatching from the eggs, but they re-emerge in the spring and their black, red and white colouring (Plate 14) makes them very conspicuous in the hedgerows. The hairs of this species are particularly irritating in both the adult and larval stages.

The caterpillars of the **vapourer moth** (Plate 14) are also quite common on hawthorn hedges and other trees in the summer. They are easily recognised by their peculiar tufts of hairs. The caterpillars spin cocoons among the leaves of the food plant. Adult moths (Plate 12) can be seen at any time from June to September. The males are fully winged and they dash up and down the hedgerows very rapidly by day and night. Much of this activity is directed to searching out the wingless females which rarely move away from their cocoons when they emerge. The moths mate on the cocoons

PLATE 11: **Butterflies.** 1 Red admiral 139; 2 Peacock 135; 3 Small copper 139; 4 Comma 140; 5 Painted lady 140; 6 Small tortoiseshell 134; 7 Holly blue 138; 8 Small white 137; 9 Ringlet, underside only, 138; 10 Orange-tip 136; 11 Green-veined white, underside only, 138; 12 Wall brown 138; 13 Hedge brown 138; 14 Large white 136; 15 Brimstone 135. Upperside on left; underside on right.

12

and the females lay their eggs there as well. The eggs remain there during the winter and begin to hatch in April, but they do not all hatch at once. It may be three months before all the caterpillars emerge, and this is why one can find both larvae and adults throughout the summer. The vapourer is one of the commonest moths in our city centres and great hordes of caterpillars can sometimes be seen crawling on the pavements under limes and other street trees after a spell of strong wind.

The garden supports numerous stout-bodied moths with rather drab grey, brown, or black front wings which are often decorated with a pair of ear-shaped marks. These moths belong to the large group known as noctuids. Many of them come to light, and the gardener will also find many of them resting on walls, fences, and tree trunks where their dull front wings afford them an efficient camouflage. Several more will be disturbed among the plants. Some of the caterpillars, such as that of the **grey dagger** (Plate 14), are well clothed with long hairs, but most are naked or covered only with scattered small bristles. Most of the species pupate in the ground, and nearly all the pupae dug up in the garden belong to this group.

The type of moth pupa commonly dug up in the garden

Most of the noctuid moths have greyish and rather 'dirty' hind wings, but there are some exceptions, such as the various species of yellow underwings. The **large yellow underwing** (Plate 12) is a very common garden insect which rests in the hedge or the herbaceous border with its bright yellow hind wings hidden away under the drab front ones. When disturbed, however, the moth takes off and flashes its yellow wings during a short, undulating flight. It then drops back into the herbage, leaving the gardener puzzling as to what it was and where it went. We can reasoably assume that a bird is equally puzzled. The caterpillar of the large yellow underwing is dark brown with paler lines running along the sides and back. There are distinct black crescents on the sides of each segment in the rear half of the animal. It reaches a length of about 6 cm and tapers fairly strongly towards the front. It feeds on a wide variety of plants and often causes some damage in the herbaceous border.

◀ PLATE 12: **Moths**. 1 Poplar hawkmoth 142; 2 Hummingbird hawkmoth 142; 3 Grey dagger 147; 4 Eyed hawkmoth 142; 5 Lackey 143; 6 Garden tiger 143; 7 Buff ermine 144; 8 Vapourer 144, a male, b female with eggs; 9 Buff-tip 143; 10 Gold tail 144; 11 Large yellow underwing 145; 12 Setaceous Hebrew character 146; 13 Cabbage moth 146; 14 Heart-and-dart 146; 15 Clay wainscot 146; 16 Dot moth 146.

Most gardeners and housewives have had cause to curse the **cabbage moth** (Plate 12), for this is the species whose plump caterpillars (Plate 14) bore right into the hearts of our cabbages and make them quite unfit for the table. Only a small part of a cabbage may actually be eaten by one of these caterpillars, but the remaining leaves are contaminated by droppings and they soon start to decay. The moths are on the wing in May and June and the caterpillars are active in June and July. A partial second generation of moths may emerge in August and further larvae will be then found in September and October. Pyrethrum-based dusts can be sprayed on to the cabbages to kill the young larvae before they burrow into the hearts, but the best method of control is to search out the brownish eggs – unfortunately usually laid singly on the leaves – and to squash them. Larvae which reach maturity pupate in the soil under the food plants and the gardener need have no qualms about treading on the pupae dug up from the cabbage patch.

The closely related **dot moth** (Plate 12) is equally common in gardens in the southern half of England and in Wales. The adult is on the wing in July and August, while the caterpillars (Plate 14) can be found on a wide variety of garden plants from August to October. The **heart-and-dart moth** (Plate 12) is another very common noctuid and, like most members of this group, it is very variable in colour. Its front wings vary from pale brown, through chestnut, to something verging on black, but the markings usually remain distinct and serve to identify the species. The moth flies in June and July in most parts of the British Isles. Its brownish caterpillar feeds from July to May and it is often discovered feeding among the weeds in the depths of winter. Although it will eat almost any low-growing plant, the caterpillar has a particular liking for lettuces in the garden.

The **turnip moth** can be distinguished from the other brown garden noctuids by its very white hind wings. It flies in June and again in the autumn and its greyish, black-spotted caterpillar feeds right through the winter. It attacks the roots of many crops, including carrots and turnips, and it also very often nibbles through cabbage stalks just above the base. The **setaceous hebrew character** and the **clay wainscot,** both illustrated on Plate 12, are two more very common garden moths. They very often come to lighted windows and the clay wainscot can be recognised very easily from indoors because it has a black mark on the underside of its body. The setaceous hebrew character flies in May and June and again in the autumn, while the clay wainscot flies in July and August. The caterpillars of both species feed on various low-growing plants.

The **grey dagger moth** (Plate 12) is quite commonly seen on old walls. When my house had grey, lichen-encrusted walls I could almost guarantee to find one or two of these moths resting there every morning in June – although I had to look hard to pick them out. The house then had a face-lift and took on a nice clean shade of cream. I have not seen a grey dagger there since and it is tempting to think that the moths know that the surface no longer matches their own coloration. The alternative explanation is that they still settle on the walls but, being conspicuous against the cream background, they are snapped up by birds long before I drag myself out of bed in the morning. The caterpillar (Plate 14) feeds on the leaves of various trees, including apples and plums. It is often common on hawthorn hedges.

Two rather well-named noctuid moths – the **old lady** and the **mouse** – sometimes hide in dark out-buildings during the daytime. The old lady gets her name because her wings are patterned with various shades of brown, arranged in a way that is reminiscent of the shawls beloved of elderly victorian ladies. She flies in July and August, often in company with the mouse moth. The latter not only has a mouse's colour: it runs like a mouse as well when it is disturbed. Its caterpillar, bright green with white stripes along its length, is not uncommon on the flowers of garden plants during April and May.

The old lady

The mouse moth

The **angle shades** (Plate 13) flies in May and June and again in the autumn. It is a very common moth, but its habit of resting with its wings rucked up makes it look very much like a dead leaf and it is often overlooked as it sits among the herbage. Its caterpillar (Plate 14) feeds on a wide variety of low-growing plants, but rarely does any damage in the garden.

The buddleia and ice-plant that are so attractive to our summer butterflies also attract many moths, one of their most abundant visitors being the **silver-Y** (Plate 13). This species, one of several with Y-shaped metallic marks on its wings, flies more by day than by night and can be seen flitting around the flowers with the tortoiseshells. It rarely keeps its wings still and we usually see it only as a greyish blur. The silver-Y is a migrant moth which arrives here in May and June and begins to breed. Its caterpillar (Plate 14) can be found on almost any herbaceous plant and it causes some damage to crops when immigration occurs on a large scale. Home-bred moths are on the wing in August and September, augmented by further immigration – this time from Northern Europe. The moths rarely breed at this time of year and many fly away to the south in September. The species does not survive here during the winter.

The **burnished brass,** a close relative of the silver-Y with brassy patches on its wings, is common in the garden from June to September. You will often see it on the flowers if you walk around the garden at night. The caterpillars feed on stinging nettles. The **herald moth** (Plate 13) is another relative and it is one of many noctuids that are attracted to ivy blossom late in the autumn. The adults hibernate in sheds and other dry places after filling up with nectar and they emerge again early in the spring.

One of the latest-flying noctuids is the **beaded chestnut,** a very variable brownish moth which can usually be recognised by a row of three fairly prominent dots along the front edge of each wing. The species is common at ivy blossom and often comes to light. Although rare in Scotland, it is abundant in most other parts of the British Isles.

The beaded chestnut moth varies from straw-coloured to a very rich brown

Leaving the stout-bodied noctuids, we can now move on to look at another large group of moths known as the GEOMETERS. The majority are rather flimsy and slender-bodied and they fly rather weakly. They get their name, which means 'ground measurer', from the behaviour of the larvae. The latter have the normal three pairs of legs at the front end, but they have only two pairs at the back. They move by anchoring the hind end, stretching the front out to find a new anchorage, and then bringing the hind end up close to the

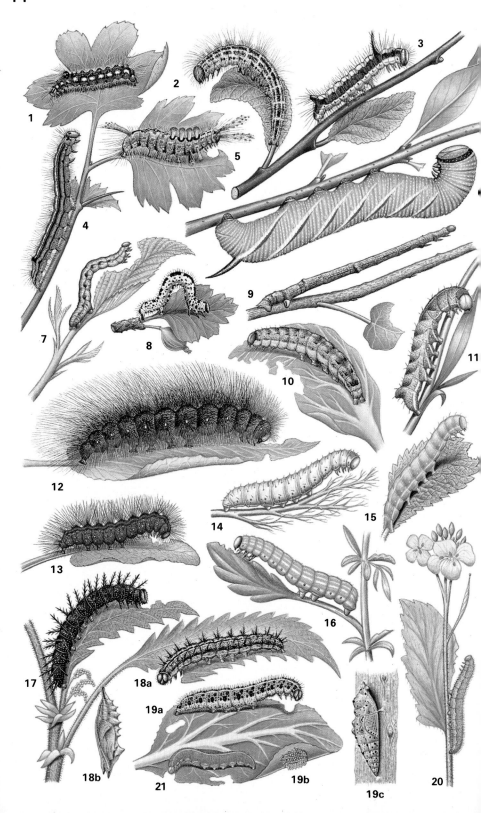

front again. In doing this, the body is arched up into a loop and the whole process gives the impression that the caterpillar is using its body to measure distances. The caterpillars are also known as loopers. Many of them are remarkably like twigs and they are very difficult to see when they are at rest on their food plants.

The striking **swallow-tailed moth** (Plate 13) is one of our largest geometers and it is common in gardens as far north as southern Scotland. It often comes to windows and to street lights in July. Its remarkably twig-like caterpillar (Plate 14) is found mainly on ivy, but it also eats hawthorn and blackthorn leaves. The brightly coloured **brimstone moth** (Plate 13) is another common visitor to lighted windows, especially where there are hawthorns nearby for the larvae to feed on. Gardeners with gooseberry or currant bushes will also meet the boldly marked **magpie moth** (Plate 13). The conspicuous pattern warns birds that the moth has an unpleasant taste and they leave it alone, but the spider does not appreciate the pattern and always attacks a magpie moth if it gets into the web. At the first bite, however, the poor old spider discovers the foul taste and immediately removes the moth from the web. The moth itself probably has some immunity to spider venom and seems to suffer no ill effects. The caterpillars of the magpie moth (Plate 14) often do much damage to currant and gooseberry bushes. They resemble the larvae of the gooseberry sawfly (Plate 9), but they are brighter in colour and they have fewer legs.

Currant bushes are also the food plant of another common garden geometer – the inaptly named **spinach moth.** This species has yellowish front wings, crossed by two or three wavy brown lines. The outer margins of all four wings are decorated with brown dots. The slender green caterpillar feeds on currant leaves in May and June and the moth is on the wing in July and August.

The spinach moth

The snout moth

Working near nettle beds in June and July, the gardener will probably come across a dull brown moth with a long point on its head. This is the **snout moth,** a very common species whose larvae feed on the nettles. The adult often comes to light. The 'snout' is formed by the enlarged palps around the mouth.

The **garden carpet** and the **yellow shell**, both illustrated on Plate 13, are two more very common geometers of the garden and the hedgerow. The garden carpet, one of several rather similar species which all sit with their wings spread out to form a triangle, can be found at any time from April to October. Its caterpillar feeds on various members of the cabbage family, including wallflowers and cultivated cabbages. The yellow shell can be beaten from nearly every hedgerow during the summer. Its larvae feed on grasses and other low-growing plants.

The **pug moths** are smaller than the carpets and they generally have rather slender front wings. The wings are held in a very characteristic position when at rest, as shown by the **currant pug** and the **lime-speck pug** on Plate 13. These are just two of the many pug moths to be found in the garden. The currant pug caterpillar is rather a slender green creature with brown lines on it and it feeds on the leaves of currant and gooseberry bushes. The caterpillar of the lime-speck pug feeds on the flowers of golden rod and many other garden plants. Both moths are on the wing for much of the summer.

Geometers of one species or another can be found flying at all times of the year, even in December and January. One of the commonest species about at this period is the **winter moth** (Plate 13). The dull greyish brown males of this species are often abundant on window panes, but the females are wingless and must be looked for on the trunks of apple trees and other fruit trees. Emerging from her subterranean pupa, she crawls up the trees to mate and lay her eggs, and her slender, green caterpillars often strip the leaves from the branches in April and May. The sticky bands which gardeners often put round tree trunks are designed mainly to trap the females and to prevent them from laying their eggs. The **mottled umber** (Plate 13) is another species with wingless females. The adults are usually to be found in November and December and their caterpillars (Plate 14) feed on a wide variety of trees in the spring. Like the winter moth larvae, they often defoliate whole branches.

Walking on the lawn or a grassy path or verge on an evening in June or July, you might see a rather limp, white object heaving itself out of the ground. This will be the male **ghost swift moth**, emerging from its pupa after nearly a year under the ground. The upper sides of the male's wings are pure white (Plate 13) and they give it a rather ghostly appearance as it dances up and down over the herbage at dusk. The yellowish brown females are attracted to the dancing males and, after mating, they scatter their eggs freely over the vegetation. The caterpillars (Plate 14) feed on the roots of dandelions, grasses, and various other plants. The **common swift** (Plate 13) has a similar life history but, unlike the ghost swift, it regularly comes to light and can often be seen whirring furiously around street lights. At rest, its wings are held tightly around the body and it looks rather like a broken twig.

Small holes in the shoots of currant bushes generally indicate the

The spider-like female mottled umber moth

The currant clearwing moth 'sun-bathing'

presence of the **currant clearwing moth.** This little insect's wings are almost devoid of scales and it looks more like a sawfly (see page 183) than a moth. Although found over the greater part of England, it is not often seen. The moth flies in June and July, but spends much of its time sunning itself on the leaves of the food plant. The maggot-like larvae tunnel in the stems of the currant bushes and pupate there when fully grown, but the species is rarely numerous enough to do much damage to the bushes.

The moths described so far all fall into an assemblage which the moth collector refers to as 'macros'. Most of them are relatively large. The other major assemblage, which contains the bulk of our species, is referred to as the 'micros'. Most of these are very small creatures and the average gardener will take little notice of them if he even sees them. There are, however, a few relatively large species which will come to his notice. Some of these are larger than some of the geometers and it is not always easy to distinguish the two groups, but the larger micros, generally belonging to a group known as pyralids, usually have relatively longer and rather spiky legs.

One of the easiest of the micros to recognise is the **white plume moth** (Plate 13), whose wings are broken up into five feather-like sections on each side. It flies in June and July and often comes to lighted windows. Only the two-lobed front wings are visible when the insect is at rest. It is common throughout England, Wales, and Ireland wherever there are bindweeds to provide food for the yellow and green caterpillars. The **small magpie moth** (Plate 13) is another very easily recognised species, found abundantly in the southern half of the British Isles. The white or pinkish larvae live in rolled-up leaves of stinging nettle and other plants. Stinging nettles are also the food of the caterpillars of the **mother-of-pearl moth** (Plate 13). On the wing in July and August, this rather shiny moth can often be seen at flowers after dark. It comes to light regularly, frequently in association with the **gold fringe moth** (Plate 13), a pretty little moth that usually comes to rest with its wings spread out and its tail stuck up in the air. It seems to be especially common in gardens near farms or thatched houses because the larvae feed on dead grasses and they are attracted to hay and straw.

The **garden pebble** is one of the less welcome micros in the garden because its larva causes much damage to cabbages and other brassicas. The moth is on the wing in May and June and again in August and September. The caterpillar is yellowish green with darker stripes along its length. It often tunnels into cabbages and cauliflower heads, and it also spins the leaves of young cabbage

The garden pebble (1½ times life size)

plants together. Although often abundant in the garden, the moth is rarely a nuisance to field-grown cabbages because it dislikes open situations.

Long stretches of hedgerow are sometimes clothed with silken webs in May. These might be the work of the lackey caterpillar (see page 143), but if you examine the webs and find them full of greyish caterpillars with dark heads you can be fairly sure that you are looking at the work of the **ermels** or **small ermine moths**. We have several species in the British Isles, but they all have white front wings dotted with black (Plate 13). The caterpillars of some species cause severe damage to fruit trees.

Our brief survey of garden moths ends with another real pest – the **codlin moth** (Plate 13), whose caterpillars so often spoil our enjoyment of a juicy apple. Adult moths first appear in May, when the apple blossom is beginning to fade, but they continue to emerge in June and July. They lay their eggs on the leaves and the young fruit and the pinkish grubs then tunnel into the fruit and feed there for several weeks. The fully grown grubs leave the apples and spin cocoons in bark crevices. Many insecticidal sprays are available to combat the codlin moth, but they are effective only if used just when the young caterpillars are hatching, and accurate timing is not easy. Removal of all loose bark from the trees is a simpler method of keeping the pest under control. This deprives the larvae of safe hiding places and allows the birds to get at them. The gardener can also try binding collars of sacking or corrugated paper around the main branches in August. Many of the grubs will spin up in this material, which can then be burned. Codlin moths sometimes come to light, but most of those that occur in houses probably come from infested fruit that has been brought in. Caterpillars emerging in the house will pupate in any convenient corner.

FLIES

The flies belong to the order known as Diptera. This name means 'two wings' and refers to the fact that the flies have only a single pair of wings. Their hind wings have become converted into the pin-like halteres or balancers, which are very well seen in the crane-flies (page 163). Some hover-flies (page 156) are able to chew up pollen grains with their mouth-parts, but the flies are otherwise entirely drinkers. Many of them suck nectar from flowers, while others go to the other extreme and lap up the germ-filled fluids from dung and other decaying material. These flies can also deal with some solid materials by pouring digestive juices over them and mopping up the resulting solutions. And then there are the blood-sucking flies, including the mosquitoes (page 161) and some midges, whose mouth-parts form minute hypodermic needles similar to those of the bugs (page 119). Apart from their overwhelming dependence on liquid foods, however, the flies are a remarkably diverse group – in terms of behaviour as well as size and shape: and the larvae are even more varied then the adults. Fly larvae are always legless, although some have a few fleshy stumps, but they are found in almost every situation and they feed on an amazing variety of materials. Some tunnel inside leaves and other parts of plants; some are aquatic and feed on microscopic organisms in the water; many live in dung and decaying flesh; some destroy the roots of our plants; some are carnivorous; and many others live as parasites inside the bodies of other animals.

The greatest variety of flies are obviously found in the wildest gardens, but even the smallest and barest garden will yield a fair number of species because many of our flies like nothing better than to sit and sun themselves on the walls of a house. Some of them annoy us by getting indoors and buzzing loudly as they try to find a way out, and a few will actually attack us or spread germs on to our food, but the majority are quite harmless as far as our gardens and crops are concerned.

Some of the sun-loving flies can be found on sunny days at any time of the year. They are attracted to south-facing walls and windows, where they sit soaking up the sunshine for long periods. Among the commonest of these 'permanent' species are the bluebottles or **blow-flies,** such as *Calliphora vomitoria* (Plate 16),

The bluebottle in typical resting position, together with its larva or maggot

which all have metallic blue bodies. They are basically carrion-feeders, and the females readily lay their eggs on exposed meat or fish in the summer. The little white eggs hatch within a day or two and produce white, carrot-shaped maggots which, if not detected, tunnel into the food and rapidly liquefy it with their digestive juices. Growth is completed within a few days and the maggots crawl away to pupate in a drier site. Each pupa is housed in a tough brown 'barrel' called a puparium, and the adult fly pushes its way out a few days later. The flies pass through several generations during the warmer months, but breeding generally stops during the winter and the adults find themselves cosy retreats when the weather is cold. The greenbottles, such as *Lucilia caesar* (Plate 16), have a very similar life history, but they are more likely to be seen sitting on vegetation than on walls, and, unlike the bluebottles, they rarely come into the house.

The bluebottles and greenbottles are often accompanied in their sun-bathing by a large grey fly with black stripes on the thorax and a fairly distinct chess-board pattern on the abdomen. This is the **flesh-fly** (Plate 16) and, except for the fact that it brings forth active young instead of laying eggs, its life history is just like that of the bluebottle. The **cluster-fly** (Plate 16), which can be recognised by the golden 'fur' on its thorax, is another very common sun-bather, especially in the spring and autumn. It gets its name because it often swarms around the windows and eaves of houses in the autumn and then enters attics and roof-spaces to hibernate in dense masses. The larva of this fly lives inside the body of an earthworm and gradually destroys it in the manner of the caterpillar-eating ichneumons (page 183).

The **common house-fly** (Plate 16) is actually far less common that it was fifty years ago, partly because of the widespread use of insecticides and also because of the decline of the horse. The house-fly breeds in dung and other filth and it was particularly abundant in the days of horse transport. It is still common enough to be a nuisance in the house, however, and it is a dangerous germ carrier because of its association with dung heaps and rubbish dumps. The house-fly does occur in the garden and it often suns itself on the wall, but it is usually out-numbered in such a situation by the very similar **face-fly** (Plate 16). Both species breed abundantly in rubbish dumps and they can be a real problem around these dumps unless the rubbish is properly covered with soil to deny the flies access to it. The dull grey **stable-fly** (Plate 16) is not too different from the house-fly in general appearance, but it has no yellow on the abdomen and it can be recognised by its prominent proboscis which it uses to pierce the skin of various animals, including us. The fly likes to sun itself, but it is not generally common in gardens unless there are farms or stables in the area. Its larvae develop in cattle and horse dung. *Mesembrina meridiana* (Plate 16) also breeds in cattle dung, but the adult is much more wide-ranging than the stable-fly and it is quite common in rural gardens. Its yellow wing-bases makes it quite conspicuous as it rests on walls and tree trunks.

Scenopinus fenestralis (Plate 16) is more likely to be found in houses and sheds than out in the garden. It is usually seen sitting quietly on windows and it has thus earned itself the name of window-fly. The wings are folded neatly over the abdomen when at rest and they reach well beyond it to give the fly a slender, cigar-shaped appearance. It is often reluctant to fly and is more likely to walk up the window pane than to fly away when touched. The larvae are thought to feed on the larvae of clothes moths, house moths, and other small insects, which they find in abundance in neglected sheds and out-houses.

The **drone-fly** (Plate 16), so named because of its remarkably similarity to a honey-bee drone, is another of the 'permanent' garden flies which can be seen sunning themselves on warm days throughout the year. It is actually one of the hover-flies, and it can be recognised as such by the false margin formed by the veins near the outer edge of the wing. It can hover in one spot for minutes on end, just as if suspended by an invisible thread, and then it can dart this way or that far too quickly for the eye to follow it. But the fly is not always on the wing: it regularly settles on walls, rocks, and flowers and pumps its abdomen up and down almost as if it were out of breath. In common with the other hover-flies, the drone-fly

The rat-tailed maggot, the drone-fly's larva

feeds on nectar and also grinds up pollen grains and swallows them. Its larva, known as a rat-tailed maggot, is one of the most peculiar of all fly larvae. It lives in muddy ponds and ditches and even in leaf-choked gutters, where it feeds on decaying material and breathes by pushing a telescopic tube up into the air.

Many other hover-flies are found in the garden from spring to autumn, and many of them display bold black and yellow patterns which make them look like wasps. This phenomenon is known as mimicry and it certainly helps to protect the flies from birds and other enemies. Every gardener must have drawn back from one of these harmless hoverflies at some time or other in the belief that it was a wasp, and the same thing happens with birds. Young birds discover what is good to eat by a process of trial and error, and they will peck at almost anything to start with. But when they have tried a few wasps and been rewarded with a painful sting, or at least an unpleasant taste, they begin to leave them alone. They obviously recognise them by the bold pattern, and the avoidance is extended to all other insects with a similar pattern. *Syrphus ribesii* (Plate 17) is one of the commonest of these black and yellow hover-flies in the garden, and it can be found in a wide variety of flowers as well as

PLATE 15: **Bees and Wasps.** 1 Honey bee 172, a worker, b drone; 2 Leaf-cutter bee 169; 3 Tawny mining bee 167; 4 White-tailed bumble bee queen 171; 5 Buff-tailed bumble bee queen 171; 6 Red-tailed bumble bee queen 171; 7 *Halictus calceatus* 167; 8 *Bombus hortorum* queen 171; 9 Carder bee queen 171; 10 Red osmia 168; 11 *Anthophora acervorum* 168, a male, b female; 12 *Prosopis communis* 169; 13 Common wasp 176, a queen, b face; 14 German wasp 176; 15 *Ancistrocerus parietinus* 175. **Digger Wasps:** 16 *Pemphredon lugubris* 175; 17 *Trypoxylon figulus* 175; 18 *Ectemnius quadricinctus* 175.

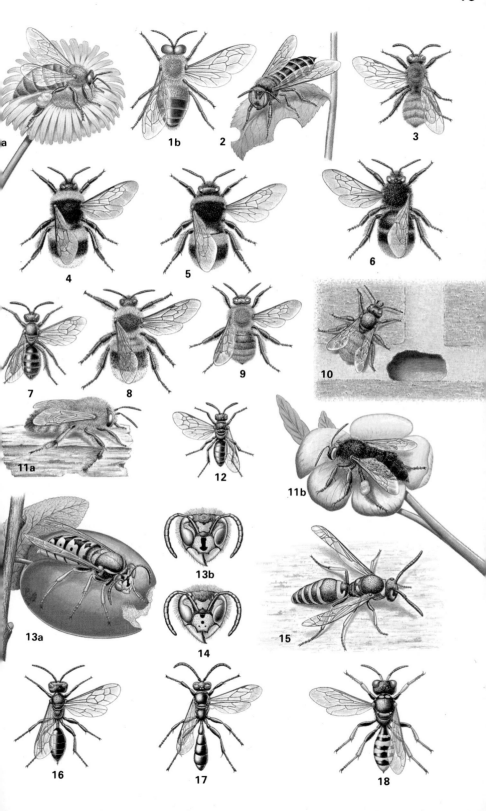

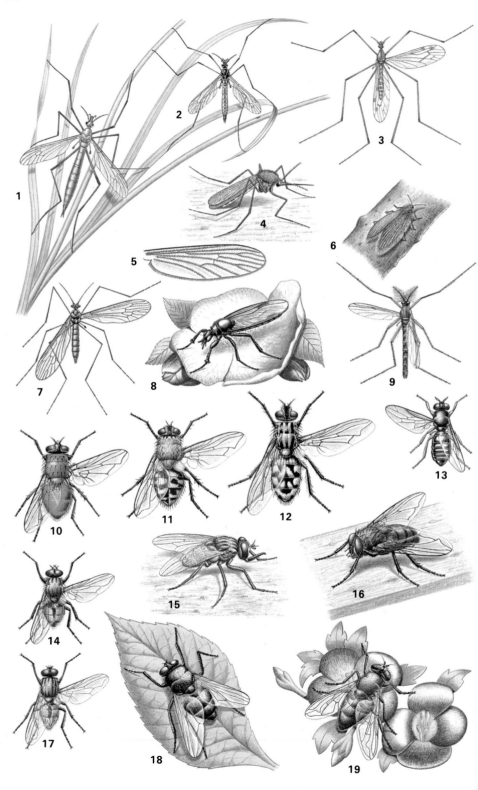

sunning itself on the leaves. *Scaeva pyrastri* (Plate 17), easily identified by its black and white pattern, is also very common. The larvae of both species feed on aphids and are therefore useful allies of the gardener. *Rhingia campestris* (Plate 17), readily identified by its snout, breeds in cow dung and it is common in rural gardens. *Melanostoma scalare* and *Neoascia podagrica* (both on Plate 17) are more slender than the hover-flies previously mentioned, and they appear very narrow when resting in flowers with their wings folded neatly over their bodies, but close inspection will reveal the false margin on the wing and show that they are true hover-flies.

One of the few hover-flies to cause damage in the garden is the **narcissus-fly** (Plate 17), a rather variable and hairy species which resembles various kinds of bumble bee. Its larva feeds in the centre of daffodil bulbs, often causing such severe injury that the whole bulb dies and decays.

Examination of apple and pear blossom in the spring will reveal numerous bees going about the important business of pollination, but it will also show that many flies play their part in ensuring our fruit crops. One of the most noticeable of these flies is *Dilophus febrilis* (Plate 16), which is sometimes called the **fever-fly**. The females often congregate on the flowers in vast numbers and sit with their smoky wings laid neatly along the top of the body, while the males, whose wings are almost clear, hover lazily around them. The larvae of this species live mainly in decaying matter, but they are known to damage the roots of various plants. The **St Mark's-fly** *(Bibio marci)* is a closely related species which is commonly found sunning itself on walls and flowers in the spring. It can be distinguished from *Dilophus* by its larger size and by looking at the front legs: *Dilophus* has a circlet of spines on the tibia, while *Bibio* has a single claw-like spine.

Aubretia, polyanthus, and other early spring flowers often attract a brown, furry fly with a very long proboscis. This is the **bee-fly** (Plate 17), a sun-loving insect and a very accomplished aeronaut. It hovers a foot or two above the ground or the vegetables and makes a high-pitched whine as it lowers itself gently down just like a helicopter coming in to land. The wings come to rest when the insect lands on the ground to sun itself, but they continue to vibrate while it feeds at the flowers. The fly thus appears to hover at the flowers, but it actually grasps the petals with its long front legs. It is a very alert and agile insect and, like many of the hover-flies, it darts rapidly away as soon as it detects any movement. The bee-fly spends its larval life as a parasite in the nest of a solitary bee such as *Andrena*

PLATE 16: **Flies.** 1 Marsh crane-fly 163; 2 Spotted crane-fly 163; 3 *Limonia flavipes* 163; 4 Common gnat 162; 5 Mosquito wing 161; 6 Owl midge 158; 7 Winter gnat 161; 8 Fever-fly 157; 9 *Chironomus plumosus* 161; 10 *Lucilia caesar* 154; 11 Cluster-fly 155; 12 Flesh-fly 155; 13 *Scenopinus fenestralis* 155; 14 Face-fly 155; 15 Stable-fly 155; 16 Bluebottle 154; 17 House-fly 155; 18 *Mesembrina meridiana* 155; 19 Drone-fly 156. The flies on this plate can be found in almost any garden, often resting on the walls and windows of the house.

(page 167), and the female can sometimes be seen flying to and fro over a patch of ground in which the bees are nesting. She drops her eggs freely as she flies and the little grubs make their own way into the bees' nests, where they feed slowly but surely on the doomed bee larvae or pupae.

One other hoverer which many gardeners will see, although few will catch and examine, is *Ophyra leucostoma* (Plate 17). This dark and very shiny fly, which is distantly related to the house-fly, hangs motionless like a tiny helicopter in the shafts of sunlight that penetrate the fruit trees in the early summer. It politely glides to one side should the gardener wish to pass, but it very soon takes up its station again afterwards. The larvae are believed to feed on a variety of decaying material.

Rotting vegetation provides food for many kinds of fly larvae, and the adults of these species can often be found in the vicinity of the compost heap. Among the most conspicuous are the shiny **soldier-flies**, such as *Chloromyia formosa* and *Microchrysa polita* (both shown on Plate 17). These flies are particularly common in early summer, when they can be found crawling slowly on the compost heap and on nearby vegetation. They also tend to appear where manure has recently been dug in, and they are also very common in waterside habitats.

Soldier-flies seem reluctant to fly, and their sluggish habits, combined with their brilliant colours, make them fairly easily identified. The group can also be recognised by the way in which the wing veins crowd together near the front margin. Species of *Dolichopus* (Plate 17) are very often associated with the soldier-flies, especially in the damper areas. The male often has very feathery middle feet, and he also has a rather elaborate genital apparatus tucked under his abdomen. *Calliopum aeneum* (Plate 17) is another common species to be seen among the vegetation in shady areas.

Clouds of much smaller flies often fly up when we disturb the compost heap. Many of these will be the brownish or grey flies with reddish eyes which are known as **fruit-flies** or **vinegar-flies**. They are especially common later in the year, when rotting fruit may be heaped on to the garden, and they are also very common in fruiterers' shops and in houses when the jam is being made. Most of them belong to the genus *Drosophila* (Plate 17). The **owl midges**, such as *Psychoda* (Plate 16), are even more common on the compost heap, and they even crawl about in the rotting material. They are very hairy insects, and their oval wings are normally held roofwise when they are at rest. Owl midges, also called moth-flies, are strongly attracted to light and large numbers come to windows on humid nights.

The **fungus gnats** are another group which abound in and around the compost heap. They are very delicate, grey flies with long, thread-like antennae and rather spiky legs. They are often found right inside the compost heap with the owl midges, and they also accompany the latter on the nocturnal visits to our windows. Among the most common are species of *Sciara* (Plate 17), which are easily identified by the tuning-fork-shaped vein in the centre of the wing.

Sepsis punctum (Plate 17) is an abundant little fly which can be recognised by its ant-like body, the prominent spot on each wing, and its habit of waving its wings slowly up and down while sunning itself on the vegetation. It can be found in any garden with a compost heap, and in a good many without one, but it is especially common in gardens close to farmland. The larvae develop in rotting material and are abundant in dung heaps, so much so that the vegetation around such places if often black with the adults when they emerge.

Platystoma seminationis (Plate 17) is a strange-looking fly which is usually found only in the wilder gardens. Very unwilling to fly, it crawls over the shrubs and other plants in a very lethargic way and holds its wings in a characteristically 'round-shouldered' attitude. The fly, whose larvae live in decaying plant material, is most common in moist and shady places. It is sometimes accompanied by some even more unusual-looking flies, known as stilt-legged-flies because of their extremely long, thin legs, Species of *Micropeza* (Plate 17) have rather flat and triangular heads, but *Trepidaria* species, which are generally more common, have rounded heads. The stilt-legged-flies prey on aphids and other small insects, while their larvae feed in decaying leaves. *Empis tessellata* (Plate 17) is another predatory species which occurs in the wilder gardens. It is sometimes common on hogweed and other umbellifers, sipping the nectar with its long beak, but always keeping an eye open for more substantial food in the form of other flies which visit the flowers. These other flies are pounced upon and then pierced with the beak, and even quite heavy flies, such as bluebottles, can be carried aloft in a slow and laboured flight. *Empis livida* is a slightly smaller relative with the same drab coloration and the same habits. It is often quite common in flower borders in spring and summer.

Several of the smaller flies are damaging in the garden because their larvae attack our crops. *Psila rosae* (Plate 17) is the common

carrot-fly, which causes severe damage to carrots in many parts of the country. The flies themselves are not often noticed, but their grubs are commonly seen projecting from freshly dug carrots. The flies lay eggs around the young carrot plants in late spring and the resulting larvae bore into the roots and turn the once-succulent carrots into little more than empty shells, especially in the lower parts of the roots. Infested plants can usually be detected at a distance because the leaves take on a rusty coloration. If the carrots are left in the ground, the larvae will eventually crawl out of them and pupate in the soil, giving rise to a second generation ready to attack the main crop carrots during the later part of the summer. As well as attacking carrots, the carrot fly larvae enjoy themselves on celery, parsley, and parsnips. Celery and parsnips also suffer from the attentions of the celery-fly, *Philophylla heraclei* (Plate 17). The larvae of this attractive little species are leaf-miners and they form extensive pale blotches where they tunnel between the two leaf surfaces. Heavy infestations kill the plants by taking all the nourishment made in the leaves. As with the carrot-fly, there is one generation in late spring and another in late summer. Both species can also exist quite happily on hogweed (see page 47) and various umbelliferous weeds.

Many of the smaller and more slender flies, including some of the smaller crane-flies, are known as gnats and midges. They very often form dancing swarms in which hundreds of individuals 'dance' up and down. These swarms generally maintain station over a prominent object, such as a brightly coloured patch of flowers or some washing on the line, and the insects take their bearings on this rather than on each other. A swarm of winter gnats regularly gathered over a yellow plastic bowl in my own garden, and I was able to control the position of the swarm by moving the bowl from place to place. The swarms generally consist only of male insects, and their function is to attract the females. The latter approach the swarms, but they rarely get beyond the fringe before they are greeted by the males and whisked away on their honeymoons.

Many of the gnats and midges are attracted to light, and among the commonest of these are the fungus gnats, the owl midges, and the little **gall midges** – tiny flies which generally have orange bodies and greyish wings with hardly any veins. Hundreds of these insects will fly into the house if you leave a window open in a lighted room on a summer evening, and many of them are killed as they fly up to the hot lamp. The gall midges nearly all spend their larval lives inside various plants, causing the tissues to swell up and produce

PLATE 17: **Flies.** 1 Bee-fly 157. 2–7 **Hover-flies,** pp. 156–7: 2 Narcissus-fly; 3 *Rhingia campestris*; 4 *Syrphus ribesii*; 5 *Scaeva pyrastri*; 6 *Melanostoma scalare*; 7 *Neoascia podagrica*. 8 *Empis tessellata* 159. 9–10 **Soldier-flies,** p. 158: 9 *Chloromyia formosa*; 10 *Microchrysa polita*. 11 Carrot-fly 160; 12 *Platystoma seminationis* 159; 13 *Dolichopus* sp. 158; 14 Gall midge 160; 15 Fungus gnat 159; 16 *Calliopum aeneum* 158; 17 Celery-fly 160; 18 Fruit-fly 158; 19 *Sepsis punctum* 159; 20 *Ophyra leucostoma* 158; 21 Stilt-legged-fly 159.

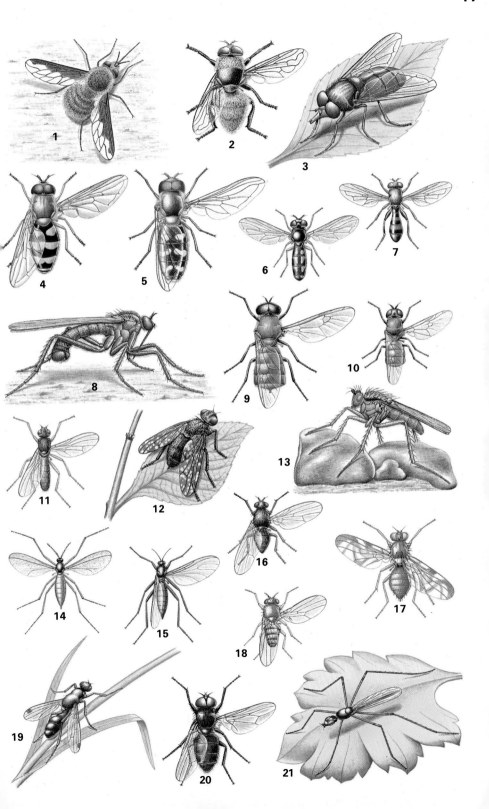

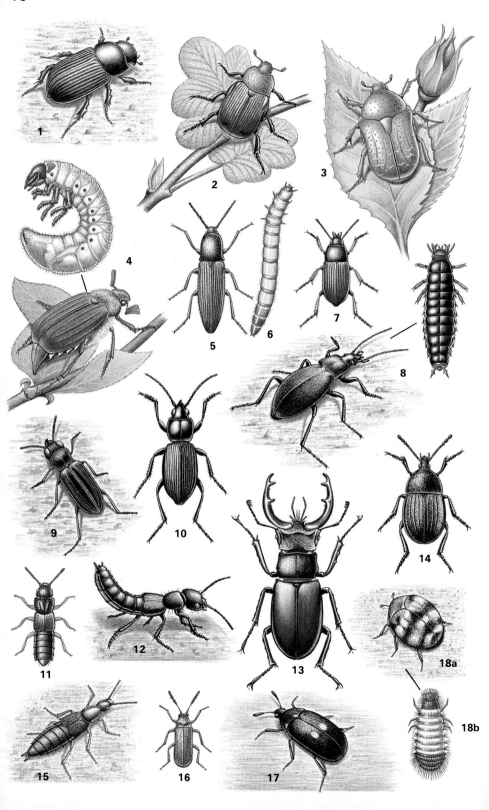

the characteristic galls. *Jaapiella veronicae* (Plate 17) is one of the most abundant species and it is responsible for the rounded, hairy galls that develop on the tips of the shoots of germander speedwell. A similar species, *Taxomyia taxi,* causes the leaves to bunch together on the tips of yew shoots. If you open either of these two galls, you will find the little orange larvae of the gall midges. Related species attack garden swedes, causing the leaf stalks to become swollen and the crown of the plant distorted.

Gnats and midges are about even in the middle of winter, and if it is not too cold they swarm in mid-afternoon and gather on the windows in the evening. Most of these hardy insects belong to the group known, not surprisingly, as **winter gnats,** and the most common species is *Trichocera annulata* (Plate 16). The winter gnats are very similar in appearance to some of the smaller crane-flies or bobbing gnats (see page 163), but they can be distinguished very easily by the short, curved vein at the hind edge of the wing. Although winter gnats are especially common in the autumn and winter, they can be found at all times of the year. Their larvae live in decaying leaves.

Chironomus plumosus (Plate 16) is our largest member of a group known as **chironomid midges,** which can be recognised at rest by the way in which the wings are held roof-wise over the body with the abdomen protruding beyond them. The males can also be recognised by their exceedingly bushy antennae. *Chironomus annularis* is another very common species, somewhat smaller but easily identified by the alternating bands of green and black on the abdomen. The larvae of the chironomids are mainly aquatic and they include the familiar red 'blood worms' which occur so commonly in water butts. The adults very often rest on house walls, especially while their wings are hardening after crawling out of the waterbutts. Chironomids are not blood-sucking insects and they are often called non-biting midges, but there are a number of less pleasant insects which do attack us and leave us with itchy arms and necks after a session in the garden.

The most familiar of these blood-sucking insects, and the only ones regularly found in the garden, are the **mosquitoes.** These are often confused with the larger chironomids, because they are of similar size and shape and because the males also have bushy antennae, but they are readily distinguished by their long beaks and by the way in which the wings are held flat over the body at rest. The wings of the mosquitoes also have more veins than those of the chironomids and they are partly clothed with minute scales. Female

PLATE 18: Beetles. 1 *Aphodius rufipes* 189; 2 Garden chafer 188; 3 Rose chafer 188; 4 Cockchafer 188, with larva; 5 Click beetle 189; 6 Wireworm 189; 7 *Amara aenea* 188; 8 Violet ground beetle 187, with larva; 9 *Notiophilus biguttatus* 187; 10 *Feronia nigrita* 187; 11 Rove beetle, *Oxytelus laquaetus* 189; 12 Devil's coach horse 189; 13 Stag beetle 188; 14 *Phosphuga atrata* 189; 15 Rove beetle, *Philonthus marginatus* 189; 16 Furniture beetle 194; 17 Fur beetle 194; 18 Carpet beetle 194, with larva.

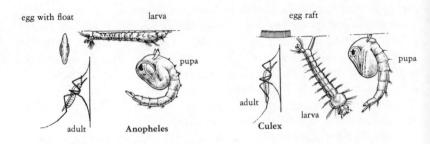

egg with float   larva   egg raft

pupa

pupa

adult

adult   **Anopheles**   **Culex**   larva

Anopheles mosquitoes (*left*) are potential carriers of malaria. They can be distinguished from *Culex* and our other mosquitoes by the attitudes of the adults at rest, and also by the resting attitudes of the larvae and pupae. *Culex* eggs are laid in a 'raft', whereas *Anopheles* eggs are laid singly

mosquitoes generally need a meal of blood before they can lay their eggs, but the males are content to feed on nectar and fruit juices and their beaks lack the piercing tips found in the females. The females lay their eggs in water or in places which are liable to periodic flooding, and the resulting larvae lead aquatic lives, feeding on bacteria and other minute organisms in the water. The larvae, with their bristly heads and elongate bodies, are familiar objects in water butts and in garden ponds – as long as there are no fish in them, for fish love mosquito larvae. The comma-shaped pupae are also very conspicuous, with their respiratory horns just breaking the surface for air. Unlike most pupae, they are very active and, although they do not feed, they wriggle rapidly down into the water at the slightest disturbance. The commonest mosquito in the house and garden is *Culex pipiens* (Plate 16), which is sometimes referred to as the common gnat. Although it often whines around in our bedrooms at night, it does not attack us: it prefers birds and it leaves us to its cousins *Theobaldia* and *Anopheles*. Most of the irritating bites that we suffer in the garden are the work of *Theobaldia annulata,* our largest mosquito, which can be recognised by its size and by the white rings on its legs. Even a thick pair of trousers or a sweater gives no protection against this insect if it decides to sample us, for its beak easily penetrates the material. Females of *Theobaldia* and *Culex pipiens* often hibernate in sheds and houses during the winter.

Gardeners in the moister parts of the country, especially in Scotland, may also suffer from the attentions of the biting midges of the genus *Culicoides*. These are minute flies, but their bite is intensely irritating, and they exist in such vast numbers that gardening is often impossible on warm, humid evenings.

The **crane-flies** or **daddy-long-legs** are among the most familiar of the flies because many are of large size and they enter our houses at the slightest opportunity, terrifying many people with their frantic buzzing and their spidery legs. They can usually be found right through the summer, from May to October, but they generally become most noticeable in August and September, when they swarm over walls and windows by night and festoon the plants by day. Their numbers sometimes reach plague proportions in country areas, and then one can hardly put a foot down on the lawn without sending a group of them buzzing noisily into the air. Two of the commonest species are the **marsh crane-fly** (Plate 16) and the very similar **common crane-fly**, *T. oleracea*. The latter has a rather silvery grey body instead of the brownish body of the marsh crane-fly, but the habits and life histories of the two species are almost identical. The females each lay up to 300 eggs in the ground during the summer, and the larvae, which are the infamous leatherjackets, feed on plant roots. They also come to the surface on humid nights and nibble the bases of the stems. The fully grown larvae pupate in the soil, and the pupae wriggle their way to the surface when the adult insects are ready to emerge. Small numbers of adults may emerge in late autumn, but most of the larvae continue to feed through the winter and do not pupate until the spring.

The leatherjacket, the larva of the crane-fly

Although the adults of these two *Tipula* species are such common insects in country gardens, they do not very often breed in the garden unless there are extensive lawns or grassy orchards. They prefer the corn fields and meadows, where they often kill the grasses and leave bare patches. The **spotted crane-fly** (Plate 16) is much more of a true garden insect, for its larvae actually prefer our cultivated plants and often damage potatoes and the roots of young brassicas. *Limonia flavipes* (Plate 16) is another quite frequent inhabitant of the garden, along with *L. nubeculosa,* a close relative which can be distinguished by the distinct banding on its legs. These two species belong to a large group of crane-flies which, unlike the *Tipula* species, fold their wings flat over their bodies when at rest. Most of this group are much smaller insects, however, and very similar in appearance to the winter gnats (page 161). Many of them are known as bobbing gnats, because of the way they bob up and down by flexing their legs when sitting on walls and other surfaces.

FLEAS

The fleas do not really come within the realm of the gardener because the adults are blood-sucking insects living as parasites on birds and mammals. Nevertheless, their life histories are such that many garden sheds and even many houses suffer from occasional plagues of fleas. The gardener may also find some of these active little creatures digging their mouths into his arms while clipping hedges containing old bird's nests, and the wildlife gardener (see Chapter 10) will certainly meet them in nest boxes. I have seen more then 700 fleas removed from a single blue tit's nest box.

The common cat flea

The adult fleas are brownish, wingless insects no more than a few millimetres long. They are extremely flattened from side to side and this unusual build helps them to run freely among the hairs or feathers of the host animal. Their long back legs enable them to make prodigious leaps, and they are very willing and able to jump from one host to another. The usual household fleas are either cat fleas or dog fleas, derived from the family pets, but bird fleas may also enter the house from nests in and around the roof. Various other fleas may also occur if there are mice around the house, and these fleas are often quite common in outbuildings. They will all bite us if they are given the chance, and only the specialist can distinguish between the various species.

Although the adult fleas are all blood-suckers, the young fleas are not. They are pale maggots and they live in the nests of the host animals – which, in the case of domestic pets, means a box or basket in the corner, or even the armchair. The maggots feed on rubbish in the nest, including the droppings of the adult fleas, and they pupate there when they are fully grown. Regular sweeping and cleaning of the pets' quarters removes the pearly white eggs of the fleas before they can hatch, so no infestation can develop. But if the animals' favourite corners are neglected, as they often are in the shed, the

164

young fleas can grow to maturity and the area may 'come alive' with fleas searching for a host animal. They will choose us if we arrive first and they may give us some irritating bites, although they will not take up permanent residence on us. Most fleas require some form of mechanical stimulus to induce them to leave their pupae. This is usually provided by the movement of the host animal in the nest, and the fleas are thus assured of a suitable host when they emerge. Human activity will also bring them out, howevever, and this explains why the gardener may be bitten when he disturbs old birds' nests.

THE HYMENOPTERA

This large order of insects includes the bees and wasps, the ants, the ichneumons, the sawflies, and a few other groups. Some of these insects are wingless, but the majority have two pairs of clear membranous wings. The sawflies (page 183) can be distinguished from the rest of the order because they lack the slender 'wasp waist' so characteristic of the other members. The ichneumons (page 183) and some other groups are parasites. The bees, wasps, and ants nearly all possess stings with which they defend themselves. Many of the wasps also use their stings to paralyse their prey. The sting is a highly modified egg-laying tool or ovipositor and it is thus possessed only by female insects. It has lost its egg-laying function, however, and the eggs pass to the outside by another route.

Many of the stinging hymenopterans, especially among the wasps, exhibit bold colour patterns – generally a mixture of yellow and black – which deter birds and other predators from attacking them. The theory behind this warning coloration is that young and inexperienced birds try the insects and get stung a few times, but soon learn to associate the bold patterns with unpleasantness and then leave the insects alone. But not all boldly marked insects are nasty. Many hover-flies (page 156) and other insects have evolved striking similarities with the bees and wasps and they gain considerable protection from this mimicry. They are sufficiently like the unpleasant bees and wasps for birds to avoid them, and many humans draw hastily back from them. Even the entomologist has to look hard to distinguish some of the mimics from their distasteful models.

The majority of insects lead independent or solitary lives in which each individual is concerned only with fulfilling its own needs. Apart from mating, the insects rarely have any contact with each other. Few of them even look after their young. Among the Hymenoptera, however, we find a remarkable development of social life, with insects living in large colonies and all working together for the good of the community. All of the ants live in this way, and so do many of the bees and wasps. The colonies all consist of one or a few fertile, egg-laying females called queens together with large numbers of their offspring. Most of these offspring are sterile females called workers. They build the nests, collect food, and look after the younger members of the community. The smooth running of the community is controlled by pheromones – chemical signals which originate from the queen and which per-meate the whole colony and automatically ensure that the workers do the right things. Males and fully developed females (new queens) are produced only at certain times of the year.

Bees

Almost as soon as the first flowers appear in the garden, the bees are out to gather the pollen and nectar on which they feed and rear their young. Bees of both sexes visit the flowers, but only the females actively gather the food and take it home. The females of many species have special pollen baskets on their hind legs. Pollen is picked up on the hairs all over their bodies and then, by clever use of the legs, it is combed into the pollen baskets. Bulging pollen baskets are a common sight on foraging bees and it has been shown that some bumble bees can carry more than half their own weight of pollen. Some bees carry pollen attached to hairs on the underside of the body.

A mining bee (*Andrena*), one of the earliest to appear in the spring

A bee sucks nectar from the flowers with its tubular tongue, but not all bees have tongues of the same length and they do not all visit the same flowers. Long-tongued bumble bees can get nectar from the deep-throated deadnettles and polyanthus and they leave the dandelions to the short-tongued bees. Some short-tongued bees, however, have discovered a way of 'stealing' nectar by biting holes in the bases of deep-throated flowers. The nectar is carried home in the honey stomach and then regurgitated. Honey bees store pollen and nectar separately, but most bees mix the two materials together before putting them into the cells.

Although it might look as if the bees get all the benefit from their association with flowers, this is definitely not so. While crawling about in the flowers, the bees transfer pollen grains from the stamens to the stigmas and so pollinate the flowers and enable them to produce fruit and seeds. The gardener, and the human race in general, therefore has cause to be grateful to the bees.

Apart from the honey bee (page 172), the earliest bees to appear in the garden are usually members of the genus *Andrena*. Some of these look rather like honey bees, but they all have short tongues and very flat abdomens. Several have prominent bands of pale hairs on the abdomen. These bees appear in March and visit the dandelions and sallow blossoms before moving on to the aubretias and rock cress in the garden. Further species of *Andrena* appear later in the spring and summer, the most striking being *Andrena armata* (Plate 15). The female of this species has a black body which is clothed on the upper side with rich chestnut-coloured hairs. She is often to be seen flying around gooseberry and black currant bushes when they are in flower. The *Andrena* species all nest in the ground and they are often called mining bees. You can often see them buzzing in and out of small holes in the garden path or in well trodden lawns. You might also see swarms of bees flying to and fro just over the surface. These will be males on the look out for mates. As in most bees and wasps, the males can be distinguished by their somewhat longer antennae – always with 13 segments compared with 12 segments in the female antennae. The *Andrena* species are all solitary insects, with each female making her own separate burrow and provisioning it with nectar and pollen. She lays her eggs in the burrow and then leaves it for good. The grubs hatch and feed on the food left by their mother, but they have nothing to do with each other and they go their own ways when they grow up. Some of these spring bees produce a second generation in the summer, but most species take a whole year to mature.

Bees of the genus *Halictus* can often be seen flying with *Andrena*. They are often quite similar, but the body of *Halictus* is much less flattened and the male abdomen is generally quite cylindrical. Female *Halictus* bees can be recognised by a little groove at the hind end of the abdomen. Most *Halictus* species have the same habits as *Andrena* and they all share the name of mining bees. *Halictus calceatus* (Plate 15) can often be seen on buddleia flowers in the summer.

The early species of *Andrena* are often accompanied by *Anthophora acervorum* (Plate 15), which is sometimes known as a flower bee. *Anthophora* looks rather like a bumble bee (page 169), but it is readily distinguished by its much more rapid darting and hovering flight. It is much more difficult to approach than a bumble bee. The flower bees have very long tongues and enjoy visits to polyanthus and other tubular flowers such as lungwort. They can also be seen hovering over the aubretia and plunging their tongues down into the flowers. The female is jet black, apart from the orange pollen baskets, but the male has brown hairs all over his body and a prominent patch of white hair on his face. He also has peculiar tufts of long hairs on his middle legs. If you watch a female on the flowers, you may be able to see the male's courtship flight. He darts around the female and then takes up a hovering station a few inches behind her. After a few seconds, during which he appears to be lining up his sights, he darts forward and grabs the female. Both bees fall to the ground and, if the female is as yet unmated, mating takes place there. If the lady of his choice has already mated, she soon lets him know and he flies off to try again elsewhere. The female digs a little burrow in the earth or in loose mortar and there makes a few little mud cells. Each cell is provisioned with honey and nectar and, after laying an egg in each, the female abandons the burrow.

The **red osmia** (Plate 15) is common in the garden in April and May, when it can be seen at the apple blossom and other flowers or merely resting on walls and tree trunks. It has a rather rounded body, especially in the male, and the female can be recognised by the two stout, black 'horns' on her face. The species makes its nest in holes in walls and tree stumps, and frequently make use of the spaces between the overlapping planks of the shed wall. Like many of the solitary bees and wasps, this species can be encouraged to

Neat sausage-shaped cells, each made from carefully cut leaf pieces, are arranged around the bottom of an unused flower pot by the leaf cutter bee

nest in the garden by fixing short lengths of hollow canes to tree trunks or to the undersides of window sills (see page 262).

The gardener is often puzzled by the appearance of neat circular and semi-circular holes in his rose leaves in June and July. This is the work of the female **leaf-cutter bee** (Plate 15), who uses the pieces to make the cells of her nest. She usually builds in dead stems of hogweed and other similar plants, but her cylindrical cells can also be found in stacked flower pots and other secluded places. One larva develops in each cell and produces an adult the following year.

Prosopis communis (Plate 15) is one of several closely related shiny black bees which appear in the summer. They are very similar to some of the smaller digger wasps (page 174) and would probably be included with them were it not for their different feeding habits. The digger wasps all feed their young on animal matter, but the *Prosopis* species all rear their offspring on pollen and nectar. The *Prosopis* species are thus definitely bees, although they are certaintly rather primitive ones. They have short, wasp-like tongues and they can only lap up nectar when it is freely exposed in the flowers. Also, being almost hairless, they are unable to collect pollen in the normal way. They have to carry it back to the nest mixed with the nectar in the honey stomach or crop. It is the existence of these primitive bees, with wasp-like anatomy and bee-like behaviour, that supports the belief that bees have evolved from some form of digger wasp. *Prosopis* bees make their nests in hollow stems, each nest containing a number of small cells. Most *Prosopis* species have yellowish markings on their faces and they are commonly called yellow-faced bees.

Bumble bees

The hairy bumble bees differ from the other bees that we have looked at in leading social lives, with numerous adults living and working in a single nest. The big bumble bees that we see buzzing rather drowsily around the garden and hedgerow in early spring have been hibernating in cosy corners during the winter. They are all young queens and they spend a few weeks eating pollen and nectar and soaking up the sunshine before seeking nesting sites. Close examination of some of these bees will show that many of them are infested with little brown mites. The infestation is some-times so heavy around the thorax that the bees have difficulty in flying, but the mites seem to do no other harm. Most of them will leave her and live freely in the nest when she makes it. The mites probably feed on scraps of pollen and other materials in the nest, but they may also take some of the honey.

Most of the bumble bees make their nests on or under the ground, frequently taking over old nests of mice and voles. South-facing hedgebanks are favourite sites and it is very common to see the bees buzzing backwards and forwards in such places looking for suitable holes. You may also see a bee spiralling around a point in ever-increasing circles. This probably means that she has found a nest hole and is circling round it to get her bearings so that she can easily find it again. Inside the nest, the queen fashions a spherical chamber with fine grass or other material. She then begins to secrete wax from glands on her abdomen and she uses this to make a little cup-like cell in the centre of the nest. The cell is partly filled with pollen and the queen then lays a number of eggs in it before roofing it over with more wax. At about this time, the queen also makes a wax honeypot and lays in a store of honey (see page 173) for when the weather prevents her from foraging at the flowers. As soon as the eggs hatch in their cell, the queen opens it up and starts to provide the grubs with more pollen and honey. The grubs pupate in silken cocoons when they are fully grown and then, perhaps a month after the eggs were laid, they emerge as adult bees. These new bees are all females, but they are smaller than the queen and their reproductive systems are not fully developed. They are workers. We don't see the queen much after this, for she stays in the nest and busies herself making more egg cells and laying eggs in them. The workers bring food in for her and for the new batches of developing grubs. Several batches of workers are reared in this way during the spring and summer and some colonies may produce more than 300 workers during the season.

After a certain period, which varies from species to species, the queen's egg-laying rate falls off and fewer new larvae are produced. The ratio of workers to larvae thus increases and each larva gets more food. This extra food causes the larvae to develop into new queens instead of workers. At about the same time, or possibly a little earlier, the queen starts to lay some unfertilised eggs. These develop in the normal way, but they give rise to male bees. The males and the new queens leave the nest and pair up and the males die soon after mating. The fertilised queens then seek their winter quarters, although it may still only be July. The old queen and the workers may linger on for a few weeks, but they are dead by the end of the summer, leaving only the sleeping new queens to continue the race for another year.

There are about 20 kinds of bumble bees resident in the British

Isles and several of them are commonly seen in the garden. Queens are on the wing in the spring, but most of the bumble bees that buzz around the garden are workers. They generally have the same colour patterns as the queens, but they are smaller. The first batch of workers, fed only by the queen, are often especially small and it is hard to believe that they and their mother, who may fly around with them for a day or two, belong to the same species. Male bees, which are rarely on the wing before the beginning of June, are generally intermediate in size between the females and the workers. They often have slightly different coat patterns and they can be distinguished by their antennae (see page 167) and by their lack of pollen baskets. The following descriptions apply only to queens and workers.

The *Bombus terrestris* queen (Plate 15) is one of the largest of our bumble bees. This species is abundant in most parts of the British Isles, although absent from northern Scotland. The queen has a rather orange tail, but the worker's tail is much paler. *Bombus lucorum* (Plate 15) is found all over these islands and may be distinguished from the previous species by the much brighter yellow bands on the thorax and abdomen. Although the tail is pure white in the southern half of the country, it becomes pinkish yellow further north and the bee also tends to be a good deal larger.

Bombus lapidarius (Plate 15) is easily recognised by its jet black body and red tail. It is one of our commonest species. *Bombus pascuorum* (Plate 15) is another widely distributed and easily recognised species. It is our only common species with a brown thorax, but it exists in two distinct forms. In southern Britain and Ireland the insect has a yellowish brown abdomen heavily contaminated with black, but in the northern regions the abdomen has very little black hair. The two forms overlap and inter-breed in northern England. *Bombus pascuorum* is very fond of deadnettle flowers, a liking which it shares with *Bombus hortorum* (Plate 15). This latter species is a rather shaggy looking bee which is common almost everywhere. It has a white tail, but can be distinguished from *B. lucorum* by having a yellow band right at the front of the abdomen and spilling over on to the hind part of the thorax. *Bombus pratorum* is a rather small species whose queen could be mistaken for a worker of *B. terrestris*. Both species have a rather rusty yellow collar around the front of the thorax, but the tail of *B. pratorum* is much redder than that of *terrestris* and the yellow band at the front of the abdomen is much less distinct or even absent. *B. pratorum* is generally the earliest of the bumble bees to appear in the spring and its colonies have usually died out by July.

171

Cuckoo bees

Several of our bumble bees find their nests invaded by cuckoo bees in the spring. The female cuckoo bee, like her namesake in the bird world, makes no nest and relies on another species to bring up her offspring. She enters the nest of the appropriate species of bumble bee, which she finds by its characteristic smell, and begins to lay her eggs there. After a while, she usually kills the rightful queen and the host workers then bring up a complete brood of cuckoo bees. These cuckoo bees are all males or fully developed females, for there are no workers. The mated females hibernate just like the bumble bees but emerge a little later in the spring – when the bumble bees have had time to start their nests. Female cuckoo bees can often be seen in the garden at this time, but close inspection is necessary to distinguish them from the true bumble bees because the cuckoos are generally very much like their host species. They

pollen basket

Hind legs of a queen bumble bee (*left*) and a cuckoo bee. The latter has no long bristles forming a pollen basket

usually are much less hairy, however, and you can see the abdomen shining through the hairs. The cuckoo bees also lack the pollen baskets on their hind legs, for they never need to collect pollen. There are six British species of cuckoo bees.

The honey bee

The honey bee (Plate 15) is a native of southern Asia and it was brought here long ago to provide us with honey, although its pollinating activities are worth far more to us than the honey it provides. If you watch a foraging honey bee you will see that it keeps to one kind of flower on each trip, and pollen is not therefore wasted by being carried to a different kind of flower. Honey bees are very highly evolved insects and their colonies go on year after year, although the individual bees do not live for very long. The queen never goes foraging, for she lacks the necessary pollen

172

baskets and other apparatus and she is quite unable to support herself. Except for a brief period when she goes off on her marriage flight, she is always surrounded by a band of devoted workers. The latter, which may number more than 50,000 in a well formed colony, do all the work except for laying the eggs. They build the combs, feed the grubs, keep the hive clean, and forage for food. Apart from a few males or drones which appear late in the summer, all the honey bees at the flowers will be workers. Although the bees sometimes escape and live in the wild, the majority of honey bees that come to our gardens live in artificial hives.

Many fine books have been written about the honey bee (see page 273) and the reader must refer to them for information on the wonderful organisation of the colony and the fascinating dances which the bees use to tell each other about the food they have found. By means of these dances, performed on the combs in the hive, the workers can give their sisters precise instructions about where to go to collect the food. It is, however, worth digressing for a short while to talk about nectar and honey – two quite distinct materials which are often confused in the layman's mind. Nectar is the sugary liquid produced by flowers. It contains several types of sugar, together with traces of proteins and salts and various aromatic substances, but the bulk of it – some 60 per cent on average – is water. The honey bees convert this rather dilute solution into honey by removing much of the water and by converting the cane sugar or sucrose, which normally accounts for the bulk of the sugar in the nectar, into glucose and fructose sugars. The conversion takes place in the hive, where the bees roll the nectar around in their mouths and mix it with enzymes. When the water content has been reduced to about 20 per cent, the material can be called honey and it is then stored in the cells. Bumble bee honey is chemically quite similar, but the bumble bees do not manipulate it in their mouths in the way that honey bees do.

Before leaving the bees, we must mention the honey bee swarms which the gardener might see from time to time in bee-keeping districts. A cloud of bees sometimes emerges from a hive when the bees feel that things are getting a bit over-crowded. It consists of the queen and a large number of workers and it usually comes to rest on a tree until the 'scouts' have found a suitable place for a new nest – or, more probably, until the local bee-keeper comes along to capture them and put them in an empty hive. Meanwhile, the original colony from which the swarm came rears a few new queens by feeding up some of the young grubs. One of these queens eventually takes over as ruler. Although a swarm of bees often creates panic in people, there is not really any danger at all. The bees are too busy looking for a new home to bother anyone, and they are so gorged with honey that they are normally unable to sting. Even when they are not swarming, the bees are generally docile creatures and rarely sting us unless provoked. Standing in the flight path of bees coming in or out of the hive is asking to get stung, and you are likely to be stung if you pick up a bee, but the insects are normally far too busy to bother about us. The large bumble bees are often so engrossed in their tasks that you can actually stroke their backs with your finger.

Wasps

Several groups of hymenopterans, not all closely related, are called wasps, but there are only two main groups as far as the gardener is concerned. These are the digger wasps and the true wasps. Some of the digger wasps are completely black and some of the smaller ones could be confused with the hairless bees such as *Prosopis* (page 169), but many diggers and all the true wasps are black and yellow and the gardener will have no trouble in deciding that these insects are wasps. The digger wasps generally have a more obvious 'waist' than the true wasps and they usually have more black than yellow on

A typical wasp at rest, showing the characteristic folding of the wings which distinguishes true wasps from digger wasps

their bodies. The diggers also have relatively large and somewhat square heads, but the best way of distinguishing the two groups is to look at the wings when the insects are at rest. The wings of the digger wasps are laid flat over the body, but those of the true wasps are folded lengthwise along the edges of the body and the bulk of the body's upper surface is exposed.

The DIGGER WASPS are all solitary creatures with life histories similar to those of the mining bees. The females of many species burrow in sandy soil, but the garden species generally excavate small nests in dead wood, such as fence posts and tree stumps, and their presence can often be detected by little piles of rather coarse

174

sawdust. They tend to choose wood which has already been invaded and softened by woodworms and other beetle grubs. Some species prefer not to dig their own burrows, however, and they often establish themselves in the hollow canes which we use in the garden. The smaller species may even use the hollow reeds on thatched roofs.

Several cells are formed in the nest, those in narrow tunnels being separated from each other by thin partitions of mud or sawdust cemented with saliva. Some species collect resin to make the partitions. The cells are then provisioned, either before or after an egg has been laid in each one. Whereas the bees provision their cells with pollen and nectar, the wasps always use animal food. *Pemphredon lugubris* (Plate 15) and most of the other black diggers collect aphids. The larger diggers, such as *Ectemnius quadricinctus* (Plate 15), generally catch flies and they can often be seen crawling on or circling round the flowers of various umbellifers such as hogweed and cow parsley. The wasps lap up nectar from these flowers, but they are always on the look out for an unwary hover-fly with which to stock the nest. *Trypoxylon figulus* (Plate 15) is one of a group which provision their nests with small spiders.

The prey of the digger wasp is paralysed by the wasp's sting, but it is not usually killed and it thus remains in good condition in the nest until the wasp grub is ready to eat it. Each cell may contain numerous victims, and the aphid-collecting diggers are clearly of great help to the gardener.

The TRUE WASPS include both solitary and social species. Several solitary species make their homes in our gardens, frequently digging out holes in vertical banks and in the mortar of old walls. They are called **mason wasps**. They collect water to soften the soil or sand and some of them use the excavated grains of sand to build tubular 'chimneys' around the nest entrances. These chimneys are often curved and, as well as keeping out the rain, they may keep out enemies such as the ruby-tailed wasp (page 179). Mason wasps generally stock their nests with small caterpillars which are caught and paralysed like the victims of the digger wasps. The masons, however, always lay their eggs before stocking the cells. One of the commonest masons in the garden is *Ancistrocerus parietinus* (Plate 15). Like the other members of its group, it has rather narrow yellow stripes, but it is easily distinguished from the diggers by the way it folds its wings when at rest. This species makes a tubular nest in a hollow stem or a crevice. The very similar wall mason often makes a quite acceptable job of re-pointing an old wall. It constructs a string of mud cells in the gap where the mortar has fallen out, and it then covers the whole lot over more or less flush with the original surface.

The social wasps are the most familiar of our wasps, for these are the ones that buzz around our tea tables and make picnics rather uncomfortable in late summer. They are *the* wasps as far as most people are concerned. Many people are distinctly frightened of them, but needlessly so, for the wasps are not really aggressive and they will not normally sting unless they are provoked. You are far more likely to be stung if you wave your arms about at a wasp than if you ignore it: the wasp will certainly ignore you if you leave it alone. It might help itself to a little jam, but this might be looked on as just reward for helping us earlier in the year. As we shall see, the social wasps destroy large numbers of insect pests.

We have six species of social wasps in the British Isles – seven if we include the large brown and yellow hornet – but only two of them are at all common in the garden. These are the **common wasp** (Plate 15) and the **German wasp**. The two species are very similar and the best way for the non-specialist to separate them is to look at the front of the face: the common wasp has an anchor-shaped mark, while the German wasp has three black dots, although the anchor of the common wasp is often reduced to some small dots. Further confirmation can be obtained by looking at the thorax: the curved yellow band around the front is of more or less even thickness in the common wasp, whereas that of the German wasp bulges prominently at the sides. Both species are widely distributed in the British Isles, but they are largely replaced by the Norwegian wasp in central and northern Scotland. The Norwegian wasp has a broad black band down the centre of its face, and it has only two yellow spots on the hind part of the thorax. Although the commonest wasp in the northern half of Scotland, it is not particularly common in gardens.

Our social wasps resemble the bumble bees (page 169) in forming annual colonies, with only the newly mated females or queens surviving the winter. The queens are much larger than the workers and they hibernate in dry corners of the shed and the house, especially in the roof spaces. People have a tendency to kill the queens that they find during the winter, but this has no effect on the wasp population of the following summer because the number of wasp nests depends on the number of available sites and less than one per cent of the queens actually manage to start a nest.

The queens usually wake up some time in April and, although

PLATE 19: **Beetles.** 1 Churchyard beetle 194; 2 7-spot ladybird 190, a adult, b larva, c pupa; ▶ 3a and 3b 2-spot ladybirds 190; 4 22-spot ladybird 190; 5 Wasp beetle 191; 6 Colorado beetle 192, with larva; 7 Cardinal beetle 190; 8 *Lema melanopa* 193; 9 *Endomychus coccineus* 190; 10 Sailor beetle 191; 11 Asparagus beetle 193; 12 Turnip flea 192; 13 *Psylliodes chrysocephala* 192; 14 Raspberry beetle 191; 15 Pea beetle 193; 16 Apple blossom weevil 193; 17 *Phyllotreta nigripes* 192; 18 *Phyllobius pomaceus* 193; 19 *Anthonomus rubi* 194; 20 Pea weevil 193; 21 *Otiorhynchus clavipes* 194.

1

2a 2b 2c 3a 3b

4

5

6 7

8

9 10 11 12

13 14 15 16 17

18 19 20 21

they can often be seen taking nectar from flowers, they soon buckle down to nest-building. Both of our common species nest under the ground as a rule, but it would be more accurate to say that they nest under cover, for they are equally content to slip under a loose slate or tile and nest in your roof cavity. Those nesting under the ground sometimes take over an old mouse hole in the hedge bank, and they very often start work under a tree stump or a fallen tree. The actual nest is made of paper, which the wasps manufacture from wood in much the same way that we do. During April and May, you can see and even hear the queen wasps gathering wood from fences and dead trees and also from the old raspberry canes and michaelmas daisy stems that you have been meaning to cut down for months. Working with the grain, the wasp uses her strong jaws to remove a thin strip of wood, and she then rolls it up in her jaws before flying off to the nest site. It is not a good plan to kill the queens at this stage of their lives, for they have already selected their homes. Killing them may reduce the number of wasps in the garden later in the year, but may also result in a noticeable upsurge of insect pests.

Returning to the nest site, the queen begins to chew the wood and mix it with saliva to form a soft pulp. The pulp is then spread out to form a narrow sheet of paper. Working entirely alone, the queen makes many journeys to and from her wood source and uses the paper to lay the foundations of the nest. Within two or three days, she has made a little umbrella-shaped dome, suspended from a root or some other support, and she has built a few small, six-sided cells on the underside of it. She lays an egg in each cell and then goes on building. The eggs hatch in a few days and the queen then has to spend much of her time feeding the grubs with chewed-up caterpillars and other insects. Unlike the solitary species, the social wasps do not use their stings to paralyse their prey: they merely pounce on their victims and bite them. The first adult workers appear in the nest about five weeks after the first eggs are laid, and the nest generally has something like thirty cells at this time. The workers immediately set about enlarging the nest, and this often involves further excavation of the soil to accommodate the extra volume. The workers also take on the task of feeding their younger sisters, while the queen 'retires' and devotes herself to egg-laying in the numerous new cells that are constructed.

The completed nest is generally rather like a large football, with several tiers of cells suspended one below the other. The whole thing is covered with a many-layered 'envelope' consisting of thousands of shell-like sections. Each section is made up of several

◀ PLATE 20: Web-spinning Spiders. 1 Garden spider 200; 2 *Meta segmentata* 203; 3 *Amaurobius fenestralis* 207; 4 *Araneus cucurbitinus* 205; 5 *Zygiella X-notata* 205; 6 House spider, *Tegenaria saeva* 208; 7 Daddy-long-legs 209; 8 *Segestria senoculata* 207; 9 *Linyphia triangularis* 210; 10 *Theridion sisyphium* 209; 11 *Enoplognatha ovata* 210; 12 *Steatodea bipunctata* 210.

The internal structure of a wasp nest, showing the tiers of paper cells

bands of paper, each band representing one load of wood pulp. The air between the various layers of the envelope serves to insulate the nest from extremes of temperature. The German wasp always collects sound wood for nest-building, while the common wasp uses rather rotten wood. The nest of the German wasp therefore consists of relatively tough grey paper, while that of the common wasp is yellowish and very brittle – so brittle, in fact, that it often collapses under its own weight when it is laid down anywhere.

The completed nest may have nine or more combs and more than 12,000 cells. During the season, the colony may rear as many as 25,000 wasps, although the average is probably nearer 15,000. These vast numbers do not all exist at one time, however, for the worker's life is fairly short. The greatest numbers are to be found in mid-August in a normal year. Despite these large numbers, the wasps are not particularly noticeable for much of the summer, except in the immediate vicinity of a nest. The wasps certainly do visit flowers and jam pots to obtain energy-giving sugar for their own activities, but they do not linger there: most of their time is spent in collecting the thousands of caterpillars and other insects needed for the brood in the nest.

Males and new queens are produced in much the same way as they are among the bumble bees. Males appear at the end of July and sit around on the flowers for long periods. The new queens do not usually appear until late August and then they mate with the males. No further grubs are raised in the nest and the colony breaks down. Freed from their domestic chores, the workers embark on a spree of feeding, and this is when they become a nuisance to us. Together with the males and the old queens, they die as soon as the colder weather arrives, but the new queens are safely tucked up in their winter quarters long before that. The old nest soon breaks down as well, with numerous scavenging insects tunnelling through it in search of the dead wasps and other food inside. These scavengers include the larvae of various small moths and the grubs of flies and beetles.

Although the wasps are more useful than harmful in the garden, it is sometimes necessary to destroy nests which are too close to the house for comfort. Local authorities will usually destroy the nests if asked, but it is not a difficult task if the entrance hole is easily accessible. Various insecticides can be used, but the simplest methods involve pouring petrol, paraffin, carbon tetrachloride, or concentrated ammonia into the hole and plugging it up. This is best done at night, when all the wasps are at home: during the day time the returning wasps are likely to take objection to your standing in front of their home.

Ruby-tailed wasps

The beautiful ruby-tailed wasps (Plate 9) are parasitic insects only distantly related to the true wasps and the diggers. They can often be seen running about on tree stumps and walls in the spring and summer, tapping their antennae on the surface as they go. They are searching for the nests of various solitary bees and wasps. When she finds one of the nests, the female ruby-tailed wasp enters it and lays an egg in one or more cells. Her thick armour renders her quite safe from the sting of the rightful occupant of the nest and when her eggs hatch the grubs feed on the young bees or wasps.

Ants

The gardener will have little trouble in recognising the ants when he sees them. They are all small yellowish, brown, or black insects with a narrow 'waist' and sharply bent antennae and, except during the mating season, all are wingless. All the ants are social insects, living in large colonies with one or more queens at the head. They make their nests in a variety of situations, but our British ants generally nest under the ground. The excavated soil is frequently piled up above the ground and the nest then extends into this mound as well. Our garden ants often nest under stones and garden paths, from which they derive a good deal of warmth during the summer. The commonest ant in the garden is usually the little black ant called *Lasius niger,* a species which even nests in and around the walls of the house. The closely related yellow lawn ant, *Lasius umbratus,* may be present also but it lives almost entirely under the ground and it is not usually seen unless one digs up the lawn. The slightly smaller *Lasius flavus* also occurs quite commonly, especially in orchards and other relatively undisturbed grassy places. This yellowish brown species sometimes nests under stones but it generally makes shallow, elongated mounds. The only other ant which is generally common in the garden is *Myrmica ruginodis,* a reddish brown ant which is readily distinguished from the *Lasius* species by its colour and also by its 'waist'. The *Lasius* species have only a single swelling on this narrow region, but *Myrmica* has two swellings. *Myrmica* also has a powerful sting, but the *Lasius* species are stingless. Pharaoh's ant *(Monomorium pharaonis)* is a very small ant that comes from warmer climates and has established itself very firmly in houses. It is only about 2 mm long and it is very difficult to get rid of.

Lasius (*left*) and *Myrmica*, showing the difference in the structure of the 'waist'

The ant colony is founded by a newly-mated female or queen after her 'marriage flight' (page 182), although some new queens enter established nests and reign jointly with the existing rulers. The new queen has wings to start with, but one of her first jobs after mating is to break off her wings by rubbing them against a stone or some other object. She has no further use for them because she will spend the rest of her life – perhaps as much as ten years – hidden away in the nest. Having removed her wings, the young queen searches for a safe hiding place where she can remain for several months while her eggs mature. She does not feed, but she draws nourishment from her now useless flight muscles. Her first eggs are laid in the spring and the little grubs soon hatch, but even now the queen does not go out to collect food: she feeds the grubs on her own saliva and, within a few weeks, the grubs produce very small worker ants. The differences between the queen and the workers are much more marked among the ants than among the bees and wasps, for, as well as being much smaller than the queen, the worker ants never have any wings.

The new workers soon set about constructing a nest and gathering food for themselves and their near-starving mother. The worker ants are just as industrious as the worker bees and wasps, but their nests are far less elaborate. Not for them the neat, six-sided cells arranged in horizontal or vertical combs: they make do

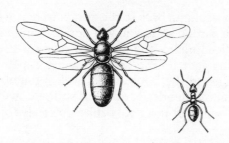

A queen ant (*left*) and a worker

with numerous chambers and passages hollowed out in the soil. But don't think that the ants are disorderly: far from it, each chamber has a particular use and the workers always seem to know what they are doing and where they are going. The queen occupies a central chamber in which she does little but lay eggs. The workers remove the eggs immediately and install them in incubation chambers. After hatching, the tiny grubs are moved to larval chambers, and the youngsters are moved again when they pupate. The larval and pupal chambers are generally situated near the surface, where they receive extra warmth from the sun. They also receive a good deal of disturbance from the gardener, for we often stick our forks into these upper chambers and scatter their occupants. But even then the workers soon bring order to the chaos: they swarm out from the passages and run around in seemingly agitated and random manner, but careful observation will show they are rapidly gathering up the larvae and pupae in their jaws and carrying them to safer quarters deep down in the nest. Crumb by crumb, the disturbed soil is re-arranged and new chambers are hollowed out: in a day or so, you would not know that anything had happened.

Our garden ants feed on both plant and animal material. They carry oily seeds and dead insects back to the nest, and they make short work of ripe fruit left lying about. They are especially fond of sweet things and a saucer of syrup or fruit juice sunk into the garden will often attract them in large numbers. The first workers to discover the food take their fill and go back to the nest to tell their sisters all about it. Then they all set out again, following the chemical 'path' already laid down. If the food is particularly good, you may see a whole column of two-way traffic leading to and from it with the ants continually stopping to 'talk' to those coming the other way. 'Talking' consists of rubbing the antennae together and may convey such information as 'Yes, this is the way: plenty of food left'.

181

If you trace such a column back to the nest entrance, which may be a small hole in the garden path, you will notice that there are several distinct tracks leading to the nest – made by the passage of thousands of tiny feet during their foraging expeditions. *Lasius niger* often forages in the house and I well remember the disappointment of finding hundreds of them sitting down to a bowl of jelly which had been put in a cool cupboard ready for my birthday tea.

The food taken back to the nest is shared with the young and with the other adults. Whole colonies can thus be destroyed, when necessary, by adding poison to the sweet foods which they love so much. Many commercial ant killers work on this basis. The ants don't do a great deal of harm, however, unless they happen to nest right underneath a plant. They will usually destroy its roots under such circumstances and the plant will wilt and die. Colonies near to the vegetable plot may also send out raiding parties to steal newly planted seeds. One must balance this, however, with the ants' usefulness in aerating the soil and destroying other insect pests.

Ants are very fond of the sugary honey-dew secreted by aphids (see page 123) and can often be seen 'milking' the aphids on roses and other garden plants. Picking their way between the aphids, the ants stop now and then to stroke one with their antennae, and the aphid responds by exuding a drop of honey-dew. But the association does not stop here, for some of our garden ants actually build 'cow sheds' for their herds on the stems of the plants. These shelters are built up from crumbs of soil, lightly cemented with the ants' saliva, and they may rise collar-like for several inches up a young rose stem. The aphids are carried into the shelters and installed on the stems there, protected from their enemies and also very handy for the ants. Our ants may even collect the aphids' eggs in the autumn and keep them safely in the nest until they hatch in the spring, when the young aphids are carried out onto the plants again. This really is a remarkable piece of behaviour, for the aphids' eggs themselves are of no use to the ants: it is almost as if the ants know that the eggs will produce aphids in the spring.

We have all experienced the somewhat annoying plagues of flying ants on summer days. These are the 'marriage flights' of the new queens and their suitors. The male ants grow from unfertilised eggs, as in the social bees and wasps, but many factors seem to be involved in the rearing of new queens. Males and queens are all winged, but they are not allowed out of the nest until the workers consider that the climatic conditions are just right. Then, when the big moment arrives, all the nests in the area erupt together and the flying ants get everywhere. Vast numbers are eaten by birds, but some manage to pair up. The males soon die, but the females are ready to begin the cycle again. Meanwhile, the old colony gets back to the mundane task of rearing workers. As an undisturbed colony can survive for many years, colonies that accept new queens from time to time are theoretically immortal.

Ichneumon flies

The ichneumon flies are parasitic hymenopterans whose grubs feed in or on the young stages of other insects. The adults are rather slender-bodied insects with relatively long antennae. Most are black or brown and the females of some species have a prominent ovipositor at the hind end. This is used to lay the egg or eggs inside the body of the victim. The host is selected by scent and, although many ichneumons are active at night, they can often be seen searching for hosts in the daytime. They fly low over the vegetation or scuttle about on the plants with their antennae waving vigorously to pick up the scent. The typical life history of an ichneumon is just like that of *Apanteles glomeratus,* which has already been described in connection with the large white butterfly (page 137).

Many ichneumons live in the garden, but only the larger species will normally come to the gardener's attention. Among the commonest are two rather similar brown species – *Ophion luteus* and *Netelia testacea* (Plate 9). Both come to lighted windows very frequently in the summer and they can be distinguished by looking at the hind end: only *Netelia* has a black tip to the abdomen. Both species parasitise various kinds of noctuid caterpillars (see page 145), but the size of the ichneumons dictates that only one grub can develop in each caterpillar. *Coccygomimus instigator* (Plate 9) is another very striking ichneumon which often comes to light. Its larvae parasitise the pupae of the snout moth (page 149) and the adult can often be seen searching for these pupae among the stinging nettles. Smaller, but otherwise very similar relatives of *C. instigator* parasitise the larvae of the large white butterfly.

Sawflies

The sawflies are hymenopterans in which the abdomen is broadly united to the thorax. In other words, there is no narrow 'waist'. They get their name because the female usually has a saw-like ovipositor with which she can cut slits in plant stems or leaves to receive her eggs. The adults are generally rather retiring insects, spending much of their time crawling among the vegetation and feeding on pollen grains, algae, and perhaps an occasional small insect. The gardener is more likely to see the larvae than the adults. They are plant feeders and they look like the caterpillars of butterflies and moths except that they have more than five pairs of stumpy legs in the hind region. Most of the larvae feed freely on the

The apple sawfly, a serious pest of apples

The saw-edged ovipositor of a sawfly

Sawfly larva

leaves, but some tunnel in the stems and other parts. Some induce the formation of galls on the food plant. Galls are swellings produced by the plant in response to the presence of some other organism in the tissues. The invading organism then feeds on the contents of the gall. The invaders may be insects, mites (see page 223), eel-worms (page 70), or fungi. Among the commonest sawfly galls are the oval red bean galls that develop on willow leaves.

Anyone who grows gooseberries will have met the greenish grey larva of the **gooseberry sawfly** (Plate 9). It could be mistaken for the larva of the magpie moth (Plate 14), but the latter is really a much more handsome creature and it also has far fewer legs. The sawfly larvae live in colonies and soon make their presence known by denuding the branches of both gooseberry and currant bushes. When they are still fairly small, they arrange themselves head to tail

Bean galls on willow leaf

Gooseberry sawfly larvae

around the edges of the leaves, and if they are disturbed they raise their tails in unison. This reaction, which transforms a seemingly peaceful leaf into a seething mass of bodies, effectively deters inquisitive birds. As they get larger, the larvae disperse and feed singly on the leaves. They can be found throughout the spring and summer, for there are three or four generations in a year. The adult insect (Plate 9) is not commonly seen, although it can be found by searching the fruit bushes. The best way to control this troublesome pest is to search out the bunches of young larvae in the spring.

The solomon's seal is another garden plant whose leaves are commonly stripped by sawfly larvae, while the roses have to contend with the larvae of several species. Some of these larvae feed just like those of the gooseberry sawfly, but others are small slug-like creatures (sometimes called slug-worms) which merely scrape the upper surfaces from the leaves. The larvae of the **apple sawfly** tunnel into apples and cause damage much like that caused by the larvae of the codlin moth (page 153). Adult apple sawflies are mainly black above and orange below, with a small orange patch at the tip of the abdomen, and they emerge in May from cocoons around the bases of the trees.

The **hawthorn sawfly** (Plate 9) is one of our larger sawflies and it is quite common on hawthorn hedges, but even this striking insect is rarely seen in the adult state. I have not seen one in my own garden for six years, and I have only once seen the green larva, but every autumn I find a number of cocoons on the hawthorns when the leaves have fallen.

Although most adult sawflies hide themselves away, some of them are regular flower visitors. They are especially fond of the hogweeds and other umbellifers in the hedge, for here their short tongues can lap up nectar as well as pollen. *Tenthredo atra* (Plate 9) and the black and green *Rhogogaster viridis* are among the most frequent species.

The current popularity of sun-lounges and other home extensions made of timber has led to the more frequent appearance of the **horn-tail** or **wood wasp** (Plate 9) around the house. This striking insect spends its early life tunnelling in coniferous trees, and the larva often survives the saw-mill and the carpenter. The adults then emerge in the new building and terrify people by their large size and loud buzzing. The female is especially awesome because of her long ovipositor, which is generally taken to be a sting. The insects are quite harmless, however. They differ from most other sawflies in that the ovipositor works like a drill instead of like a saw.

Beetles

With something in the region of a quarter of a million species, the beetles are by far the largest group of insects. Rather more than 4,000 species are known in the British Isles but, although many of them turn up in the garden from time to time, very few are in any way restricted to garden habitats.

Beetles are generally recognised very easily because the front wings are hardened and modified into protective shields called elytra. These elytra usually cover the whole abdomen, but they are very short in the rove beetles (page 189) and they are absent altogether from the female glow-worm. Only the hind wings are used for flight, but most beetles prefer to keep their feet firmly on the ground or on the vegetation and they do not very often fly. They scuttle away when disturbed, or else they just drop to the ground and play possum, with their legs held tightly against the body. Many

A typical ground beetle

beetles have no hind wings at all, and their elytra are fused together and immovable. It is possible that some of the beetles will be confused with the Heteropteran bugs (page 127) to start with, but the elytra of the beetles always meet and form an obvious junction in the mid-line, whereas those of the bugs always overlap. In addition, the beetles all have biting jaws and never have the piercing beak which is so obvious in most bugs.

The beetles can be found almost everywhere, for their tough elytra give them added protection and allow them to inhabit places which are denied to other winged insects. Many of them, for example, live in the soil and under stones, while others spend their lives groping their way through piles of stored grain and flour. Water beetles use the spaces between their elytra and their bodies as re-chargeable air cylinders which enable them to spend long periods under the water. Associated with their wide range of habitats, the beetles also make use of a very wide range of foods –

186

animal and vegetable, living and dead. Many have a remarkable metabolism which enables them to survive without free water, and it is this ability which has led to the establishment of grain weevils, carpet beetles, and other species as pests in food stores and domestic premises. In general, the larvae of beetles eat much the same kind of food as the adults, and both stages therefore cause damage. The larvae themselves are very variable, ranging from the very active young of the ground beetles to the legless grubs of the weevils (page 193). Most of the plant-feeding beetle larvae are rather stout and slow-moving, bearing three pairs of legs at the front of their soft and often brightly coloured bodies.

One group of beetles stands apart from the others which are found in the garden. This is the group known as the GROUND BEETLES – fast-moving, predatory species with rather long legs and a fairly characteristic angular shape. They also bear fine, sensory bristles on various parts of the body, but these are not easily seen without a lens or at least a close examination. Many ground beetles have a beautiful metallic sheen when seen from certain angles, but the majority are of a rather sombre hue and generally look black when we see them in the garden. The gardener usually meets them while digging or lifting stones and logs, but the best way to find the ground beetles is to go out with a torch at night, when they can be seen scampering about in search of slugs and other tasty morsels. The beetles are also attracted to water and not infrequently perish in steep-sided garden ponds into which they blunder at night. Many of the species have no hind wings, and their elytra are frequently fused into a single unit.

The **violet ground beetle** (Plate 18) is a common and very conspicuous species which often scuttles away from the wood-pile or from beneath large stones. It may also take up residence in the garden shed, especially if the latter has damp floors. The species can be recognised by its black elytra and by the bluish or violet shine on the margins of the thorax. The closely related and equally common *Carabus nemoralis* also has purplish edges to its thorax, but its elytra are brassy green with purple margins. The genus *Feronia* contains several very common shiny black species which can be found in the garden. *Feronia nigrita* (Plate 18) is completely black, while *Feronia cuprea* usually has a very distinct coppery sheen, and it can also be recognised because the two basal segments of the antennae are red. *Notiophilus biguttatus* (Plate 18) is one of the few ground beetles which are active in bright sunshine. This shiny little insect is often seen sunning itself on paths and rockeries, but it is difficult to catch because of its great speed and its ability to 'melt' into the tiniest hole or crack in the ground. *Amara aenea* (Plate 18) which has a smoother outline than most ground beetles, also enjoys the sunshine and often sunbathes on low-growing spring flowers.

The other beetle groups include vegetarian and carnivorous species, but most have relatively shorter legs than the ground beetles and they are generally much slower moving insects. Many are harmful in the garden, and among the most destructive are the maybugs or cockchafers and their relatives. These beetles belong to a very large group called lamellicorns, and they can all be recognised by their antennae: the last few segments bear prominent flaps which can be drawn together to form a club or separated to give the antennae a fan-like appearance. The bumbling **cockchafer** (Plate 18), which frequently crashes onto windows and car windscreens in the evenings in May and June, is far too common in the eyes of the farmer and forester, and it causes considerable damage in the garden as well. The adult beetles strip the leaves from trees and shrubs, while their fat, white larvae spend three or four years nibbling away at the roots of a wide variety of plants. They are especially damaging to the roots of cereals and other grasses.

The **garden chafer** (Plate 18) is a smaller relative of the cockchafer which can be identified by the greenish thorax. Adults abound in late June, when they chew the leaves of numerous plants and cause much damage to fruit trees. The larvae are like those of the cockchafer and they have the same habits, but they complete their life cycle in one year. A third species, known as the summer chafer, is locally common in June and July. It is about 15 mm long and entirely orange-brown in colour. The unmistakable rose chafer (Plate 18) is about in May and June and most likely to be found lying contentedly in roses and other large flowers. Its larvae resemble those of the cockchafer and cause similar, although less widespread damage to pasture.

The **stag beetle** (Plate 18) is one of the wood-feeding lamellicorns which spend their larval lives tunnelling in old trees and stumps. The cutting down of many of our woodlands, and the replacement of others with conifers, have made this striking insect much rarer today than it was in the past, but it still keeps going in some tree-dotted parks and hedgerows and it is not uncommon in some suburban areas where it finds the numerous fences to its liking. Only the male bears the great 'antlers' which are really over-grown jaws, and he uses them, just like the male deer, to fight over the females. Male stag beetles can sometimes be seen flying around in the early evening, but the females less often take to the wing.

Many of the lamellicorn beetles are dung-feeders, and they include the famous scarabs and tumble-bugs which roll balls of dung about before burying them. The **dung-beetles** are clearly not normal garden inhabitants, but *Aphodius rufipes* (Plate 18) is a very common visitor to houses in rural areas because of its strong powers of flight and its fascination with light: it very often flies in through open windows in the summer, and then frequently collides with something and falls to the ground to spin noisily round on its back in frantic attempts to right itself.

The **click beetles,** easily recognised by their narrow, bullet-like shape, are another group which the gardener could well do without, for their larvae are the notorious wireworms which live in the soil and attack the roots of our plants. The wireworms (Plate 18) have very tough coats and they vary from yellow to rich brown in colour. They take four or five years to mature, and during this time they feed on decaying matter as well as on the roots of a wide variety of plants. The adult beetles nearly all have a self-righting mechanism which they bring in to play if they fall on their backs: they arch their backs and a small peg, which normally rests on the edge of a cavity on the underside of the thorax, slips off the edge and springs forcefully into the cavity, causing the familiar click and throwing the beetle into the air at the same time. Success may not be immediate, but the beetle usually lands right-way-up in the end. *Athous haemorrhoidalis* (Plate 18) is one of several very common garden click beetles, which vary from greyish brown to black and which all have similar histories.

Phosphuga atrata (Plate 18) is a flesh-eating beetle which is quite common in the more neglected parts of the garden, where it rests under logs and stones by day. It will eat dead animals of all kinds, but its favourite diet seems to be live snails. The **devil's coach-horse** or **cock-tail** (Plate 18) is another carnivorous species which feeds on a variety of living and dead animals. It can be found under stones by day, but it wanders freely over the paths at night and often enters sheds and houses, especially the older buildings with damp floors. The beetle assumes a rather sinister attitude when disturbed, curling the abdomen up and over the thorax and opening its large jaws in a threatening fashion, but it is actually quite harmless. The devil's coach-horse is one of a very large group of beetles called rove-beetles or 'staphs', which all have very short elytra. Many smaller members of this group occur in the garden, especially in and around the compost heap, where they feed perhaps partly on the decaying material and partly on the associated fly maggots and other insects. *Oxytelus laquaetus* and *Philonthus marginatus,* both shown on Plate 18, are two of the commonest species in such places. Although these beetles have very short elytra, their hind wings are usually well developed and many of the smaller species fly very well, often getting into our eyes as they fly about on hot summer days.

The most familiar of the carnivorous beetles are undoubtedly the brightly coloured LADYBIRDS, which give us so much help in our battles against the aphids and scale insects (see page 119). Ladybirds, whose bright colours warn birds that they are unpalatable (see page 165), are found in almost every garden, and very often enter sheds and houses in large numbers to hibernate in the autumn. There are several 'garden' species, of which the largest and commonest is the 7-spot ladybird (Plate 19). This glossy, round insect can be seen on almost any kind of plant, seeking out the aphids and chewing them up in rapid succession. The female lays small batches of yellow, skittle-shaped eggs on the undersides of the leaves, and the little bluish larvae (Plate 19) chew their way out about a week later. During a larval life of about three weeks, each youngster eats several hundred aphids, and it then pupates openly on a leaf (Plate 19). The adult ladybird emerges about a week later and begins the cycle again. Several generations are thus produced in a year. The **two-spot ladybird** (Plate 19) is smaller than the 7-spot and much more variable in appearance: it may be red with two black spots (the normal form), or it may be black with four red spots, and there are several varieties in which the spots are linked together to form intricate patterns. The underside and legs, however, are always black. The little **22-spot ladybird** (Plate 19) is also very common in the garden, and often abundant on my own gooseberry bushes in early spring. It is easily recognised by its black and yellow colour, but it actually has more than 22 spots if you count those on the thorax as well as those on the elytra.

Endomychus coccineus (Plate 19) could easily be mistaken for a ladybird at first, because of its black and red colouring, but it is not closely related to the ladybirds. It is a fungus-eater which is most frequently found under the bark of old logs and trees. A well-kept garden might not harbour this insect very often, but I usually find plenty of specimens on some old plum trees which I keep more for decoration than for plums.

Librodor hortensis is another red and black species which is often found crawling on tree trunks, especially where sap is flowing from a wound, and on house walls in the spring. Much more striking are the **cardinal beetles**, of which *Pyrochroa serraticornis* (Plate 19) is the most common. These beetles, whose larvae tunnel in old tree

Librodor hortensis, a black beetle with red spots

stumps, can often be seen sunning themselves on the trunks or basking in flowers in the spring. *Pyrochroa coccinea,* which is quite common in southern England and in parts of Wales, differs from *P. serraticornis* in having a black head.

The **wasp beetle** (Plate 19) alarms many gardeners because of the wasp-like way in which it scuttles about. It is actually quite harmless, but by mimicking the wasps in this way it avoids being eaten by birds (see page 156). The wasp beetle belongs to the group known as longhorn beetles because of their long antennae. The larvae develop in living and dead tree trunks and the adults that we see scuttling on the trunks are probably searching for somewhere to lay their eggs. At other times the beetles can be seen sipping nectar from hogweed and other similar flowers.

The hogweed is also a favourite feeding place for *Cantharis rustica* (Plate 19) and its relatives, popularly known as soldier beetles or sailor beetles, according to which part of the country one happens to be in. But it is not the hogweed itself which interests these beetles, for they are mainly carnivorous and they prey on the smaller insects which are attracted to the flowers. The reddish colour of most of these beetles has given them the name of 'blood-sucker' in many regions, but they are quite harmless to us because they cannot pierce our skin with their jaws. The bold colours indicate that the beetles are unpalatable to birds.

The adult **raspberry beetle** (Plate 19) is not a commonly seen insect, but its larva must be known to all raspberry addicts. On most days during the raspberry season there is a tea-time exodus from my house to the raspberry patch where, bowl in hand, each member of the family picks his or her own tea. Returning to the table, we heap on the sugar and cream – usually far too much of each – and then we watch for the little yellow grubs to appear. Those which we actually see are discarded but many are undoubtedly eaten. This additional protein does not mar the taste of the fruit in any way, and it does not seem to harm the raspberry beetle population either, for there are always plenty more next year. Those grubs which escape us pupate in the ground and emerge as adults the following spring. The adults nibble the raspberry buds and the females then lay their eggs in the flowers. The larvae hatch in about ten days and tunnel into the developing fruits, causing them to become stunted and distorted and therefore useless for marketing.

The small holes and pale blotches that develop on the leaves of cabbage seedlings and other brassicas almost as soon as they appear above ground are the work of some shiny little beetles called **flea beetles**. They are generally dark in colour and you can see them quite easily if you get down to examine the seedlings, but if you get too close they will leap away and you will see why they are called flea beetles. Their amazing jumping ability stems from the very fat and powerful hind legs, which can often be seen jutting out from the sides of the body. *Phyllotreta nigripes* (Plate 19) is one of the commonest of the several species which inhabit the garden, and it attacks docks and various other plants as well as brassicas. The adult beetles hibernate among dead leaves and other debris and they emerge in the spring to feed on the young seedlings and also on any of the previous year's Brussels or broccoli plants which are still in the ground. The females lay batches of eggs throughout the summer, and both larvae and adults feed on the leaves. Adult beetles can be found on the plants until well into the autumn, often feeding together in large numbers before moving off to find snug winter quarters. *Phyllotreta nemorum* (Plate 19), which is sometimes known as the turnip flea, is another very common flea beetle. It attacks a wide variety of brassicas, but is especially troublesome on turnips and radishes. Its larvae tunnel in the leaves. *Phyllotreta vittula* is very similar to *P. nemorum,* but it is slightly smaller and the yellow bands on the elytra do not curve inwards.

Psylliodes chrysocephala (Plate 19) is yet another common brassica flea beetle, but the brassicas are not the only crops to be affected by these little pests. *Psylliodes affinis,* which is similar to *P. chrysocephala* except that the thorax and elytra are yellowish brown, is the potato flea beetle. Adults of this species chew little holes in the potato leaves, while the larvae feed on the roots.

The flea beetles belong to a very large group known as LEAF BEETLES, which are nearly all shiny insects and which are almost all leaf-feeders at some stage in their lives. One very distinctive feature, although it cannot normally be seen without a lens, is the lobing of the third segment of the foot and the reduction of the fourth segment to a minute structure between the lobes. The most famous of the leaf beetles is the **Colorado beetle** (Plate 19), which is so destructive to potato crops on the Continent. Constant vigilance by the British authorities has so far prevented the beetle from establishing itself here, but the threat is always there and any discovery of the adult beetle or its fat, pink larvae must be reported immediately.

Lema melanopa (Plate 19) is a very common leaf beetle which hibernates in roof spaces and sheds as well as in garden debris of all kinds. When it wakes up in spring it enjoys sunning itself on house walls, and then it goes off to lay its eggs on couch grass and some of the other coarser grasses. The larvae strip the 'flesh' from the grass blades and they often cause serious losses among cereals. The **asparagus beetle** (Plate 19) is a close relative of the previous species and is a frequent visitor to asparagus plants in the southern half of England.

Bruchus pisorum (Plate 19) is the **pea beetle,** a serious pest of cultivated peas. The adult beetle hibernates under bark, in sheds, or in similar secluded places and emerges in the spring to sun itself on walls and tree trunks. Eggs are laid on the developing pea pods and the tiny larvae bore their way in to reach the seeds. Usually only one fat, legless grub develops in each seed, but the affected pea is completely destroyed. These larvae should not be confused with those of the pea midge, which are slender and legless and which occur in large numbers under the skin of each pea, or with the larvae of the pea moth, which have black legs and which live only one or two to each pea.

The WEEVILS are relatively small beetles in which the head is drawn out to form a slender snout or rostrum. The jaws are at the end of the snout, and the antennae usually join it about half way. Numerous species live on our garden plants and weeds. Several species of *Sitona* (Plate 19) can be found walking on paths and walls. They are all very similar and they are known as **pea weevils,** for they attack leguminous plants. They are responsible for the U-shaped holes eaten out from the edges of the pea leaves in the spring and again in mid-summer. The larvae attack the nodules on the roots of the plants. The beetles also attack broad beans and clovers. *Phyllobius pomaceus* (Plate 19) is abundant on stinging nettles. The shiny green colour of fresh specimens is due to a covering of minute scales, but these are easily rubbed off and older specimens reveal a good deal of the black body colour. *Anthonomus pomorum* (Plate 19), recognised by the very prominent teeth on each front leg, is the apple blossom weevil which severely reduces apple crops in some years. The female lays her eggs in the unopened flower buds, and the larvae then destroy the buds before they open properly. *Anthonomus rubi* (Plate 19) is a related species which attacks strawberries and raspberries in the same way. *Otiorhynchus clavipes* (Plate 19), one of our largest weevils, is often found on fruit trees.

Carpet beetles, such as *Anthrenus verbasci* (Plate 18), are more likely to be found in the house or the garden shed than in the garden, although the beetles do enjoy feasting on the flowers of the hogweed and other umbellifers. The larvae, known as woolly bears because of their dense fur coats, are scavenging creatures which feed on wool, feathers, and other animal debris. Their natural habitat is in the nests of birds and rodents, but they do very nicely in piles of old woollen rags in the shed and they also do a certain amount of damage to carpets underneath and behind heavy and rarely moved furniture such as pianos. The **fur beetle** (Plate 18) is a relative of the carpet beetles and it has much the same habits, although it rarely does as much damage. The adults of both beetles are often found on the windows. Control of the carpet and fur beetles revolves largely around regular spring-cleaning to prevent the build-up of damaging populations.

The **furniture beetle** or **woodworm** (Plate 18) is another insect which is more often seen in the house than in the garden, but it is really quite common out of doors. Its natural habitat is in dead wood, and our fences and sheds are just as acceptable to it as floor boards and furniture or tree stumps in the wood. It is, of course, only the larva which does the damage to our timber, but we don't normally know anything about the infestation until the little 'worm holes' appear at the surface. By then the damage is done, for these are the escape holes of the adult beetles, but treatment of the timbers will reduce the risk of a further generation of larvae getting to work on the wood. The adult beetles can often be seen crawling on window panes in older houses during June and July.

The last species in this very brief survey of 'domestic' beetles is the **churchyard beetle** (Plate 19). This jet black species, which is also known as the cellar beetle, is most often found in cellars and outhouses, including stables. It might easily be mistaken for a ground beetle (see page 187), but it has none of the sensory bristles found on the ground beetles and a further distinction is that the hind feet have only four segments. Ground beetles have five segments on each foot. Both adult and larval churchyard beetles feed on decaying vegetable matter which they find on their nocturnal ramblings.

194

CHAPTER 7

The Spiders and their Allies

THE spiders and their numerous relatives make up the class known as the Arachnida. This is yet another large division of the arthropod phylum and it gets its name from the Greek word *arachne*, meaning spider.

The typical arachnid has four pairs of walking legs and its body may or may not be divided into two distinct regions. There are no antennae, but the spiders and some other arachnids have a pair of palps at the front which look and behave like antennae. They help the animals to feel and smell their way about and to find food. They also help male spiders with their courtship, which is, as we shall see, a rather dangerous business. Arachnid palps are not always like antennae, however: those of the scorpions and false scorpions (page 220) form prominent claws which are used to catch food.

There are no real jaws, but just in front of the palps there is normally a little pair of pincers, called *chelicerae,* which may help to

The house spider, common in and around the house and garden shed

tear the food to pieces. These pincers are much modified in the spiders to form the poison fangs. Arachnid mouths are all very small and, with a few exceptions, the animals cannot ingest solids. They either suck the juices from their food, or else they use their chelicerae and the bases of their palps to crush and liquefy it.

195

Digestive juices may be poured into or over the food to break it down before it is taken into the mouth.

As well as the animals already mentioned, the arachnids include the harvestmen (page 214), the mites and ticks (page 221), and a strange assortment of creatures from tropical lands and from the seas.

Spiders by the million

Most people will agree that the spiders are the most disliked of all the creatures that occur in the house and garden, and many people will admit that their aversion to these common creatures is much stronger than a simple dislike: it is a positive fear. Arachnophobia, which is the word that has been coined for this fear of spiders, seems to me to be more common among the ladies, although I have no idea why this should be so. Discussions with my arachnophobic wife have not shed any light on the problem: she will happily pick up a slimy slug or a spiky stick insect, and centipedes don't bother her in the slightest, but a spider in the room is a different matter. Returning after a day or two away from home, I have found the bed moved into all sorts of funny places 'to get away from that thing on the ceiling'. Repeated stressing of the harmless nature of our spiders does nothing to alleviate the fear in the confirmed arachnophobe.

Despite this widespread dislike or fear of spiders, few people will actually bring themselves to kill the animals. Cups, jam jars, and dusters are brought out to catch them on walls and ceilings, and the spiders are then deposited gently outside. Such acts are more likely to be triggered off by ancient beliefs that killing spiders brings bad luck than by the knowledge that spiders are useful creatures, but you have only to look at the numbers of flies and aphids trapped in a spider's web to realise that spiders *are* useful and that it *is* a good plan to spare them.

The spider's body has a narrow waist which clearly divides it into two regions – a *cephalothorax* at the front and an abdomen at the back. The cephalothorax is protected by a fairly tough shield called the carapace. This carries six or eight eyes at the front and its hind region often has a distinct hollow or *fovea*, surrounded by a series of grooves. There are the normal four pairs of legs, although their lengths vary a good deal in relation to the size of the body, and a pair of palps at the front. The palps of male spiders are distinctly clubbed and this allows us to distinguish the sexes very easily. The male uses his palps to fertilise the female, depositing a packet of

Left, the face of a wolf spider (*Pisaura*), showing the eight eyes typical of most spiders and the poison fangs. *Right*, the spinnerets at the hind end of the house spider.

sperm in the clubbed end of one palp and then inserting it into the female's body. Some male spiders also use their palps to signal their intentions to the female (page 213).

All the spiders are carnivorous, and feed almost entirely on living animals. Their prey consists mainly of insects and other small arthropods, which are caught in a variety of ways and subdued with the venomous fangs. Each fang is like a curved needle and it is hinged to a stouter segment at the base. When the spider bites its prey, the two fangs are sunk into the victim and venom is pumped into the wound from a little hole near the tip of each fang. The venom varies a good deal in composition and it may kill or merely paralyse the prey. Some of the world's spiders are, of course, very poisonous and their bite can be fatal even for a man, but none of our British species is at all dangerous. Some of our larger species may pierce the skin if they are picked up and they manage to get their fangs into the more tender creases of the hand or fingers, but the effect of the venom is localised and rarely more irritating than nettle stings. The majority of our spiders are far too weak to get their fangs into us.

The other major feature of spider biology is, of course, the production of silk. Although not all spiders make webs, their lives all depend on silk in some way or other. They all wrap their eggs in silken cocoons, and many species remain in contact with their silken threads throughout their lives. The silk is made in a number of glands in the spider's abdomen and it reaches the outside through the spinnerets at the hind end. Each spinneret carries a number of minute nozzles through which the silk actually emerges, but the spider cannot force the threads out like toothpaste. The silk must be drawn out from the nozzles, and the spider frequently does this with its hind legs. You can see this happening very easily if you watch a spider spinning a web or wrapping up a fly. On other occasions the spider will attach the thread to some object and then walk away, or merely fall, so that the silk is drawn out behind it. Most people are familiar with the way in which spiders use this 'life-line' trick when disturbed. Paying out a thread as it goes, the spider falls down out of harm's way and waits until the danger has passed. It then climbs back up the life-line and, true to Nature's admirable waste-not, want-not system, it eats the thread as it goes.

There are three or four different kinds of silk glands in the spider's body, each connected to its own nozzles and each producing a different kind of thread. Each kind of thread has a different use. Female spiders possess a particular kind of silk gland whose silk is used only for wrapping up the eggs. These egg cocoons vary a great deal from species to species. Many are fluffy little yellow balls stuck into crevices or under window sills, others are smooth and

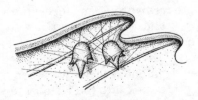

The little sputnik-like egg cocoons of *Theridion pallens*

rolled in the soil for camouflage, while the wolf spiders (page 212) carry their cocoons around with them. One of the most unusual egg cocoons is that of the little *Theridion pallens*. This spider, which lives in oaks and various other trees, is only a couple of millimetres long, but the spiky cocoons which it attaches to the leaves may be more than twice this size.

Many kinds of spider, especially those that feed on flying insects, pass the winter as eggs. The young spiders hatch in the spring and are often seen in dense swarms on walls and tree trunks when they leave their cocoons. There may be three hundred or more baby spiders in such a batch, and they could not hope to find enough food if they all stayed together for very long. After a day or two, they pull out a little thread of silk and raise their abdomens to the wind. The latter may be sufficient to draw even more silk out and then to carry the little spider away to begin an independent life. Very few of these little spiders ever reach the ground again, but sufficient manage to avoid birds and other enemies to keep their populations going from year to year.

Spiders are extremely numerous in the countryside and in the garden. W. S. Bristowe, one of our leading authorities, has estimated that an English meadow in late summer may support over two million spiders to the acre. Most of these are very small, and such high populations are not found in many other habitats, but it still adds up to a tremendous weight of spiders in these islands. Bristowe has further estimated that the weight of insects eaten each year by these spiders is greater than the weight of our human population.

There are nearly 600 kinds of spiders living in the British Isles and, although they have a wide range of habits and habitats, a good many of these can be found in our gardens. Detailed identification of the species is beyond the scope of this book, but I have attempted in the following pages to describe the major groups that the gardener will meet and to mention some of the commoner and more conspicuous species of the garden.

The web builders

The web-building species are the most familiar of our garden-dwelling spiders because they attract our attention with their delicate webs. These are of many different kinds, and they are built in almost every possible situation. They are strung along fences and across doors and windows, they are draped over walls and bushes, and they carpet the grass. Funnel-shaped webs poke out from crevices in walls and tree trunks, while every neglected corner supports its triangular platform of cobwebs. The spiders sometimes incorporate their own shelters into their webs, but the prime purpose of the spider web is to catch food and in this respect the spiders stand almost alone. Apart from man, the only other animals that make traps are a few caddis fly larvae, which spins silken nets among the water plants and wait for the current to bring them their dinner, and the ant-lion larvae. The latter live in the warmer parts of the world, mainly where the soil is sandy, and they excavate little conical pits in the ground. The larvae live at the bottom of these pits and their huge jaws wait for ants and other small insects to tumble in.

It is thought that the webs evolved in the first place as simple extensions of the spiders' egg cocoons or resting places. Spiders which habitually left strands of silk lying about might well have caught insects in them. This would obviously have been an advantage, and these spiders would have survived preferentially over their tidier relations. The habit would have been passed on from generation to generation, and refinements would have been built in until an efficient web had evolved. The early web-builders probably lived mainly on crawling insects and other arthropods, just as many of the more primitive spiders do today, and it is quite possible that the presence of so many spiders and their webs actually stimulated the evolution of wings among the insects. When once they had achieved the power of flight, the insects were much safer from spider attack, but the forces of natural selection then favoured those spiders which left odd strands of silk draped over the plants. These strands would have brought down the occasional flying insect, and the scene was set for the gradual evolution of these scattered strands into the elaborate webs that we see today.

The most attractive webs are undoubtedly the more or less circular orb webs made by spiders of the family Argiopidae. These are the webs that are strung out along our fences and stretched between the plants. Spangled with dew on an autumn morning, they are among the most beautiful sights in any garden. Some of the largest of these orb webs are made by the **diadem** or **cross spider** (Plate 20), which gets its name from the cross-shaped pattern of white dots on the abdomen. This species, which is certainly one of our more conspicuous arachnids, is also called the **garden spider**, although it is by no means confined to garden habitats. Specimens can be found at nearly all times of the year, but they do not really become obvious until July or August, when they are fully grown. The plump female then has a body about 12 mm long, but the male, as in nearly all the spiders, is considerably smaller. If you go round your garden at night and look at the webs with a torch, you will see the garden spiders sitting patiently in the middle of their webs. They will probably still be there in the morning if you look for them early enough but, unless they are in a very sheltered position, they will gradually leave their webs and seek the seclusion of a bark crevice or an overhanging leaf. But don't think that the web has been abandoned: if you look carefully at the hub of the web you will see a single thread running away from it, and if you follow the thread you will find the spider holding tightly to the other end. The arrival of an insect in the web will see her streaking down the signal thread and on to the hub. There she spreads out her eight legs and immediately knows in which direction to go for her dinner. The struggles of the insect stimulate the spider to bite it and, assuming that she is not disgusted by its taste, she will begin to wrap it up with silk. A thick band of silk is drawn from the spinnerets by the back legs and, with deft movements which are utterly fascinating to watch, the spider turns her victim round and round and winds the silk on just as if she were winding it on to a spool.

The garden spider is not a fussy eater and she will accept almost any kind of insect, large or small. The sticky threads of her web are quite strong enough to trap and hold a wasp and the spider herself is quite capable of dealing with such a victim. The bold warning colours of the wasps (see page 165) are quite lost on her. There are, however, certain creatures which the garden spider will reject, and reject very quickly. Harvestmen, for example, are very quickly released from the web if they become trapped, and so are magpie moths (page 149). Having tasted one of these unpleasant animals, the spider usually rushes off to clean her fangs on some nearby leaves. (This convention of referring to spiders as feminine might give the impression that only the female spider acts in this way, but male spiders have to feed as well and their actions are just the same as those of their mates.)

Although spider silk is very elastic and remarkably tough for its size – the strands in the garden spider's web are no more than about $0 \cdot 003$ mm in diameter – the webs do not last very long when buffeted by winds and subjected to the daily struggles between spider and prey. Most garden spiders probably remake their webs every day before retiring to their shelters.

When building a web from scratch, the spider must first establish a bridge thread from which the rest of the web is suspended. She may do this by attaching the thread to a chosen point and then trailing it behind her as she walks along a branch or a window sill to another chosen point. Alternatively, she may up-end her abdomen and allow the wind to carry away a thread until the end becomes attached to a neighbouring support. The spider then glues down her end and tests the line for strength. Whichever method she uses, she will then strengthen the bridge line by moving along it several times and laying down more threads. She then spins another thread which she attaches to two points on the bridge line in such a way that it hangs down like a slack washing line. Having done this, the spider drops on another thread from the centre of the sagging line and attaches the new thread to a convenient point. The result of this is that the sagging thread becomes pulled down into a taut V, and the base of the V then becomes the centre of the web. The spider then completes the frame by attaching threads to surrounding objects, and proceeds to spin the radii of the web (see fig: 1, overleaf). These radii are of various lengths, because of the irregular shape of the frame, but the spider makes a remarkably fine job of arranging them. The exact number varies, but garden spider webs have about thirty radii on average, with the younger spiders gener-

Stages in the construction of an orb web (see text)

ally having more radii in their webs than the adults. The angles between the radii are not constant, but the spider uses her legs as 'rules' to ensure that the radii are all about the right distance apart.

Having constructed the radii, the spider makes herself a little platform at the hub of the web and then, leaving a little gap around the platform, she moves outwards on a spiral course and lays down what is known as the temporary spiral (fig: 2). This is a very open spiral of silk and its function is to strengthen the radii and give the spider something to walk on while she carries out the final stage of construction – the formation of the sticky spiral which actually traps the insects (fig: 3). A different kind of silk is used now, and it is coated with gum from special glands situated among the silk-producing ones. The spider works from the outside of the web and you can watch the wonderful way in which she uses her legs to measure the distances and to stretch the silk and glue it down to the radii in exactly the right places. Stretching the silk as it is laid down causes the gum to break up into tiny droplets, which are accentuated early in the morning when they glitter with the dew that they attract. The temporary spiral is rolled up and usually eaten as the spider moves round with the sticky spiral, but the little platform is left in the centre of the finished web (fig: 4). The sticky threads do not always form a single spiral: the web is very often markedly asymmetrical, with many more sticky threads below the hub than above it. These extra threads are laid down in the form of over-lapping arcs. Toothed claws on her feet enable the spider to guide herself very efficiently along her threads, and oily secretions ensure that she does not become stuck to her own glue.

The entire web-building procedure is instinctive or inborn and the spider is never taught to how to do it – most spiders, in fact, never even see their parents. Each stage of the process simply triggers off the next stage automatically and the spider cannot modify the web if anything goes wrong. A few spiders may patch up broken webs under certain circumstances, but damaged webs are usually completely rebuilt apart from the frame. The whole process of destroying the damaged web and re-building it may take the spider less than an hour– a truly wonderful rate of working, even if the spider *has* been programmed for it. Further information on the construction of orb webs may be found in two delightful books: *The Spider's Web*, by Theodore H. Savory, and *The World of Spiders*, by W. S. Bristowe.

Male and female garden spiders both spin webs when they are young, but the adult male gives up eating in favour of courting. This is a dangerous business for him because the female is larger than he is and would pounce on him if he blundered into her web unannounced. He approaches stealthily and signals his presence by plucking her web, but he is always ready to drop down on a life-line if she attacks him. And she usually does at first. He may have to make the approach many times before subduing her and enticing her on to a special mating thread that he has spun. His palps are already charged with sperm, and at last he manages to insert one into the female's body. After further courtship, he may be able to insert the other one and then, if he is lucky, he makes his escape. It is often said that the female eats her mate after mating, but this is not always true. Male garden spiders usually mate with several females in the late summer and they seem to have no trouble in getting away from their first few mistresses. It is later in the autumn, when they are worn out by exhaustion and lack of food, that the males are likely to be eaten. This is no great loss to the species, for the males are very near the ends of their lives at this stage in any case, and when they are eaten their bodies go to help nourish the eggs which they have fertilised.

The mated females are also near the ends of their lives in October and they leave their webs to deposit their eggs and cocoons in sheltered nooks. The eggs are protected by a mass of coarse yellow silk and these cocoons can be found during the winter in bark crevices, under fence rails and window sills, and in various other secluded places. The eggs hatch in the spring and the youngsters emigrate on their silken threads as we have already seen. Some of them may grow up by the autumn, but the majority take two summers to reach maturity.

Even more common in the garden than the garden spider is a related species called *Meta segmentata*. Its web is often abundant in the lower parts of the hedgerow and in the herbaceous border, and it can easily be identified because it has no central platform such as we saw in the web of the garden spider. In addition, whereas the garden spider's web is usually more or less vertical, that of *Meta segmentata* is usually slung at an angle – generally somewhere between 30° and 70° to the horizontal. The spider can often be seen in the centre of the web, but it is more often sheltering under a nearby leaf and maintaining contact with its snare by a slender signal thread. *Meta segmentata* is a smaller and more slender creature than the garden spider, the female being no more than about 8 mm long*. The carapace is basically light brown, with a slender, U-shaped mark looking rather like a tuning fork. The abdomen is variable in colour, but the pattern is fairly constant (Plate 20).

Meta segmentata is adult in late summer and autumn and probably hibernates in the adult state, for adults are also commonly found in the spring. The species has a rather unusual courtship behaviour and, in contrast to other members of the family, the males are almost as large as the females. A male takes up station alongside a female's web and drives off other males that come too close, but he makes no advance towards the female until an insect arrives in the web. Both spiders then move towards the insect, but the male makes sure that he advances in such a way that the insect remains between him and his intended. His front legs are larger than hers, and he uses them to ward her off. He may even chase her a little way, but then he returns to the insect and may 'gift wrap' it with a few strands of silk. When the female approaches again, he allows her to tuck into the meal and, while she is busy, he spins his mating threads around her. It is then fairly easy for him to entice her on to the threads and to mate with her. As in the garden spiders, each male probably mates with several females, and each female receives several suitors.

Meta menardi is a close relative of *Meta segmentata,* but its habitat is quite different. It is known as the cave spider but, as well as caves, it inhabits cellars and damp, dark outbuildings. It can also be found in inspection chambers connected with the sewers. Its web is often more or less horizontal in such places and it catches woodlice and other small creatures which fall on to it. The cave spider is about 13 mm long, with a light brown carapace and a chestnut coloured abdomen, but its egg cocoons are much more obvious than the spider itself. Attached to the walls or roof of the spider's home by silken stalks, they hang among the webs like small white hens' eggs. Each cocoon may reach a length of about 2 cm – much more than the length of the spider itself.

The orb webs that hang from your window frames and brush against your hair when you go into the garden shed are usually the work of another very common spider called *Zygiella X-notata.*

*The lengths given for the various spider species on the following pages refer to females unless otherwise stated.

The egg-cocoon of the cave spider hanging in the web

These webs are almost always spun in a corner or under a ledge where the spider can make a tubular retreat. The webs of young *Zygiella* spiders are much the same as other orb webs, but the webs of the adults are very easily identified because the spiral threads are missing from two sectors. The radius dividing these two empty sectors serves as the signal thread leading to the spider's retreat. In addition, the webs are often markedly asymmetrical, with many more sticky threads below the hub than above. *Zygiella X-notata* herself (Plate 20) is a fairly plump spider up to about 1 cm long. Her abdomen often has a pinkish tinge and always carries a broad leaf-like pattern. She is mature from late July onwards and she later leaves her little yellow egg cocoons securely tucked up in the corners of our window frames or under the eaves of sheds and houses. *Zygiella atrica* is a very similar spider, and her webs are similar as well, but she prefers to spin up on shrubs and she is not common in the garden. The rather flat and very dark spider which spins in the same sort of corners as *Z. X-notata,* and which drops menacingly down from its webs at night, is *Araneus umbraticus.*

Araneus cucurbitinus (Plate 20) is a bright green spider only about 5 mm long and it spins its orb web in a variety of trees. The web is often very small and stretched across a single leaf, such as that of an apple or lilac tree. The spider herself is beautifully camouflaged as she sits in or by the web.

If you examine an old wall or the overlapping boards of an old shed at any time of year, you will almost certainly find the webs of one or more of our three *Amaurobius* species. The webs are white and lacy and they look not unlike small and rather ragged doilies stuck to the wall. There is a hole in the centre, leading to the spider's retreat deep in a crevice between the bricks or the boards. These spiders belong to a group known as the cribellate spiders, because they have a special spinning organ known as a cribellum.

This is a somewhat oval plate just in front of the spinnerets and it is covered with tiny pores leading to specialised silk glands. The spiders also possess a distinct comb of hairs, known as a calamistrum, on each back leg, although both cribellum and calamistrum may be reduced in adult males.

When spinning her snare, *Amaurobius* produces two straight threads from one pair of spinnerets and passes the threads from the other pair through the combs. The hind legs are then vibrated rapidly and the silk threads are thrown into wavy bands over the straight ones, almost as if the spider were knitting. The cribellum exudes a very sticky material which is then laid across the wavy bands, and the whole arrangement forms a narrow ribbon. It has a

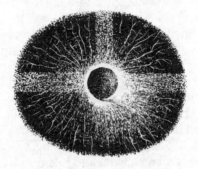

The tangled web of *Amaurobius* on an old wall with the spider's retreat in a crevice where the mortar is missing

slightly bluish tinge when freshly spun. These ribbons are not arranged in any regular pattern, and the spider adds a few more each night. The web thus tends to become very tangled and untidy. It is, however, a remarkably efficient trap for both crawling and flying insects, whose feet become completely enmeshed in the lacy threads. The spider always bites her victims in the leg, and then drags them back into her retreat to enjoy them at her leisure. Pulling a web out from its crevice will reveal just what the spider has been eating, and it will also show you just how easily the lacy threads stick to your fingers. You will find that the web contains the remains of flies, earwigs, woodlice, and many other small creatures. There will also be several spider skins, but these will not all be from her victims: some will be the outgrown and cast-off skins of *Amaurobius* herself. You may even find some very small pink spiders in the web, and these will probably be specimens of *Oonops* *pulcher,* an inquiline* which lives on the scraps from the larger spider's table.

Our three species of *Amaurobius* are all quite large spiders when fully grown, with the front end of the carapace raised well above the rest. There is a marked fovea or pit in the carapace, with several grooves radiating from it. Both *Amaurobius fenestralis* (8 mm long) and *A. similis* (up to 12 mm) have pale brownish abdomens heavily mottled with black towards the back (Plate 20). *Amaurobius ferox* is a much darker species, often almost black, with an abdominal pattern resembling a skull and crossbones. It reaches a length of about 14 mm and, unlike the other two species, its legs are not marked with light and dark bands. *Amaurobius similis* prefers slightly drier conditions than the others and can be found on dry walls and sheds. Although widely distributed, it is less common in the north of the country. *Amaurobius fenestralis* inhabits the same sort of places, but will tolerate damper conditions. It is also found in the corners of window frames and under loose bark. *Amaurobius ferox* prefers much damper places and can be found at the foot of old walls, in log piles, and in cellars. It was the commnest spider to be found lurking under the floorboards when my old house was being renovated. Like *A. similis, A. ferox* becomes rarer in the north. Adults of all species can be found at any time of the year.

Segestria senoculata (Plate 20) is another widely distributed wall-living spider, living in the same sort of sheltered habitats as *Amaurobius.* She builds a silken tube in a cavity between the bricks or stones, but her presence can be detected by the dozen or so 'trip wires' that radiate out from the tube entrance. As soon as some

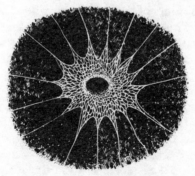

The web of *Segestria senoculata*, easily identified by the radiating 'trip wires'

*An inquiline is any animal which lives in the nest or home of another species without having any obvious effect on this other species.

poor creature blunders into one of these stout threads, the spider is out to pounce on it with her large chelicerae.

The triangular hammocks or cob-webs that festoon every corner of the garden shed and seem to appear in a room almost as soon as the duster is put away belong to the long-legged **house spiders** of the genus *Tegenaria*. These are the spiders that dart out from under the furniture and cause panic in the family just as you settle down in the armchair for the evening. They also seem to take their exercise on the bedroom ceiling just as you are about to put the light out, and they appear to lurk behind every box in the garden shed. House spiders are especially noticeable in the late summer, for this is when they are fully grown and at their speediest. The spiders are generally a dirty brown colour, with heavily mottled abdomens and with prominent spinnerets protruding from the hind end. Males and females are about the same size. We have three common species in our houses and sheds, the most widespread being *Tegenaria domestica*. With a body length of about 10 mm, this spider is found all over the British Isles, but only rarely seen away from human habitation. *Tegenaria saeva* (Plate 20) is a much larger spider. Up to 18 mm long, this is the species which frightens people in their houses more than any other. She is very common in the southern half of Great Britain, but rare in the north of England and absent from Ireland. She is much less restricted to houses and other buildings than the previous species, but garden-dwelling specimens often invade the house in the autumn. *Tegenaria parietina* is the largest of the three domestic species. Her body is about the same size as that of *T. saeva*, but her legs are much longer. This makes her very frightening as she runs across the floor at great speed and legend has it that spiders of this species terrified Cardinal Wolsey at Hampton Court. This spider, found only in the southern half of England, is sometimes known as the Cardinal spider.

The webs of these house spiders may reach enormous sizes when they are built in undisturbed sheds. That of *Tegenaria saeva* may span the two or three feet between rafters. One corner of the web is always rolled up to make a tubular retreat, from which the spider can run out on to the sheet when an insect gets tangled in it. The webs are not sticky, but the spiders add more and more threads as they move about on them and the insects' feet get hopelessly tangled. The spiders' egg sacs are hung up near the web or else firmly attached to the walls beside it.

If the house spider's legs are long, then those of *Pholcus phalangioides* are very long (Plate 20). This species, which is found in sheds and houses in the southern half of England and Wales and

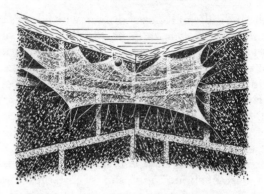

A large sheet web of the house spider (*Tegenaria*)

in Ireland, is well named the daddy-long-legs spider. It makes a rather diffuse three-dimensional web which clothes walls and ceilings rather like scaffolding. Insects and other spiders which stumble into the trap soon find themselves bombarded with more silk, which *Pholcus* throws at them with her long legs. This spider can be found at all times of the year, but it becomes inactive during the winter. The female can often be seen carrying her egg cocoon around in her jaws during the summer.

Theridion sisyphium (Plate 20) is one of the commonest spiders in the garden, although it is only about 4 mm long and therefore far less conspicuous than some of the other species. Mature spiders can be found from June onwards, spinning their webs among the shrubs and the plants of the herbaceous border. These webs are usually well above the ground and, like those of all the members of this family (the Theridiidae), they consist of a sort of three-dimensional trellis. The threads in the central region are sticky, and the spider makes a little conical tent in the upper reaches. When an insect flies into the web, *Theridion* rushes out and throws more silk over it with her hind legs until it is completely immobilised. Even quite large prey is tackled by this fearless little spider. She lays her eggs during the summer and wraps them in a bluish green cocoon which she then keeps in her tent. Her subsequent behaviour is really remarkable, because she actually feeds her offspring for several days. At first, she feeds them with drops of fluid from her mouth, and later she may sit down and share a fly with them. W. S. Bristowe describes how she punctures a fly in several places to allow the youngsters to suck out the fluids.

Several related species occur commonly in the garden, all of them with the typically bulbous abdomen which looks too large for the rest of the body. *Enoplognatha ovata* (Plate 20) is very common and, with a greater or lesser amount of carmine markings on her abdomen, she is one of our prettiest spiders. Her web can be found among all kinds of plants, while she herself spends most of her time sheltering in a curled-up leaf, very often nursing her greenish blue egg cocoon. *Achaearanea tepidariorum* is an alien species, but it is commonly found in greenhouses in this country. The carapace is pale brown and the abdomen, as in many other species of this genus, is heavily mottled. *A. tepidariorum* is an aggressive species and, with a length of about 7 mm, she is our largest member of the genus. Her bulb-shaped egg cocoons are hung up in her trellis.

Steatodea bipunctata (Plate 20) is a closely related species whose webs are most commonly found in and around sheds. The central part of the trellis usually forms a rather open platform extending out from a window sill or similar object, and a number of straight threads pass obliquely down to meet the wall. The web is designed primarily to capture crawling insects, and it is the lower ends of these oblique threads that are sticky. An insect walking into one of them gets stuck and *Steatodea* rushes out from her retreat under the sill or in a corner to deal with it.

During the autumn, our shrubs and hedgerows are adorned with the slightly domed sheets of *Linyphia triangularis* (Plate 20). The sheet is quite densely woven and it is supported by a maze of 'scaffolding' above and below. The spider hangs upside down from the lower surface of the sheet. Small insects, such as leaf-hoppers (page 126) or midges (page 160), that blunder into the upper scaffolding fall onto the sheet and, although the threads are not

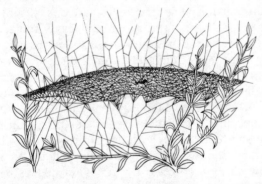

The up-turned-hammock-like web of *Linyphia triangularis*, with the spider hanging upside down near the centre

sticky, they impede the insects' progress sufficiently for the spider to be able to run along and bite them through the sheet. *Linyphia triangularis* is related to the tiny money spiders that land on us whenever we go out in the autumn. These tiny creatures exist in enormous numbers and their sheet webs – remarkably large when compared with the size of the spiders – cover almost every square inch of our grasslands during the autumn and early winter. The spiders seem to indulge in their aeronautical activities mainly in sunny weather, when the ground heats up quickly. Up-currents tug at their silk threads, and up go the spiders. They can travel many miles in this way, but many of them are snapped up by birds and never come down again.

Crab spiders

Leaving the web-spinning spiders, we can now move on to look at some of the other groups, which either go out and hunt their prey or else lie in wait and ambush it. The crab spiders belong to the second group. They are well named, for most of them have squat bodies and their first two pairs of legs are usually much longer and stronger than the others. They dart about with a distinctly crab-like action. Crab spiders usually take up station in flowers or among leaves to wait for their insect prey, and many of them are very well camouflaged in their normal situations. The unsuspecting insect alights and is immediately grabbed by the crab spider's strong front legs. Several species of crab spiders can be found in the garden, mainly belonging to the genus *Xysticus* (Plate 21). Up to about 7 mm long, adults of this genus can be found from April until late summer. The amorous male takes no chances with his chosen mate, grabbing one of her legs and then fastening her down with gummy threads before attempting to mate with her. He is away before she manages to disentangle herself. After mating, the female lays her eggs and surrounds them with a cushion-like cocoon on which she then sits guard until they hatch.

Jumping spiders

If you have a sunny fence or wall, especially an old one with a good coating of algae and lichen, you may well find the little **zebra spider** enjoying the sunshine there. This black and white spider (Plate 21) belongs to a group known as jumping spiders. These spiders hunt rather like cats, stalking their prey and then pouncing on it when they get near enough. Good eyesight is obviously necessary for such activity, and if you look into the face of a jumping spider you will see four large eyes looking back at you. It is rather like looking at the front of a miniature car and seeing two headlights and two slightly smaller side-lights. The spider's other four eyes are much smaller and much further back on the carapace.

The jumping spiders are adult all through the summer and you can find them on rockery stones and on paths as well as on walls and fences. You might even be lucky enough to see the male's courtship display, which is a sort of tick-tack signalling with the front legs, designed to appease and stimulate the female. The zebra spider is found nearly all over the British Isles, but many of our other jumping spiders are restricted to southern regions.

Wolf spiders and other hunters

Most gardeners will have met the ground-living wolf spiders. Several species live in our gardens, all of them greyish brown and rather hairy spiders about 6 mm long. Their front and back legs are noticeably longer than the others. *Pardosa amentata* (Plate 21) is one of our commonest and most widely distributed species. In the garden, the wolf spiders live under low growing plants such as pinks and aubretia, but they come out whenever possible to sun themselves on stones and paths. They seem to need plenty of light and warmth at ground level, and none of them ever lives in completely shaded habitats. They are most noticeable during the spring and early summer, when each female is carrying a little round egg cocoon. The cocoon is attached to the spider's spinnerets and she has an instinctive desire to hold on to it. If you remove the cocoon, she will search around for it until she finds it, and if she can't find it she will often pick up a small pebble or shell as a substitute to satisfy her instinctive drive. This parental care continues after the eggs have hatched, for the young spiders spend a few days riding on their mother's back before they scatter to lead their own lives.

Wolf spiders run down their prey and catch it with their long front legs. Courting males have to signal their intentions to the females from afar, and they employ a form of semaphore or tick-tack with their enlarged palps. Without this signalling behaviour, they would probably be attacked by the females.

If you have a hedge or wall with plenty of dead nettles or other herbaceous vegetation growing in its lee, you may well find the brown *Pisaura mirabilis,* sunning herself in her characteristic position on the leaves (Plate 21) or darting after insects. She is especially noticeable in such places in May. The courtship of this species

A male wolf spider using his swollen palps to signal his intentions to a nearby female

A female *Pisaura mirabilis* with the silken 'tent' in which her offspring spend the first few days of their lives

is again very interesting, for the male catches a fly and presents it to the female to keep her occupied while he gets on with the business of mating. The female carries her egg cocoon around with her for a few weeks in June, holding it in her jaws and dragging it along under her body. When the eggs are about to hatch, she fixes the cocoon to a leaf and spins a conspicuous tent over it. The young spiders spend their first few days in the tent with their mother standing guard outside.

Pisaura and other wolf spiders have no permanent homes, but most of the hunters have a home base from which to make their forays. These home bases are usually in the form of silken chambers under stones or logs, and they are often found when tidying up in the garden or shed. *Drassodes lapidosus* (Plate 21) is one of the fiercest of these hunters and, like many of the others, she comes out at night. With her projecting spinnerets and reddish brown carapace, she could be mistaken for *Dysdera crocata* (Plate 21), which often lives in the same area. *Dysdera* has only six eyes, however, and her jaws are much larger than those of *Drassodes*. Both spiders reach lengths of about 15 mm as a rule, but *Drassodes* is sometimes much larger. *Drassodes* hunts a wide variety of prey and can deal effectively with spiders much larger than herself. *Dysdera* feeds mainly on woodlice, which she pinches between her huge jaws. She is especially common in greenhouses and frames, where the temperature is often a bit higher than that of the surroundings.

As one final example of our garden and household spiders, we can look at one of the strangest of them all, the **spitting spider** (Plate 21). One of the six-eyed spiders, it is one of our rarer species,

213

confined to southern England and rarely found outside houses and warm sheds or greenhouses. It is well worth searching for to witness the remarkable way in which it catches its prey. The spider walks slowly over the walls and when it is about 6 mm from its prey it raises the front end of its body and fires two sticky threads from its jaws. The prey is immediately pinned down by two sets of zig-zag threads. This gummy material is produced in glands inside the spider's domed cephalothorax, and the spider must oscillate its jaws extremely rapidly during the firing in order to produce the zig-zag effect.

The spitting spider with its pinned-down victim

A typical harvestman, showing the one-part body, the very long legs, and the eyes perched up on a turret on top of the body

HARVESTMEN

Tidying up the garden at the end of the summer, you will undoubtedly come across several long-legged, rather globular animals lurking under the pinks and other clumps of low-growing plants. These small animals are harvestmen. They are often known as harvest spiders, and they are frequently confused with the spiders, but the two groups are not closely related. Harvestmen are very common on the ground and among low-growing vegetation, and several species can be found on trees and walls. They are abundant in hedgerows and in the wilder and shrubbier gardens. They get their name because they are to be found in their greatest numbers at harvest time, although few species are actually found in the corn fields. The animals were also called shepherd spiders in bygone days but, although various amusing suggestions have been put forward, there is no straightforward explanation for such a name.

Harvestmen belong to a group of arachnids called the Opiliones. Like the spiders and the other arachnids, the harvestmen have four pairs of walking legs, but the resemblance between the harvestmen and the spiders ends right there. Whereas the spider's body is clearly divided into two regions by a narrow waist, that of the harvestman is virtually in one piece, with only a slight groove

214

marking the division between the front and hind regions. A closer look will reveal that the eyes are two in number and borne on a pimple-like turret on the top of the animal. This arrangement is quite unlike that found among the spiders. Although perched up in a commanding position, and looking out to both sides of the animal, the harvestman's eyes are not renowned for efficiency. They detect light and shade, and probably pick out a certain amount of movement, but sight is much less important to the harvestmen than the senses of smell and touch. These senses are centred on the leg-like palps, which spring from close to the mouth, and on the second pair of legs. If you watch harvestmen going about their business, you will see them tapping the ground and leaves with these limbs, picking up scents and feeling their way around obstructions. The second pair of legs are always longer than the rest among the harvestmen, and this is one of the easiest features by which the animals may be recognised.

Unlike the spiders, the harvestmen spin no silk and they have no venom. They are quite harmless creatures (as, indeed, are our British spiders), but the larger species still manage to induce a certain amount of panic among the ladies when they stride boldly across the threshold on their stilt-like legs.

Like many of the soft-bodied invertebrates that we have seen in the garden, the harvestmen are basically nocturnal creatures and they soon scurry for shelter again if they are disturbed during the daytime. This behaviour is associated with their rather thin skins, which are not water-proof and which allow the animals to lose too much water in dry air. The harvestmen are much more dependent upon water than the spiders and, although they get plenty of moisture in their food, they need to drink regularly. They make great use of dew, and I have often seen them drinking from the little beads of rain water trapped on the rough-cast walls of my house.

The harvestmen are almost entirely carnivorous animals, eating the flesh of a wide range of other small creatures, both alive and dead. Their presence under your clumps of prize pinks need not cause alarm, for they are not harming the plants and they are probably guarding them against attack by caterpillars and other vegetarians. Apart from caterpillars, the harvestmen eat millipedes and centipedes, spiders, mites, woodlice, and a wide range of small insects. Some of the ground-living harvestmen eat slugs and snails, and many species take an interest in fungi and decaying material of all kinds. The sense of smell is particularly important in finding food, tasty morsels being discovered in the first instance by the long second pair of legs, Harvestmen can lose two, three, or even four of their legs without much loss of mobility, as long as they do not lose both members of the second pair. Deprived of the sensory functions of both of these legs, the harvestmen cannot normally survive for very long.

Having found a suitable meal, the harvestman walks over it and pins it down with its legs and palps. It then brings its smallest limbs into play. These are the chelicerae or pincers right at the front. The hard bases of these limbs help to crush the food if necessary, and the little pincers tear off small pieces and crush them even further. The juices oozing from the food, together with the smallest particles, are then sucked into the mouth. After dinner, the harvestman settles down to the washing up. The legs and palps, which usually become soiled during the meal, are gently drawn through the pincers to remove all traces of dirt. This is especially important for the palps and the second pair of legs, because their numerous sense organs must be kept clean at all times. A harvestman with legs caked with dirt is rather like a man with a heavy cold and a bunged-up nose – the sense of smell is greatly impaired. And we have seen how important the sense of smell is to the harvestman. The cleaning up process usually takes place at night, but you may well see it during the daytime, especially in a shaded part of the garden or after a shower. The performance put on by the longer-legged species is a real pleasure to watch – a miniature ballet, in fact, with graceful movement and perfect control of all eight legs. Rising 'on point', the animal lifts one leg at a time and, starting at the base, draws the whole limb through the pincers. The limb being cleaned gradually curves round into a large circle as the tip approaches the pincers and then, when it is released, it straightens gracefully and returns to its normal position.

Water is necessary for the final stages of the washing-up – the cleaning of the pincers themselves – and you can often see harvestmen around the edge of a puddle, dipping their front ends into the water and waving them around. This removes the dirt from the pincers, and also gives the animals a chance to drink.

Mammals, birds, lizards, beetles, centipedes, and spiders have all been known to attack and eat harvestmen but, with the possible exception of the hedgehog, these predators don't take a very great toll of the harvestmen. Invertebrate predators, notably the spiders, are strongly repelled by the unpleasant secretions from various glands on the harvestman's body, and they usually let go as soon as they take hold of the animal. Nevertheless, many harvestmen perish in spiders' webs because their legs become inextricably tangled and they starve to death. Some birds also reject the harvestmen because of the foul-tasting fluids. I have seen several house sparrows and blue tits home in on harvestmen sitting on the wall and then appear to drop them straight away. The explanation could be that the birds were slightly off target and succeeded only in dislodging the harvestmen, but birds don't usually miss and it seems more likely that they don't like the taste of the harvestmen. The repellent fluids of the British harvestmen are not normally detected by our own rather inefficient noses, but some biologists claim to detect a slight nutty odour when several harvestmen are confined in a small container. The secretions also appear to affect the harvestmen themselves, for they become very drowsy and lethargic when crowded together. They recover very rapidly when they are separated again.

Harvestmen nearly all have a second line of defence involving the loss of one or more legs when they are caught. Muscular movements cause the legs to snap off at one of the joints near the base, leaving the enemy holding a twitching leg while the harvestman makes good its escape. Unlike the spiders, however, the harvestmen cannot regenerate their legs. They must therefore take care not to lose too many.

Several of the harvestmen that you find wandering about in your garden may be carrying little red blobs on their legs and bodies. These look like little lumps of sealing wax at first sight, but closer examination reveals that the blobs have legs. They are, in fact, mites – yet more members of the group we have already seen running over slugs' bodies and weighing down bumble bees in the spring. Most of these red mites will be young individuals living parasitically on the harvestmen. Attaching themselves to their hosts, these young mites plunge their anchor-like mouthparts through the soft joints and suck out the body fluids. The adult mites are more often found in the soil and leaf litter, where they get their nourishment from decaying matter. Adults are found on harvestmen from time to time, but they are using the larger animals merely as taxis to get from place to place. This 'hitch-hiking' behaviour is called phoresy. The mites do not appear to harm the harvestmen, even when several young mites are busily sucking fluids from one individual. Mite-infested animals still seem able to move about and feed without difficulty.

The sexes are very much alike among the harvestmen, although the females of some species have somewhat larger bodies than the males. The reproductive organs are tucked away for most of the time under a shield-like plate on the lower side of the animal. Mating is a much more straightforward business than among the spiders, with little or no courtship on either side. A mature male meeting an adult female turns to face her and almost immediately copulates with her. He then leaves in search of another willing female. Such goings on are rarely observed by the gardener, or even by the biologist, because they generally take place during the night. The subsequent egg-laying by the female is also primarily a nocturnal activity, but it is much more likely to be seen because the females do occasionally venture forth to lay their eggs after a daytime shower. The eggs are rarely much larger than the full stops on this page and the female harvestman uses her long ovipositor to place them in tiny crevices in the soil or under loose bark. Some females can produce several hundred eggs, but they do not lay them all at once. Batches are laid at intervals, and the females very often mate again between laying each batch. The majority of our British harvestmen mature towards the end of the summer and go on laying their eggs into the autumn. These eggs do not hatch until the spring, and the cycle then starts again. There are, however, other types of life cycle, as we shall see in the next section.

The British harvestmen

Only twenty-two species of harvestmen have been recorded in the British Isles, and an amateur with patience and a good lens could soon learn to identify them all. Several are very local creatures, however, and only about half of the species are likely to be found in gardens. Looked at from the ecological point of view, taking only their preferred habitats into consideration, the harvestmen fall quite easily into three major groups: those that live in the surface layers of the soil and in leaf litter, those that live among low-growing plants, and those that live on shrubs and trees. There is a certain amount of overlap between the last two groups, because the tree-living species may drop down in dry weather and the low-level species may climb higher under very humid conditions, but this does not invalidate the distinction. As one would expect of animals that spend their lives on the ground or among the vegetation, our harvestmen are all of sombre hue, brown and black being the dominant colours.

The only really common soil-dwelling species, and the only one likely to be turned up in the garden, is a little black creature called *Nemastoma bimaculatum* (Plate 21). As in all the soil-dwelling harvestmen, its legs are relatively short – a clear adaptation to habitat, because long legs would certainly be a hindrance in the confined spaces of the soil. *Nemastoma* thrives under stones and logs, and also gets under the bark of fallen trees. Look out for it if you bring in firewood from the garden: I have rescued several specimens from a fiery fate when they have crawled from logs stacked by the fire. This species, like other soil-dwelling ones, has no definite breeding season because conditions do not fluctuate much from month to month in their chosen homes and food is always available in the form of mites and springtails. Adult specimens of *Nemastoma* can be found at all times of the year.

One of the most likely harvestmen to be lurking under your pinks is *Oligolophus tridens*, a slightly flattened creature in which the saddle-shaped mark on the upper surface has parallel sides. Just behind the head, and just about visible to the naked eye, there is a trident of three forward-pointing spines. *Oligolophus spinosus* (Plate 21) is another stout species with a forward-pointing trident of

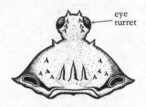

The upper surface of the body of *Oligolophus tridens*, seen from the front (head and legs removed) to show the trident of spines

spines, but the saddle is not parallel sided and it is terminated by a distinct black line. With a body length between 7 and 11 mm, this species is considerably larger than *O. tridens*. *Oligolophus spinosus* may be found lurking under vegetation, but it is more often to be seen on the lower parts of walls and tree trunks.

Phalangium opilio (Plate 21) lives in similar places. It has a well marked saddle, a shiny white underside, and no trident. The male is very easily identified by the large 'horns' at the front (Plate 21). These are the greatly enlarged chelicerae or jaws. *Mitopus morio* is the commonest and most widely distributed of the British harvestmen. It can be found among all sorts of low-growing vegetation. The animal is very variable, but it can usually be recognised by the rather dark saddle which tends to look rather like an hour-glass. There is a trident of spines just behind the head, but it is very indistinct.

Moving to slightly higher levels in the vegetation, we find that *Leiobunum rotundum* (Plate 21) is the most abundant of the harvestmen. It has a very small brown body, especially in the male, and enormously long black legs. This is the harvestman that most often wanders into houses, and this is the one that normally gets called daddy-long-legs, although, as we have seen, this name should really be applied only to the crane-flies (page 162). *Leiobunum* strides over the leaves of bushes and other plants and is often active by day as well as at night. It very often rests on walls, with its long legs radiating out like fine cracks in the plaster.

Opilio parietinus is another very common species on garden walls and fences and it seems especially attracted to outside toilets and public conveniences. It resembles *Phalangium* in having no trident of spines behind the head, but it has a poorly defined saddle and it has a very speckled underside, quite unlike the pure white belly of *Phalangium*. *Platybunus triangularis* is the only one of our harvestmen that is common in the spring. Its eggs are laid during the summer and they hatch relatively quickly. The species passes the winter in the immature state, when it is known as a pullus. It is found mainly in deciduous woodland and is only an occasional inhabitant of the garden.

FALSE SCORPIONS

These tiny but very fascinating arachnids live mainly on the ground and they usually escape detection because of their very small size – our native species are all under 4 mm long. If you do see one, however, you cannot fail to recognise it by its little greyish body and its relatively enormous pink 'hands'. These 'hands', with their two tweezer-like fingers, are properly called pedipalps and they are well supplied with sensory hairs. As well as catching the false scorpion's food, they help it to find its way about. When the animal is walking forward, it moves very slowly with the pedipalps held out like antlers in front. If it bumps into anything, or if you touch it with a piece of grass, the pedipalps are drawn in and the animal shoots rapidly backwards. False scorpions are carnivorous creatures, feeding on mites, springtails, and other small insects. In most species, the 'hands' possess poison glands and the prey is very soon killed or paralysed when it is caught. The poison produced by the false scorpions is very strong, but the animals themselves are far too small and weak to be able to harm anything much larger than their normal prey. They normally lie in wait for their food, grabbing it when it comes into range. They often grab hold of the hairs on flies' legs, and use the flies as 'taxis' to get to new pastures. This is another example of phoresy (see page 217).

The majority of our 26 species of false scorpions live among leaf litter and other decaying vegetation. Several can be found on the rubbish heap, and it is here that they usually meet and climb on to their aerial taxis. Only females appear to take rides in this way. Some species live in birds' nests, and they may find their way into sheds and houses if you have nests in or around the buildings. One

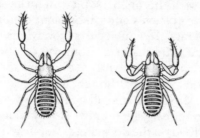

A false scorpion moving forward with pedipalps extended (*left*), and on the retreat with pedipalps withdrawn

species is often found in hay and straw, and if you keep rabbits you may well be keeping this false scorpion as well. Others may turn up among old sacks and papers stored in the garden shed, and one, known as the book scorpion, is often found among the books on neglected shelves. It feeds on the booklice (see page 128) which thrive in such places. The various species of false scorpion all look very much alike and their identification is a matter for the expert.

MITES

The mites are very small arachnids belonging to the group known as the Acarina. This is not a natural group, but a convenient 'dustbin' erected by the biologists to contain an assortment of small arachnids which look alike in many respects but which are not closely related. The body is generally rather globular and there is no division into sections such as we find among the spiders. Adults normally have four pairs of legs, but the young stages have only three pairs. Some of the larger mites could be confused with small harvestmen (page 218), but the second pair of legs are never the longest among the mites. The Acarina also contains the blood-sucking ticks, but these animals are likely to come to the gardener's notice only if he searches the cat or the dog.

Mites are extremely abundant creatures and they live in almost every habitat. Huge numbers live in the soil and leaf litter, many

221

live as parasites on or in larger animals, while others feed freely on plants. Some cause galls to develop on various plants, while yet more live in houses and infest stored foods such as grain and flour. Others live in water.

The soil mites will not be seen during the course of normal gardening because they are so small, but they are there in the garden, sharing with the microscopic fungi the important role of breaking down dead leaves and other plant material and releasing food for new plants. If you have a good lens, or better still a microscope, put a little material from the compost heap under it and take a look. You will probably see several soil mites, bizarre as any science-fiction monster although, in reality, they are less than a millimetre long. Most of them will be the shiny, globular creatures known as beetle mites, which crawl slowly along on their short, spiky legs. They feed on the decaying material and on the associated fungi. You may also see some more active mites, and these will probably be predatory species hunting the slower-moving beetle mites.

Beetle mites do occasionally leave the soil and climb walls, sometimes congregating in dense masses on the windows of sheds and houses, but the mite that you are most likely to see in such places is the clover mite (Plate 21). This is a brownish or dull red mite, about the same size as the beetle mites but more flattened and with much longer legs. The mites feed during the summer on grasses and clovers, but during the autumn they seek out crevices in which to lay their eggs and hibernate. Bark crevices are normally used, but if trees are not available the mites will swarm up walls and enter windows. They do no harm, but large numbers can be a nuisance. The vacuum cleaner is probably the best way to get rid of them, and a second treatment may be needed in the spring to remove those that did find a cosy nook for the winter. These mites are especially noticeable on new housing estates, where extensive lawns enable the mites to build up large populations.

Bright red, velvety mites are often seen scurrying over garden paths and walls during the summer. These velvet mites (Plate 21) are somewhat larger than the clover mites and they are predatory species, feeding on various small insects and other arthropods. They are often called red spider mites, but this name really belongs to several much smaller and much more damaging mites which live on various kinds of fruit trees. These are related to the clover mite and they get their name because they clothe the leaves on which they are feeding with a fine silk web. One of the most serious of these pests is a species called *Panonychus ulmi*, a brick red creature which is sometimes so numerous that affected trees are completely defoliated and killed. This mite has an interesting history in that it was not really a problem until the 1940s. DDT then came into use and vast quantities were sprayed onto our orchards. It killed the insect pests all right, and it killed the insects which had previously kept the spider mite in check, but it did not do much harm to the spider mite itself. Freed from its enemies, the mite was able to increase its numbers and become a real pest. Newer pesticides can keep the mite in check, but it is still a serious threat to fruit growers. In addition to the food it takes and the mechanical damage it does, the mite spreads a number of serious diseases.

The gall-causing mites are even smaller than the soil mites and they are not visible to the naked eye. Their effects are only too well known, however, to anyone who grows black currants. The familiar 'big bud' is a gall caused by these tiny creatures invading a normal bud and stimulating abnormal growth. Various sprays can be used to keep the mite in check, but the enlarged buds should be removed and burned. The end of this troublesome pest is in sight, however. The gooseberry, which is a not-too-distant relative of the black currant, is resistant to the mite and plant breeders have managed to transfer this resistance to black currants. Mite-resistant bushes will probably be available before long. Other mite-induced galls that might appear in the garden hedge include the spiky nail galls on lime leaves and the little red pustules on maple leaves.

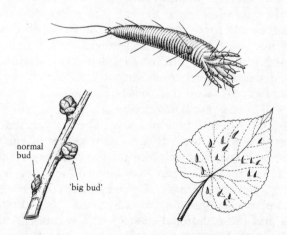

normal
bud

'big bud'

A typical gall mite (very highly magnified), together with two kinds of mite-induced galls: big-bud of blackcurrant (*left*) and nail galls on lime leaves

CHAPTER 8

Birds of the Garden

BIRDS, like insects, are very mobile creatures and they are free to come and go almost wherever they please. As a result of this mobility, most of our British birds have probably been seen in a garden somewhere. Some of these birds, such as the heron that drops in for a meal at the garden pond, are obviously nothing more than casual visitors, but many others occur sufficiently regularly for us to regard them as truly garden birds. Relatively few species actually 'prefer' gardens in the sense that they are more commonly found in gardens than elsewhere, and very few species would suffer if we all disappeared and left the birds to their own devices, but there are, nevertheless, a number of species which are very charactistic of gardens and which will breed there if conditions are suitable.

A few migratory species, such as the swallow and the house martin, may take up residence during the summer months, and occasional fieldfares (page 241) or other winter visitors may settle in the garden in the winter, but most of our truly garden birds are resident species that stay with us throughout the year. Their numbers fluctuate greatly, however, and tend to rise during the winter when territorial behaviour is generally in abeyance and the birds flock together wherever they can find food. The bird-watcher or bird-gardener (see Chapter 11) can exert a considerable influence in this respect by putting out food regularly in the winter months. Birds soon learn the whereabouts of good food and they will congregate in such places. If food is put out at a fixed time each day, the birds will even get to know this and they will actually be waiting in the garden for dinner time to arrive. The bird-gardener can also influence the types of birds that visit the garden. Crusts of bread thrown from the window will interest the house sparrows and the starlings, but other birds do not take much notice of such plain food unless they really are hungry. The way to encourage these other birds is to provide interesting mixtures of seeds and fat, together with fruit and the occasional treat of meal-worms or fishermen's maggots. Such feasts will attract not only the common garden birds, but also some of the more unusual species that live in the surrounding areas.

224

Although it is easy to attract many kinds of birds to a garden by putting out a suitable range of foods, the birds will take up permanent residence only if the garden offers them suitable cover and a certain amount of privacy. Town gardens and backyards rarely support anything other than the familiar house sparrow and perhaps a few starlings and feral pigeons, but only a few trees and shrubs are necessary to transform such ornithological wildernesses into thriving bird communities. The trees or shrubs need not all be in one garden, of course, for birds are no respecters of human territorial boundaries. A group of small gardens each with a small tree are just as acceptable to the birds as a single larger garden with several trees. Walls covered with ivy or some other creeper also help to attract the birds. Blackbirds and blue tits are among the first to join the house sparrows as the garden develops and sprouts a few trees or shrubs. Slightly more mature gardens, with hedges or shrubberies, will attract thrushes and dunnocks, together with robins, chaffinches, and greenfinches. Extensive areas of lawn may attract starlings in some numbers and also provide a stage for the amusing antics of the pied wagtail. Really mature gardens, especially if they are large or occur in groups, as on a large and mature estate, will support many more species and it is probably true to say that such habitats are richer in terms of bird species than any other area of similar size.

Although all these birds are permanent residents in the sense that they visit the garden every day to feed, they do not necessarily nest in the garden. House martins often nest under the eaves very close to bedroom windows, and we often hear of robins or blackbirds which have built their nests in constantly-used sheds and garages, but birds generally resent disturbance and they usually keep to the denser shrubs and hedges and other less frequented parts of the garden when they are nesting. If the garden does not provide the seclusion required, the birds will not nest there. It is usually fairly easy to detect the presence of a nest in the garden by following the path taken by the parent birds going home with beakfuls of food, but it still may not be easy to find the nest itself. Many of our birds build exquisitely camouflaged nests right in the centres of shrubs and hedges and it has always been a source of wonder to me how these birds can zoom into the middle of a dense thorn hedge without being speared to death. It is always tempting to look into a nest to see how many eggs there are or how the young are getting on, *but this temptation should be resisted at all costs.* Pulling branches aside to peer into a nest may well damage the foundations of the nest, and the parent birds will often desert a nest if its surroundings have been interfered with. If you have a nest in the garden, be content with the thought that the birds have considered your garden a good enough place in which to rear their young and with the knowledge that you will, in due course, be treated to the spectacle of the young birds going out for their first flying lesson.

Resident birds

The **house sparrow** (Plate 22) is surely the most abundant bird in every garden and the gardener may well be forgiven for thinking that it is the commonest of all our birds. In fact, over the country as a whole, it is heavily outnumbered by the chaffinch and the blackbird and probably by the starling and the robin as well. These other birds are equally happy in the woodlands and wild country and they are distributed all over the land. The house sparrow, on the other hand, is very much tied to human activity and its distribution is very patchy. Although abundant where it does occur, it has been estimated that more than 80 per cent of the country is devoid of house sparrows. The areas in which the birds do occur are built-up localities, farms, railway yards, docks, and waste land – anywhere, in fact, where they can find easy food. House sparrows are natives of the African grasslands, although they have now followed man to nearly every part of the world, and, as suggested by their stout beaks, they feed primarily on grain and other seeds. Grain is an important commodity in nearly all human communities and the house sparrow was not slow to cash in on this fact. Grain still forms an important part of its diet, but the bird is more than happy to supplement this with bread and other manufactured foods which man scatters around him deliberately or accidentally. The house sparrow has become so dependent upon man that it really would suffer if we all disappeared and it might even become extinct in this country. There is no likelihood of this happening at the moment, however, for recent population estimates suggest that the sparrow is constantly increasing its numbers and keeping pace with expanding urbanisation.

The house sparrow is an intensely sociable bird with no territorial behaviour except in the immediate vicinity of its nest. Living in places where food is abundant, it has no need to stake out a territory and defend it in the way that many other garden birds do. Throughout the year, the sparrows can be seen hopping around in the garden and mingling with each other with little sign of aggression. They might have an occasional tussle over a crust of bead or chase each other noisily through the bushes, but relationships are, on the whole, very friendly. The birds do not usually form very large flocks, however, and, while it is rare to see just one or two house sparrows together, it is equally rare to see groups of more than about fifty individuals.

The birds make their nests in or very close to buildings, but the nests are not evenly distributed through the built-up areas. A group of houses at one end of a street may support several nests each, while similar houses at the other end of the street may have no house sparrow nests at all. The house sparrow thus forms distinct colonies. Such colonies are always close to adequate feeding grounds and the birds never have far to go for food. This means that, although the individual birds do not have territories, each colony does have an area which it can more or less call its own. The area may be all the gardens of a street or housing estate, or it may be the whole of a small village, but the nests will always be concentrated in one part of the range. The nests themselves are very often built in roof spaces, but they are also tucked behind gutters and drain pipes or among climbers. They are rather untidy, with long wisps of straw hanging out in all directions, but they are very warm and cosy. Each consists of a mass of grass or straw, in the centre of which, completely protected from the elements, is a feather-lined chamber.

When once they have mated, the house sparrows usually remain faithful to their partners for life, and they also remain faithful to their nests. If one member of a pair dies, whether cock or hen, the other retains ownership of the nest and simply acquires a new spouse from among the young, unmated sparrows. The new spouse inherits the nest if the older partner dies, and so the nest remains in use for many years, even though its inhabitants gradually change. The nests are always being added to and they sometimes reach enormous sizes. One in the roof of my house was as large as a pillow, and probably just as comfortable, when it was finally removed during building operations.

Two or three broods, each consisting of three to five young, are raised in the nest between April and July and the squawking youngsters make quite good alarm clocks at this time of the year if they are nesting close to a bedroom window. The youngsters all stay around the family home for a while, often roosting in nearby hedges and making a good deal of noise about it. At the end of the breeding season, however, the house sparrows of agricultural areas all tend to go off to the grain fields. But they don't venture far from cover and they are continually flitting back into the hedges and trees as one or other of the birds takes fright and gives the alarm. After the harvest, the sparrows gradually drift back to their homes and, unlike most birds, they often return to their nests and use them as roosts throughout the winter. Unmated individuals roost in the nearby trees and hedges or in barns and other tall buildings.

The **blackbird** (Plate 22) needs little introduction to the gardener, for few gardens are without at least one pair. The cock has glossy black plumage and a bright yellow beak, while the hen is dark brown and has a brown beak. Her spotted breast, although not always very obvious, reveals a close relationship with the thrushes. Albino specimens occur quite frequently, and so do piebald individuals with white wings and black bodies or vice versa.

The blackbird's stout beak is well able to deal with a variety of foods, including insects and fruit. The birds like fruit of all kinds and are often responsible for stripping red currants and raspberries from the plants. Blackbirds also make short work of ripe apples and pears that fall to the ground, hollowing them out and leaving little more than the skin. When fruit is not available, the birds find much of their food by rummaging about on the ground and they make a great deal of noise as they search the dead leaves in the shrubbery or the hedge bottom. The beak is also well suited for doing battle with earthworms (see page 66).

Blackbirds start courting each other at about Christmas time, but the cocks do not really start to defend territories until the end of February. This is about the time when they burst into their sweet and rather mellow song, which is usually produced from the top of a tree or from a prominent chimney stack and which is very different from the shrill alarm call. The latter warns the whole community of approaching danger.*

The nest is usually built in a thick hedge or bush, although it may be high in a tree in an area well stocked with cats. The outer part of the nest cup is woven from stout grasses, hair, and mosses. Inside this there is a mud cup, and this is finally lined with more grass. The eggs are bluish green, heavily mottled with brown, and there are usually between three and five in a clutch. Two or three broods may be reared from March to July.

Outside the breeding season, the birds remain basically solitary and never congregate in large flocks as many other birds do. This is especially true of the females, which often start to keep territories as early as October, although they are not very successful at keeping out intruders. Several blackbirds may be seen feeding together

*Because of the difficulty of describing bird song in words, no descriptions of the songs are being given in this book. Readers are recommended to listen to the recordings of garden birds listed on page 273.

where food is plentiful, but the relationship between them is little more than mutual tolerance. The nearest they get to social behaviour is when a number of males congregate and 'show off' during the winter. Even here, they may congregate initially to feed or drink, but they amuse themselves with simple displays and dances and with mock fights. The birds may be feeding on various parts of the lawn, and one may suddenly run or hop rapidly towards another in a half-hearted attack. The threatened bird runs or hops away a few yards, and the process may then be repeated. The birds soon forget all about it, however, and start feeding again.

Apart from its very musical song, the first indication that a **song thrush** (Plate 22) is about the garden may be an intermittent tapping from the rockery or the garden path. This is the thrush at work at its 'anvil', hammering snail shells on to a stone to break them and get out the juicy flesh. Follow the sound, and you will see the thrush holding a shell in its beak and bringing it down quite forcibly on to the stone. It is usually quite easy to watch the activity, for the thrush gets very engrossed in its work. Examination of the 'anvil' after the bird has left will reveal the remains of numerous snails, for the bird usually selects one place and brings all the snails to it for treatment. Garden snails and the white-lipped and brown-lipped banded snails (see page 76) are the most frequent victims, but the bird also eats plenty of other invertebrates and, like the blackbird, it is very fond of fruit.

The song thrush or throstle is less common than the blackbird in every habitat and it is usually missing from the most built-up areas. It is even less sociable than the blackbird and you will rarely see more than one in your garden at any one time. The cock's powerful song can be heard at nearly all times of the year and it serves to maintain the territory at all times. The nest is built in the same kinds of places as that of the blackbird and it is constructed in a similar fashion, except that it does not have an inner lining of grass. The eggs, which are sky blue with a few black spots, are laid directly on the lining of mud and dung which the hen moulds to shape with her own body.

The **mistle thrush** (Plate 22) is larger than the song thrush and it has more grey on the head and wings. It also has more rounded spots on its breast. Although it will come to gardens if dried fruit is put out on the ground, it normally frequents only the larger gardens where there are mature trees. It is often seen in town parks. The mistle thrush's nest is rather like that of the blackbird, but it is normally built in the fork of a tree. The birds are very territorial in the breeding season and are quite aggressive in the vicinity of the nest, but they become quite sociable at other times and often form quite large flocks in the fields. Slugs, insects, and fruit are the mainstays of the mistle thrush's diet, but it does little harm to cultivated fruit. It tends to move out into open country in the summer and it feeds largely on wild fruits.

Our most popular and easily recognised bird is undoubtedly the **robin** (Plate 22), whose red breast and perky behaviour can be witnessed in the garden throughout the year except perhaps in July. True to its inquisitive nature, the robin always seems to be around when the gardener is busy, and one does not have to leave the spade in the garden for long before the bird comes to perch on it. He acts as if he owns the garden – and he does as far as other robins are concerned, for the robin is the most territorial of all our birds and only the coldest weather and the direst hunger will cause him to tolerate the presence of another robin other than his mate. The hens are equally aggressive in defending their territories and many of them sing just as vigorously as the cocks. Territories are usually staked out in August and September, just after the birds have moulted, and they range up to about two acres in area. The loud warning song is often enough to keep trespassers at bay, but the occupier will back up this threat when necessary by puffing out his red breast and displaying it prominently to the intruder. If this show of strength is not enough, the birds may actually fight. Robins start to pair up at about Christmas time, when the hens enter the territories of the cocks and pester them with displays and songs until they (the hens) are finally accepted. Each hen then has to learn the boundaries of her new home, which she does quite quickly because neighbouring robins are always ready to chase her back if she ventures over the line. The hen builds the nest alone in March or April. She usually selects a site fairly low down in a bush or hedge, but she is always pleased to accept a ready-made hollow or platform and she really will nest in an old kettle concealed in the hedge. The nest is made of dead leaves and moss and lined with hair and it contains five or six creamy white eggs with red speckles. Two broods are usually reared each year between March and June. The territories break down in June when the last young have flown and the birds all start to moult, and the robins are rarely seen at all in July because they hide away while they are moulting.

Robins eat a very wide range of foods, including insects and other invertebrates, seeds, and fruit, and they are regular visitors to bird tables as long as these are not too far from bushes or other cover. Although bold and fearless when it comes to defending its territory and investigating the gardener's activity, the robin does tend to be somewhat agoraphobic and it rarely ventures far out into the open.

The **dunnock** (Plate 22) is one of our commonest birds and it is found wherever there is a reasonable amount of scrub and undergrowth. It is one of those birds that have benefitted from human activity because it enjoys the hedgerows and other similar habitats that man has created. Its rather drab brown plumage is rather similar to that of the hen house sparrow, but the dunnock has much more grey on its throat and breast. The bird was known as the hedge sparrow for a long time, and this name is still commonly used, but one look at the beak will show that the bird is not a true sparrow.

Dunnocks feed on insects in the spring and summer, but their staple diet in autumn and winter consists of the seeds of plantains, chickweed, and other weeds. Much of the food is picked up in the hedge bottom or under the bushes, for, like the robin, the dunnock dislikes moving too far away from cover. It can be enticed on to the lawn to feed, but it does not very often visit a raised bird table. The dunnock is definitely a loner and it rarely mixes either with other dunnocks or with other species, although the occasional dunnock can sometimes be picked out among a group of house sparrows in the garden.

The nest is usually built fairly near the ground in thick hedges and shrubs, although the birds also make use of stacked wood. The outer part is made of twigs, but there is a central cup lined with moss or hair. Two clutches, each with four or five deep blue eggs, are normally laid each year.

The **wren** (Plate 23) is another small brown bird and the non-bird-watcher might confuse it with the dunnock at first. It is much smaller than the dunnock, however, and it is a much cleaner-looking bird because it lacks the black and grey of the dunnock. Its most obvious feature is its cocked tail. Like the dunnock, it is a bird of the hedge and the undergrowth, but it also frequents old walls and buildings if these provide it with the nooks and crannies which it enjoys. The wren is an avid hunter of insects and spiders, using its slender beak to extract them from bark crevices and to pluck them neatly from the leaves. Most of its hunting is done within a few feet of the ground and the bird can be seen darting in and out of the undergrowth rather like a mouse.

Each cock wren maintains a territory throughout the year, although several birds may congregate in a communal roost in cold weather. The cock bird builds several nests in his territory in the spring, using mosses and leaves to make neat little domed structures tucked into well-concealed places. His shrill song, remarkably loud for such a small bird, and his vigorous display attract a female who then inspects the nests and selects one for her nursery. She lines it with feathers and, after mating, lays about six white eggs with brown spots. The cock bird temporarily loses interest at this point and goes off to see how many more wives he can acquire and instal in his nests. He usually manages to persuade at least one more to take up residence, but he has nothing to do with incubating the eggs and he does not return to his nests until the youngsters are well feathered and nearly ready to fly. He then helps with the feeding and, when the youngsters are able to leave the nest, he often leads them on tours of the surrounding vegetation.

The finches are basically seed-eating birds and several species can be seen pecking away in the garden during the year. Large numbers can sometimes be attracted in the winter by putting out mixed bird seed. The birds are all equipped with rather stout and powerful beaks which are well suited to cracking hard seed coats and crushing the kernels. The enormous beak of the hawfinch, one of the rarer garden visitors, is even able to crack open cherry stones. Many finches are brightly coloured and they often have conspicuous white or yellow bars on their wings. They can usually be recognised in the air by their undulating flight. It is almost as if they are following imaginary telegraph wires, rising at intervals as if to the poles and then sagging noticeably between these high points.

Several species of finch are now actively increasing their ranges in this country, spreading out from their natural habitats into both agricultural and built-up areas. Like the house sparrow, the finches benefit from human activity and human waste. They are often abundant on rubbish dumps and waste ground where weeds flourish and provide them with plenty of seeds.

The **chaffinch** (Plate 22) is primarily a bird of the woodlands, but it is a common garden visitor and it often breeds in the more mature gardens which are well endowed with shrubs and hedges. Like many other birds, it is more common in the garden in the winter, when it has to extend its activities in order to find enough food. Adult chaffinches feed almost entirely on the ground and you do not see them swaying precariously on thistles and other plants in the way that some other finches do. The seeds of grasses, including cultivated cereals, are particularly important in the chaffinch's diet, and so are the seeds of docks and crucifers. The seeds of composites, such as dandelions and thistles, are not eaten very much. Insects and other invertebrates play a more important part in the diet of chaffinches than in the diets of other finches, and young chaffinches are fed entirely on invertebrates – mainly aphids and caterpillars.

Unlike our other resident finches, the chaffinch is a territorial bird and each cock lays claim to an acre or more of land early in the spring. His song attracts a mate and she soon gets to work to make a very neat nest with moss, lichen, grass, feathers, and spider silk. She then lays three to five greyish green eggs, attractively mottled with red or brown. A second clutch may be laid later in the spring. The territorial behaviour of the chaffinch is almost certainly associated with the need to find insects for the young. The insects are spread fairly evenly over the vegetation and each pair of birds must have a territory large enough to ensure a continuous supply of food while the young are being reared. Many of our resident chaffinches retain their territories and remain more or less solitary throughout the year, although they wander into unclaimed areas to feed and often meet up with two or three other chaffinches there. The large flocks of chaffinches that are seen in woods and on farmlands during the winter are made up of immigrant birds which come to us from Scandinavia.

The **goldfinch** and the **greenfinch**, both illustrated on Plate 22, are natives of the forest edge and they thus enjoy gardens with shrubberies and hedges. Their nesting habits differ, however, for the goldfinch nests high in the trees and the greenfinch prefers the shrubs. Tall and overgrown hedgerows are favourite nesting sites for the greenfinch, especially if they consist of evergreen shrubs. Both species take a little insect food in the spring, but they feed mainly on the seeds of herbaceous plants. The goldfinch is particularly fond of thistles, teasels, and burdock, and it also attacks dandelions in the spring: the birds can be seen tearing the flowers to pieces long before the seeds have ripened. Alder seeds are eagerly sought out in the winter, but many of our goldfinches fly off to the continent in the autumn. The greenfinch enjoys the same kinds of food as the goldfinch, together with the seeds of grasses and various cruciferous weeds such as charlock. It is also very fond of peanuts and it is a frequent visitor to the bird table. It is a rather aggressive bird in such situations and often pushes smaller birds aside.

Young goldfinches and greenfinches are fed almost entirely on seeds and the birds do not therefore have the strongly territorial behaviour of the chaffinch. Suitable seeds are not evenly distributed in space or time and the birds have to move from one feeding ground to another as the different plants start seeding. The seeds are abundant when they do occur, however, and numbers of birds can feed together. The goldfinches and greenfinches usually nest in small colonies of four or five pairs and, although each pair defends a small area around the nest, the birds are quite sociable when they are feeding. The colonies are usually situated within easy reach of good feeding grounds, but the birds may have to travel considerable distances during the year in order to visit the various sources of seeds.

Outside the breeding season, the goldfinches and greenfinches become even more sociable and form quite large flocks. These can often be seen scouring the fields and waste grounds for seeds during the winter. Whereas the cock chaffinch obtains a mate by advertising in song, these other finches behave more like humans. They get friendly with each other in the non-breeding flocks and a bond gradually develops between a cock and a hen. Although remaining part of the flock throughout the winter, the pair go off more and more on their own, often visiting the garden to feed. The bond between them is strengthened by the cock's display and by the furious games of chase which they play through the shrubs, and the birds eventually settle down to nest.

The **bullfinch** (Plate 22) is primarily a woodland bird and, until recent years, it was rarely seen far from well-wooded country. Today, however, it has spread deeply into built-up areas and it frequently breeds in large gardens and town parks. It is one of the softer-billed finches and it feeds on softer seeds than most of the other finches. Buds play a very important role in its diet in the spring and, despite the male's brilliant colours, it is not a bird that one should encourage into the garden or the orchard. Bullfinches cause severe damage to currants and gooseberries during the winter, often removing so many buds that the crop is lost. Similar damage occurs to pears and plums, but cherries and apples are less affected. Some insect pests are eaten, but this does not make up for the crop damage. Bullfinches nest in thick hedgerows and undergrowth and their breeding biology is similar to that of the previous two species, with pairs forming in the winter flocks and then gradually going off on their own.

The **siskin** is another woodland finch that has been spreading in recent years and coming more and more into gardens. Resident in Scotland and Ireland, it has usually been a winter visitor to most other parts of the British Isles, but it is now showing more and more reluctance to return northwards in the spring. This is associated with the spread of coniferous plantations which provide it with both nesting sites and food. During the winter, the siskin is especially fond of alder and birch seeds, but it seems to be turning its attention to weed seeds in many areas and this is why it is becoming more common in gardens. The male is not unlike the cock greenfinch, but is easily distinguished by its black crown and chin.

Gardens with large lawns are often visited by the well-named **pied wagtail**, a sprightly black and white bird whose long tail bobs conspicuously up and down as it walks daintily over the grass in search of insects. The bird is especially common around farms and near lakes or ponds, obtaining a good living from the swarms of flies and midges found in such places. The shallow waters around the edges of lakes also provide the bird with the bulk of its food in the winter, when flying insects are scarce. Pied wagtails nest in holes in walls and trees and they rear two or three broods between April and July.

Well-timbered gardens often attract the lively little **tree creeper** (Plate 23), a woodland bird which is easily recognised by its curved beak and its very white belly and also by its behaviour. Keeping its stiff tail feathers pressed firmly against the bark, its scuttles nimbly up the tree trunks, usually taking a spiral course and stopping frequently to probe for insects. Having reached the top of a tree, the bird never turns round and comes down again: it always flies down to the base of a neighbouring tree and starts to climb again. The tree creeper usually nests in large cracks in trees, behind loose bark, or in dense growths of ivy.

In the southern half of Britain, the tree creeper is often joined by the **nuthatch** (Plate 23), another nimble climber, perhaps even more agile than the tree creeper because it can run both up and down the trunks. It extracts insects from the bark, but it feeds primarily on seeds. Large seeds and nuts are picked up and wedged in bark crevices, and the bird then hammers them vigorously with its beak until they break open. Nuthatches are also very happy to display their agility on bags of peanuts hung from trees or bird tables.

The other famous birds of the tree trunks are, of course, the WOODPECKERS. All three of our British species will visit gardens and bird tables. The **green woodpecker,** easily recognised by its green back and red head, is very fond of ants and it often feeds on the lawn. The **lesser spotted woodpecker** (Plate 23) is widely distributed in the southern half of Great Britain, where it inhabits woods and orchards. It tends to keep to the more slender branches of the trees, often hanging completely upside-down while pecking at insects. The **greater spotted woodpecker** is somewhat larger and more boldly marked with white and it prefers the larger trunks and branches.

Close behind the robin in terms of popularity comes the little **blue tit** (Plate 23). Like its relatives, it is basically a woodland bird, but it is a very adaptable species and it has not been slow to take full advantage of the conditions created by man. It is one of the most characteristic garden birds, occurring wherever there are a few trees and a bit of cover in which it can nest. The blue tit feeds mainly on small seeds and insects and it does a great service by ridding our gardens of large numbers of aphids, but it has also acquired other tastes through its association with man. It is particularly fond of fat and cheese and it gives the bird-watcher a great deal of pleasure with its antics at the bird table. Its habit of piercing our milk bottle tops and stealing the cream is less amusing, although we cannot help admiring the way in which this little bird and various others have learned to make use of this new source of food. The blue tit nests in holes and crevices in walls and trees and readily makes use of nest boxes. It will also build among dense ivy and other creepers on a house. The nest is made of leaves and moss and lined with hair and feathers. There is usually only one brood, but each pair may rear as many as seven youngsters.

The **great tit** (Plate 23) is slightly less common than the blue tit in most gardens, but it is nevertheless an abundant species. It has a black cap instead of the blue cap of the blue tit, and it also has a prominent dark stripe down the belly. Its habits are very much the same as those of the blue tit. The **coal tit** (Plate 23) is primarily a bird of coniferous forests and plantations, but it often takes up residence in gardens containing or within easy reach of conifers. Even a single conifer may be enough to attract a breeding pair to the garden. The birds can be recognised by the white patch on the back of the head. Marsh and willow tits sometimes pass through the garden as they forage along the hedgerows, and so do long-tailed tits, but these birds are far less closely connected with man than the blue tit and the great tit.

The **starling** (Plate 23) is often painted as a rather dull and uninteresting bird, but it is neither of these. Although its plumage is basically black, it is beautifully speckled with paler colours and it has an iridescent sheen which varies from green to blue and purple according to the angle of the light. The starling is also a very sociable being with a distinct liking for the company of other starlings. Like the house sparrow, it has taken great advantage of man's activity, and it has been increasing its numbers considerably in the last hundred years, both in Britain and elsewhere. At the end of the 19th Century, the species was introduced to North America and it spread so rapidly that it is now thought to be the most abundant wild bird in the world. There are probably more than 1,000 million starlings alive at the moment.

Starlings are most often seen in the garden during the winter, when our resident population is swollen by an influx from the continent and the starling is probably the most numerous bird in Britain. The birds strut around the garden in small groups and, although they are not really aggressive towards other birds, the smaller species do tend to get out of their way and let the starlings get the pick of the food. Like blackbirds, the starlings are very fond of pecking at apples, but they will eat almost anything and they make valiant attempts to hover while pecking at fat and other materials hung from the trees. Early in the winter afternoon, the starlings begin to gather in the trees. Groups from neighbouring gardens, or perhaps a whole village, come together in a convenient tree or group of trees and they become very noisy. When the assembly is complete, the whole flock flies off to a communal roost where they may be joined by numerous other flocks from an area covering as much as twelve hundred square miles. Such roosts may contain more than 50,000 staarlings and they are situated in small woods or spinneys, in reed-beds, or on buildings. Roosting on buildings is actually a rather recent habit, but it is an annoying one because the droppings from thousands of birds soon damage the buildings and the noise from the birds is also rather unpleasant.

During the breeding season, the starlings are rather less sociable and they spread their nests fairly thinly over the countryside, avoiding only extensive woodlands and most of the moorland areas. The nests are built in holes in trees and buildings and they are made rather untidily from straw and other grasses. About six pale blue eggs are laid on the inner lining of feathers. Although the nests are fairly well spaced out as a rule, the birds still enjoy each other's company and can be seen feeding socially in the fields, often together with lapwings and other birds.

PIGEONS of several kinds may visit the garden from time to time. Gardens in heavily built-up areas are most likely to attract the **town** or **feral pigeon** – the one that is so common in Trafalgar Square and other city centres. This is a descendant of the rock dove that inhabits some of our wilder and rockier coasts, and it still has the rather conspicuous white rump of its wild ancestor. Its colouring varies a good deal, however, as a result of a domestic interlude in its history. Rock doves were domesticated long ago and many breeds of pigeon have been produced from them, and the hordes of town pigeons that are with us today are the descendants of various domesticated birds that escaped and established themselves in the wild. Town buildings are not too different from rocky cliffs and the pigeons had no difficulty in making themselves at home in urban

Feral or town pigeon (left), wood pigeon (centre), and collared dove

areas. The tons of food thrown down for them in our parks and squares obviously help to keep their numbers up, but the town pigeons are very able scavengers and they would still make a good living from backyards and street markets even if we did stop feeding them.

The **wood pigeon** (Plate 22) is a real pest in country areas and it seems to be increasing as a result of the spread of coniferous plantations which provide it with good nesting sites. Large flocks feed in the fields, taking huge quantities of grain and green crops such as peas and beans. During the winter, many of the birds visit exposed gardens and reduce the broccoli and other greens to bare stalks. The wood pigeon is much larger than the town pigeon and it has a clear white bar on the top of each wing in flight. The town pigeon has black bars on its wings.

A third pigeon has made its appearance in our gardens in recent years. This is the **collared dove,** readily identified by its greyish brown plumage, black wing tips, and neat black collar. It is a native of India, but during the last seventy years it has completed a remarkable invasion of Europe, from Turkey to the Outer Hebrides. It was first recorded in Britain in 1955, but it is now breeding nearly all over the country and still multiplying fast. Like the house sparrow, the collared dove thrives on human company and it is most frequently seen in parks and gardens and around farms. It feeds largely on grain and could become a serious agricultural pest, but it also eats buds and berries. Like the wood pigeon, it usually nests in coniferous trees, making a rough platform of sticks and grasses. It may rear several broods in a year and this has undoubtedly contributed to its rapid increase.

Summer visitors

Many insect-eating birds come to us for the summer months, during which time they rear their young and get fat on our abundant insect population. They cannot survive our cold and almost insect-less winters, however, and, by the end of September, most of them have flown off to sunnier climates where they can be sure of food for the next few months. But they will be back in the spring and we will all be waiting for our first swallow or cuckoo to tell us that winter is behind us and summer is on the way. Most of our summer visitors spend the rest of the year in central or southern Africa and biologists still puzzle over how they find their way, especially as the youngsters often travel by themselves some time after their parents have left. They are obviously not shown the way by the older birds. The return journey may involve a certain amount of memory, but a round trip of more than 10,000 miles is still an amazing achievement. Some martins and swallows even return to the very nests which they used the previous year.

Relatively few of our summer visitors actually settle down in the garden, although several can be seen flying through or over it. The whitethroat and the lesser whitethroat, dunnock-like birds with a distinct white patch on the throat, sometimes nest in thick hedges and they may be accompanied by the blackcap, but our other warblers generally prefer the greater seclusion of woods and thickets. The garden warbler – what a misnomer that is – is one of the species that are least likely to nest in the garden.

The **spotted flycatcher** (Plate 23) is the only summer visitor which is really characteristic of our gardens. It is rather a drab bird as far as its colouring goes, but it makes itself quite conspicuous by its behaviour. Each individual adopts a perch on a tree or some other support and waits for insects to come along. The perch is usually chosen to be near a hedgerow or some other shelter where insects congregate and the bird then darts out periodically to pluck a victim from the air and return to its perch. Large numbers of insects are caught in this way with very little effort. Spotted flycatchers nest in holes in walls or trees or else among creepers if there is a suitable support for the nest. Mosses and grasses are used to make the nest, which is lined with hair and feathers before the mottled greenish grey eggs are laid.

The **house martin** (Plate 23) likes to make its mud nests under the eaves of our houses and, not liking to go too far from home, it tends to stay over if not actually in our gardens. Like the swallow and the swift, it catches its food in its wide open beak while

239

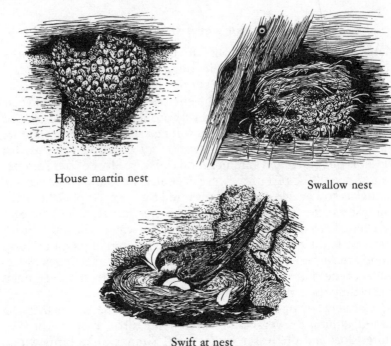

House martin nest

Swallow nest

Swift at nest

swooping to and fro through the air, but the three species do not compete with each other because they normally feed at different levels. The swallow collects most of its food within about 100 feet of the ground, but the house martin frequently feeds at 500 feet and the swift flies even higher.

House martins collect mud for their nests from the edges of ponds and puddles and often have difficulty in getting enough material in a dry spring. It is worth soaking a small part of your garden each day so that the birds can make use of the soil. As long as the old nests are not in too bad a state, the birds will use them again, but house sparrows often take over the nests before the migrants get back and the returning martins then have to make new nests.

Swallows certainly swoop across our gardens in the summer, and they may even perch on our telephone wires and television aerials, but they are less associated with gardens than the house martin because they do not usually nest on ordinary houses. They prefer to make their cup-shaped mud nests on top of beams and rafters and they most often nest in farm buildings. Such situations provide them with plenty of insects as well, but the birds will also nest in church towers and porches, in railway stations, and in garden sheds

PLATE 21: **Spiders**: 1 Zebra spider 211; **2** Wolf spider, *Pardosa amentata* 212; **3** Wolf spider, *Pisaura mirabilis* 212; **4** *Dysdera crocata* 213; **5** *Drassodes lapidosus* 213; **6** Crab spider, *Xysticus* sp. 211; **7** Spitting spider 213. **Harvestmen**, pp. 218–20: **8** *Oligolophus spinosus*; **9** *Leiobunum rotundum*; **10** *Phalangium opilio*; **11** *Nemastoma bimaculatum*. **Mites**, p. 222: **12** Clover mite; **13** Velvet mite.

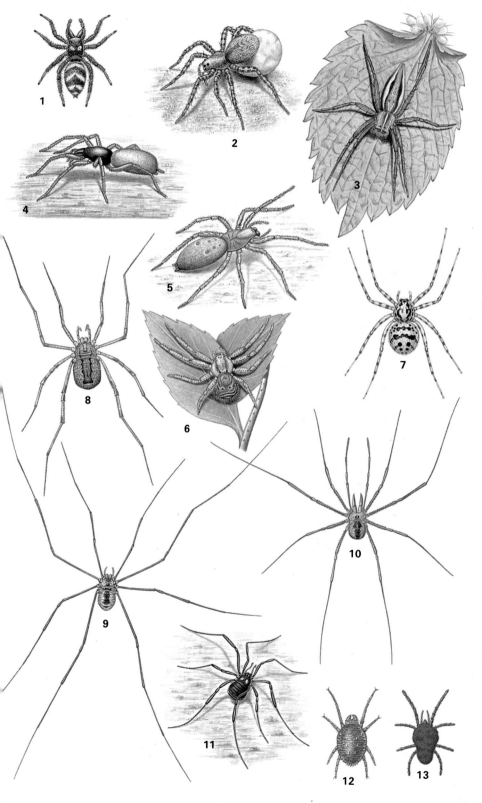

and out-buildings. The swallow (Plate 23) can be distinguished from the house martin by its longer and more deeply-forked tail, and also by its rich blue sheen and its red throat, although these last two features are less easy to see when the bird is in flight. Swallows are particularly fond of swooping low over water and collecting the midges there, and they often drop down to scoop up a mouthful of water as well.

Swifts are much larger than the last two species and almost completely black. They never land on the ground and they spend nearly their whole lives on the wing. They may even take short sleeps while gliding down from great heights. Spending their time so far up in the air, the swifts cannot be regarded as garden birds except that they sometimes nest under the eaves of houses. Their nests are made of feathers and other materials picked up in mid-air and cemented together with saliva.

Swift in flight

Winter visitors

Our winter bird visitors come to us from more northerly regions where winters are too severe for them to find food. The most famous are the ducks and waders that come south in search of open water, but there are also several smaller birds among our winter visitors. The fieldfare (Plate 22) is one of the most abundant of these and it is the only one which regularly visits the garden. It feeds mainly on invertebrates and fruit and it finds most of its food in the fields and hedgerows, but in really cold weather it comes into our gardens and it makes short work of any apples that are lying about under the trees. Its close relative, the redwing, is often associated with it, especially out in the hedgerows. The redwing looks rather like a song thrush, but it has a red patch on the side of its body and a prominent white stripe running through the eye.

◀ PLATE 22: **Birds**. 1 Goldfinch 233; 2 Greenfinch 233; 3 Chaffinch 232; 4 Bullfinch 234; 5 Robin 230; 6 Songthrush 229; 7 Mistle thrush 229; 8 Fieldfare 241; 9 Blackbird 228; 10 House Sparrow 226; 11 Dunnock 231; 12 Wood pigeon 238.

CHAPTER 9

Garden Mammals

THE mammals are the furry animals – the animals that have hair and feed their youngsters with milk. They are among the least conspicuous animals in the garden and many gardeners will never see them at all. This is partly because they are mainly nocturnal, but also because of their remarkably acute senses of smell and hearing: a mouse will usually be off to his home in the hedge or in the bottom of the wall before you have even started down the path. But the mammals do not disappear without trace and it is possible to learn quite a lot about the mammals in your garden merely by looking at the footprints, droppings, and nibbled plants that they leave behind them. Gardens with walls or hedges and old sheds are most likely to provide homes for mammals, but even if the animals don't actually live on the premises they will visit the garden regularly, and it is surprising what can turn up to examine your handiwork from time to time.

Gardens in wooded regions are often visited by deer, which are

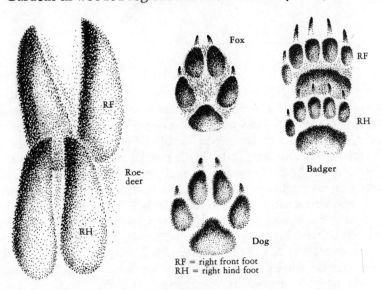

RF = right front foot
RH = right hind foot

Footprints of roedeer, fox, badger, and domestic dog

242

among the largest of our wild animals and which often make short work of cabbages and lettuces. Flower gardens also suffer from the activities of these mammals. Foxes very often visit gardens, even in urban areas, and if they can't unlock the chicken run they might well rummage around in the dustbin for tasty scraps. They usually leave behind them a very strong musky smell. Badgers normally shun human habitations, but they have been known to visit new housing estates built on their former hunting grounds. I know one such estate with a badger's footprint clearly preserved in a concrete path. These large mammals must, however, be regarded as unusual garden visitors. The resident mammals are all much smaller. With the exception of the occasional weasel scampering through the flower beds, all of our garden mammals are likely to be either insectivores or rodents.

The insectivores include the hedgehog, the shrews, and the mole. Although the name actually means 'insect-eaters', the insectivores are not particularly fussy about their food and they certainly don't look to see if it has six legs before they eat it. Worms, slugs, snails and woodlice are all eaten eagerly along with beetles, caterpillars, and assorted insect grubs. These creatures are all readily dealt with by the insectivores' numerous small, but very sharp teeth.

The hedgehog

The hedgehog or hedgepig (Plate 24) is the largest of our insectivores, with a weight of about a kilogram. Its spiny coat, composed of greatly modified hairs, makes it instantly recognisable. The animal is common over most of the British Isles, although less frequent in the Highlands than elsewhere, and the large numbers mown down on our suburban roads show that high populations must exist even in built-up areas. Gardens, especially the untidier ones and those with thick hedges, provide ideal homes for these fascinating creatures.

The hedgehog is certainly the easiest mammal to find and watch

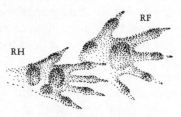

Footprints of hedgehog

in your garden, although it is rarely seen in the daytime. Its five-toed footprints are easily identified but, because of the animal's preference for leafy hedge bottoms and similar places, the footprints are not frequently preserved. The long, tapering droppings are also easy to identify, but these are usually lost among the leaves as well. The most obvious sign of the hedgehog's presence is the continuous grunting and the rustling of leaves as the animal rummages about for food on summer evenings: he is not called the hedgehog or hedgepig for nothing. The animals even squeal like pigs on occasion. They can be found at any time of night but, in the two gardens in which I have done most of my hedgehog watching, they have always been most active in the two hours before midnight.

Garden hedgehogs find plenty to interest them in the compost heap, in the shrubbery, and in the well-established herbaceous border. They feed there on worms, slugs, beetles, and other juicy tit-bits. They will roam freely over the lawn on moist nights to pick up the adventurous earthworms, and from the noise of the munching one would think that the animals were eating potato-crisps rather than soft earthworms. Hedgehogs will also eat frogs and lizards and they are not above taking eggs and small birds from their nests. They have often been seen visiting cows lying in the fields and they have been accused of sucking milk from them, but such an accusation is without foundation. I cannot imagine any cow taking kindly to a sharp-toothed, bristly hedgehog trying to steal her milk. The hedgehogs probably lap up milk that has oozed from the udder, but it may be that the inevitable beetles crawling on the cow dung are the real attraction. Plant material is not ignored by the hedgehogs and fallen fruit is especially attractive to them in the autumn. They will readily come to saucers of milk or kitchen scraps put out in the garden in the evening, and regular provision of such food may well encourage the animals to take up residence in the garden if they are not already living there. They will make themselves snug retreats among the leaves in the hedge bottom or some other out of the way corner, or even in the compost heap. Although gamekeepers still persecute the hedgehogs for their egg-stealing activities, there is no reason for the gardener to feel hostile towards the animals: the worst they are likely to do is to wake him up in the middle of the night.

When you first come across a hedgehog in the garden it will probably erect its spines and sit quite still. Further disturbance may cause it to roll into a ball, but if you don't make sudden noises, the animal will soon decide that you are harmless and it will continue its business. Its eyesight is not at all good and it takes little notice if you shine a torch on it. It has a very keen nose and it finds its food mainly by smell, but it is apparently unperturbed by human odours and it is possible to watch a hedgehog from as little as a yard away as long as you are quiet. But do keep your eye on the creature, for it has an annoying habit of slipping quietly away as soon as the watcher's gaze is averted.

The hedgehog has a surprising turn of speed when necessary, and a remarkable ability to scale walls and fences. Getting down is no problem either: the animal merely rolls into a ball and drops to the ground. The spines are flexible at the base and they cushion the animal's fall without digging into him when he hits the ground. The spines also protect the animal from its enemies, especially when it is rolled into a ball, but they do not give it complete protection. Badgers know how to get the hedgehog to uncurl, and then they attack the spine-less underside. Some foxes also know how to deal with hedgehogs. Useful as they are, the spines do have one drawback in that the hedgehog cannot groom itself as most mammals do. Consequently, it is always heavily infested with fleas.

The hedgehog's courtship is quite a public affair, fascinating to watch and also to listen to. The two animals leap about and run around each other like playful puppies and this activity is usually accompanied by much grunting and loud squealing. I have watched courting hedgehogs in my garden on several occasions and remember one particularly noisy performance which woke several of my neighbours. Windows were opened one by one and the hedgehogs had quite an audience on that warm August night. Mating may occur any time from May to August and the young are born about 32 days later in a cosy nest of leaves, grass, and moss. There are generally four or five babies in a litter, and some hedgehogs may produce two broods in a year. The babies are blind and helpless when they are born and their spines are very soft. They are fed and looked after entirely by the mother and they grow very quickly. They start to leave the nest when they are about a month old, often walking along in single file behind their mother.

A mild winter might see hedgehogs out and about in December and January, but the animals usually go into hibernation at the end of October and remain asleep until March or April. Before going to sleep, the animals feed themselves up very well and you might even see them out in the daytime ensuring that they get enough food. They then retire to their nests deep in the leaf litter or underground cavities and settle down to sleep. But this is no ordinary sleep: as in all other hibernating mammals, the temperature of the body falls and the breathing rate and heartbeat slow down almost to a stop. In this condition, the animal uses very little food to keep its body ticking over and the reserves accumulated in the body are sufficient to see it through the winter. Any hibernating hedgehogs which are discovered during winter gardening activities should be left alone whenever possible. They will wake up if they are disturbed and, although they will find another retreat and go back to sleep again, the process of waking from such a deep sleep uses up such large amounts of energy that the animals may not then have enough food reserves to see them through the rest of the winter.

The shrews

The shrews are small mouse-like insectivores that can be distinguished from mice by their very slender, pointed snouts and by their small ears which are more or less concealed in the fur. The shrews have five toes on each foot, but the mice have only four toes on the front feet and so the tracks of the animals, usually seen only in muddy ground, are also quite different. There are, in addition, marked differences in the teeth of the two groups of animals and this feature will allow the gardener to identify the occasional skulls that he unearths. The only two shrews likely to be found in gardens on the mainland of Britain have red tips to their teeth, but white-toothed species occur in the Channel Islands and the Scilly Isles.

Skull of shrew

Footprints of shrew (*top*) compared with those of mouse

The two shrews likely to be found in the garden are the **common shrew** or ranny (Plate 24) and the somewhat smaller, but otherwise very similar **pygmy shrew**. The common shrew rarely has a body length of less than 65 mm, while the pygmy shrew's body is rarely more than 60 mm long. These figures hold true throughout the active lives of these animals, for they do not grow a great deal when once they leave the nest. Both species are widely distributed in Great Britain, but only the pygmy shrew is found in Ireland. Both

246

animals prefer rough ground with dense grass or other vegetation. The common shrew makes winding tunnels through this vegetation at about ground level, but it also tunnels through the soil on occasion. The pygmy shrew probably makes few tunnels for itself and generally makes use of the runways of its larger cousin and of the voles (see page 252). Apart from this, however, the two species are very much alike in their behaviour.

Garden-dwelling shrews are most likely to make their homes in the hedge bottom or in the longer grass of the orchard. Their nests are loose balls of woven grasses placed at or just below ground level. They are very energetic little creatures and they are active by day as well as by night. Short periods of rest alternate with longer periods of activity which are almost entirely taken up with feeding. Some shrews eat more than their own weight of food each day. Their food consists mainly of earthworms, beetles, spiders, and woodlice, but they also nibble at fruit and seeds and they take fresh carrion, including the dead bodies of their own kind. Foraging shrews can be heard uttering soft squeaks from the herbage at any time of day. They usually keep under cover during daylight hours, but they venture out into the open more at night.

Most female shrews produce two litters each year, with about six youngsters in each litter. The litters are usually produced between April and September and the young animals breed in the following year. The adults all die in the autumn after breeding, when they are between a year and 18 months old. The dead animals can often be seen lying around the garden in the morning. Winter shrew populations consist entirely of young animals less than a year old. They do not hibernate.

Domestic cats often kill shrews, but the shrews are rather distasteful and many cats refuse to eat them after killing them. Owls and other birds of prey take shrews in some numbers, as shown by the numerous shrew skulls found in the pellets coughed up by these birds.

The mole

The velvety black mole (Plate 24) spends nearly all of its life tunnelling in the soil and it is only occasionally seen on the surface. Its immensely broad and powerful front legs are used to dig the tunnels and the excavated soil is piled up on the surface at intervals to make the well-known mole hills. When the animal is tunnelling within a few inches of the surface, however, it merely heaves the soil up with its back and produces a continuous ridge on the ground.

In association with its subterranean habits, the mole has very weak eyes and no ear flaps. Its fur lies easily in any direction, and so the mole has no trouble in moving backwards along its tunnels. Some wide tunnels are used as main roads by many moles, but each individual normally keeps to its own tunnel system. It is a tight fit in its own tunnels and this helps to keep its fur sleek and clean.

During the winter, moles feed almost entirely on earthworms, but they vary their diet in the summer with slugs and insect larvae such as leatherjackets (see page 163). Much of the food is caught in the tunnel system, but the moles do sometimes come out in search of food especially on damp nights. Like the shrews, they cannot go without food for very long and they hunt at all times of the day and night, with only short periods of rest between each burst of activity. Food is usually stored in times of plenty and this ensures that the moles do not all starve if food is scarce. The 'larders' are usually filled with earthworms, whose front ends are bitten off to prevent them from getting away. These food stores may not be used, however, in which case the worms gradually regenerate their front ends and disperse.

Moles are most abundant in woodlands and permanent grass-lands where the soil is undisturbed. They do not usually take up residence in gardens unless there are large expanses of lawns or orchards. Gardeners living near woodlands or meadows can expect occasional visits from moles, however, especially during the summer when the young moles are dispersing and looking for new homes. This is the time when they may push up a ridge right across the lawn, or even gouge out a shallow, open furrow. Mole-catching was once a worthwhile occupation, but with mole skins now out of favour there is little reward for the mole-catcher and the animals are increasing in many places. Mole hills are unsightly on the lawn, but the animals do no harm otherwise. They destroy large numbers of useful worms, but they make up for this by making their own drainage and aeration systems.

THE RODENTS

The rodents are the most numerous of all the mammals, in terms of species as well as in terms of individuals. Most of them are rather small mammals, among the best known being the rats and mice. The group also includes the voles, the squirrels, and the porcupines, together with the beaver and the guinea pig. They are all basically vegetarians and they feed by gnawing at the plants with their sharp front teeth and then grinding the fragments with their cheek teeth.

The upper and lower jaws of a rodent each carry two rather long and often strongly curved front teeth called incisors. The upper pair are always well in front of the lower pair. The front of each incisor tooth is covered with a very hard orange enamel, but the rear surface is much softer and it thus wears away much more rapidly. The teeth thus maintain sharp, chisel-like edges at the front and they are always fit for gnawing. They grow continuously from the base thus making good the wear at the front and maintaining a more or less constant length. The incisor teeth are separated from the cheek teeth by a long gap. The animal can draw its lips into this gap and cut the front teeth off from the rest of the mouth. In this way, it can gnaw through wood and other inedible materials without getting the pieces in its mouth. The cheek teeth have fairly broad grinding surfaces, but they are very variable and their detailed structure is often used to separate closely related species.

Mice and rats

Three kinds of **mice** are likely to turn up in the garden and all might be confused with the shrews (page 246) at first. The surest way to distinguish them on sight is to look at the ears: the shrews have very small ears almost completely hidden in the fur, but the mice all have quite prominent ears. In addition, the shrews tend to have much shinier coats. The mice are even more likely to be confused with the voles (see page 252), but here again a look at the ears will separate them: the voles have small ears and much shorter and blunter snouts than the mice. They also have shorter tails.

The commonest rodent in the garden is probably the **wood mouse** (Plate 24), also called the long-tailed field mouse. This neat little creature lives in almost every kind of habitat and it is especially fond of hedgerows. It will also take up residence in the house or the garden shed, especially if there are no house mice about. The animal normally makes runways in and below the leaf litter in the garden hedge and it makes nests of shredded grass just under the ground. It is almost entirely nocturnal and doesn't even venture out in bright moonlight. Wood mice will eat insects and other small animals, especially in the spring, but they feed mainly on plant material. They will climb high into the bushes to reach juicy fruit and buds, and they will move out into the open to eat seeds and seedlings on the ground. Wood mice are usually to blame when your peas and beans don't show up. I have found that it is useless to sow peas in my own garden before about the middle of April because the wood mice take the lot as soon as they are in the ground. Sowing after that time is usually successful, presumably because the mice can find plenty of other food by then without having to dig for it. Wood mice also play havoc with apples and potatoes stored in out-buildings. Seeds and other easily transported foods are often taken back to the nest and stored, especially in the winter, and the wood mouse's abode can usually be identified by these little caches of food. The animals breed throughout the summer and often in the winter as well if they find cosy quarters.

The **yellow-necked field mouse** is rather similar to the wood mouse, but it is usually a little larger and its under parts are a purer or cleaner white than those of the wood mouse. The most obvious difference between the two species, however, is to be found on the throat: the wood mouse usually has a yellowish patch in the mid-line, but the yellow-necked field mouse normally has a distinct

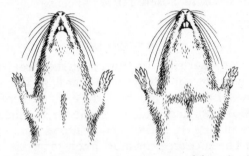

Underside of head and shoulders of wood mouse (*left*) and yellow-necked mouse, showing the difference in the extent of the yellow 'collar'

collar of yellow reaching from one shoulder to the other. The habits of the two species are very much the same, but the yellow-necked field mouse does not usually dig its own tunnels and it seems to enter houses more readily than the wood mouse. The yellow-necked field mouse is widely distributed in Wales and southern England, but it is absent from Ireland and Scotland.

The **house mouse** (Plate 24) is much more closely linked to human activity and habitation than the other mice, but it is not particularly common in the garden. It is much more likely to be found in the house or shed or in the farmyard, although it does spread out along the hedgerows and fields in the grain-growing areas. Its distribution is closely linked to that of the grain and other dried foods which make up the bulk of its diet. Large colonies often grow up in ricks and grain stores and the mice do immense damage. In and around the house, the mice make their nests in roof and wall cavities and under floors. They build the nests with shredded-up material of all kinds and they rear up to ten litters per year. The average litter consists of five or six babies and the animals can thus build up large populations very quickly. House mice living out in the country often have white underparts, but those in and around the garden are generally a rather dirty grey all over and easily distinguished from the wood mice and field mice.

The **brown rat** (Plate 24) is, like the house mouse, an alien species. It originated in eastern Asia and, after the opening up of trade routes across Asia, it followed man to all parts of the world. It arrived in Britain early in the 18th Century and very soon ousted the black rat which had been here for about four centuries. Black rats are now found only in the vicinity of ports, where their numbers are constantly being reinforced by newcomers brought in on ships. The brown rat is rarely found far from human activity and its main haunts are farms, rubbish tips, and sewers. It was originally a grain-feeder, but it is now a real scavenger and it can survive on a very wide range of both plant and animal material. It finds little to interest it in the average garden, however, and is most likely to be seen in those gardens with chicken runs or with neglected out-buildings. The former often provide the rat with food, and the out-buildings provide shelter. Brown rats are active burrowers and their nests are generally underground. Several tunnels may lead into the nest from various directions. A female may produce up to five litters in a year, each with perhaps ten babies, and so the animals can soon overrun an area if they are not controlled. Domestic cats and dogs probably account for large numbers of young rats, but an adult brown rat is a formidable adversary even for a man.

The brown rat occurs in several colour forms, including the white ones commonly bred as pets and as laboratory animals. Black individuals are quite common, but they can be distinguished from the black rat by their ears and by their much larger size and shaggier coats.

Head of black rat (*left*) and brown rat showing differences in ears

The voles

Voles are mouse-like animals, but they have shorter snouts and shorter ears than the mice and their cheek teeth are built to a very different pattern. The cheek teeth of the mice are not really very much different from our own, but those of the voles are columnar and they form a prominent wall along each side of the jaw. Their large grinding surfaces are well suited to pulverising the tough roots

Hazel nut opened by wood mouse (*left*) compared with one opened by vole. The mouse always leaves a ring of tooth marks around the opening, but the vole does not

Jaws and teeth of mouse (*top*) compared with vole

and grass stems on which most of the voles feed. The voles are generally less nocturnal than the mice and their squeaky voices, louder than those of the shrews, are commonly heard in the middle of the day.

The usual vole found in the garden is the **bank vole** (Plate 24), which, like the wood mouse, generally makes its home in the hedge bottom. It may also take up residence at the bottom of a wall as long as there is plenty of permanent vegetation there to give it cover. The nest is often below ground, but it may also be in a concealed hole in the wall or in a hollow stump in the hedge. The bank vole is in several ways intermediate between the rest of the voles and the mice, and it shows this in its feeding habits. It is much more catholic in its tastes than the other voles and eats far more insects than they do. It also likes succulent fruits and it often damages bulbs in the garden. Gardens with well-grassed orchards or with nice unkempt grassy verges outside may also harbour the **short-tailed vole**. This is a much darker species than the bank vole and it has a shorter tail. It makes most of its runways on the surface of the ground, right down among the bases of the grasses on which it feeds. It often makes its nest under planks of wood and other similar objects lying in the grass.

The bank voles run or scuttle along quite fast on their short legs, but do not leap in the way that mice do and this may be why our cat catches more voles than mice. Voles brought to the door during the year far outnumber the shrews and mice, although the living populations of these animals are probably much the same. There is another explanation, however, and that is that the cat actually prefers the voles. She certainly eats them more readily than the mice and shrews, but she always leaves the stomach for some reason or other. Even if there is no other trace of the vole I usually know if one has come to a sad end because the little black, kidney-shaped stomach will be lying around on the lawn. Such behaviour is apparently quite common in cats, and they often leave the stomachs of other prey as well.

The grey squirrel

Gardens with large deciduous trees growing in or around them will probably be visited by the grey squirrel (Plate 24), a sprightly little animal which is one of our few diurnal mammals. It is not a native species, however, and arrived here from North America towards the end of the 19th Century. It rapidly spread to most parts of England and Wales but it is less common in Scotland and Ireland.

Popular belief has it that the grey squirrel killed off most of our native red squirrels, but there is no evidence to support this idea. The fact is that the red squirrels were already declining rapidly when the grey squirrel arrived and, although they recovered in some places, they have never been able to drive out the grey squirrels when once the latter have established themselves. The red squirrel is now holding its own only in the larger stretches of coniferous forests and plantations. These areas are unsuitable for the grey squirrel because it needs a high proportion of hardwood seeds in its diet. Other foods eaten by the grey squirrel include

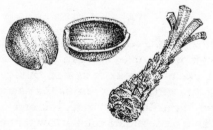

Hazel nut and pine cone attacked by squirrel

253

fruit, bark, bulbs, fungi, insects and other small animals, and the occasional bird's egg. This food is collected anywhere between the ground and the tree tops and the squirrels find quite a few acceptable items in the garden. They are much more fearless than the red squirrels and they are often quite bold in the garden. They would become quite tame if they were encouraged, but feeding or otherwise encouraging the grey squirrel is a crime because it is such a serious pest in our woodlands and plantations. It does a great amount of damage by stripping bark from the trees and deforming them.

The squirrel's nest is called a drey and it is a rather untidy affair made of twigs, leaves, and grass. It has a domed roof and it is normally wedged into the fork of a tree. A female squirrel raises one or two litters a year in her drey, each litter averaging three youngsters. The dreys are also used for sleeping in throughout the year but many squirrels make themselves leafy platforms further out on the branches for summer nights. Although the squirrels may go to sleep for several days on end in the coldest weather, they do not really hibernate. They are active on sunny days in the winter and they feed partly on nuts and other foods which they have buried here and there in the autumn.

Gardeners living in the Chilterns, in an area bounded roughly by Luton, Oxford, and Slough, may meet another introduced rodent which is very much like the grey squirrel on first sight. This is the **glis-glis** or **edible dormouse** (Plate 24), which was introduced to Tring Park in 1902 and which has since been spreading slowly out into the countryside. The glis-glis is smaller than the grey squirrel, however, and it is a nocturnal creature. Its natural home is in the deciduous woodlands, but it often comes to gardens and orchards in the autumn and fares very well on the apples. It sometimes takes up residence in a loft or roof space where its nocturnal activity can be a source of great annoyance until it finally beds down for its winter hibernation.

The weasel

The weasel (Plate 24) is the commonest of our predatory mammals or carnivores and it often comes into gardens in search of the voles and mice which make up the bulk of its diet. But it is not often seen because, although it is often about during the daytime, it generally keeps out of sight in the dense herbage. It is an extremely slender animal and well able to negotiate the narrow tunnels and passages used by its prey. So lithe and elastic is its body, that the weasel is said to be able to get through a wedding ring, although it is hard to get the animal to perform such a trick. The animal is most likely to be seen standing up on its hind legs and sniffing the air with a rather haughty expression on its face. It may increase its height by standing on a log or a large stone.

Its dependence on the small rodents for food means that the weasel is found mainly in the wilder gardens with dense hedges and plenty of long grass. Mother and youngsters hunt together for a few weeks in the summer, but adult weasels usually hunt alone. They are very courageous hunters and they readily attack rats and rabbits three times their own size, but they stick mainly to the mice and voles. It has been estimated that a male weasel will catch and eat up to 500 of these small rodents in a year. Female weasels, at about 60 grams, weigh only about half as much as the males and they kill fewer prey, but the weasel population as a whole obviously plays an important part in controlling the rodents.

Bats

As soon as the weather warms up and the evenings draw out in April, the bats wake up from their long winter sleep and start flitting over our gardens each evening. They are the only mammals that can really fly, although some foreign squirrels and other mammals can glide from tree to tree on outstretched flaps of skin. The bat's wings are formed from a large membrane of skin which embraces the front and hind legs and the tail and which is supported mainly by the greatly enlarged fingers of the front limbs. The rest of the bat's body is quite like that of a mouse – hence the alternative name of flitter-mouse – with large ears and exceedingly sharp teeth.

The European bats are all insect-eaters and they catch most of their food on the wing, although they will occasionally swoop down to snatch a large moth or beetle from the ground or from the vegetation. Many bats have a definite beat, which might be the air space in front of a row of houses, and they patrol it ceaselessly, turning abruptly at the ends and flying back. They deviate from the path to snap up passing insects, but they otherwise seem to keep to a fairly well defined route. Such a beat or territory is sometimes defended against other bats, which are chased off as soon as they get too close. Small insects are eaten in flight, but a bat will often alight on a favourite perch to deal with larger victims. It does not have to alight, however, for many species can fold the tail membrane forward to form a 'feeding bowl' in which the prey can be held while the bat's teeth get to work on it. Many bats have two distinct periods of activity – one in the evening during the hour or two just after dusk, and the other just before sunrise. For the rest of the time, the bat sleeps hanging upside down on the wall or ceiling of some secluded hide-out. Their natural homes were hollow trees and caves or crevices in rocks, but tall buildings are equally acceptable

Typical bat in flight (*right*) and at rest

now. The animals often abound in church towers and sometimes get into the lofts of houses. Their droppings may accumulate and become a nuisance, but the bats probably help to destroy the furniture beetle or woodworm. There is certainly very rarely any need to get rid of these interesting lodgers if they are living in your roof.

Any of about 14 species of bats may be seen hawking up and down over the garden, but only the expert can identify them without catching them – and catching them is extremely difficult. One's best chance is to watch the bat for some time and map out its beat. Standing at one end of the beat, it is sometimes possible to net the animal in the split second during which it is almost stationary while making its abrupt turn. The difficulty in catching bats stems from their amazing agility. Bats are not quite as blind as we are sometimes led to believe and some of them have perfectly good eyes, but they find their way about mainly by sending out very high-pitched sounds and listening to the echoes bouncing back from near-by objects. This system is known as echo-location and it is so highly developed that the bats can distinguish between telegraph wires and flying insects and take appropriate action. Their co-ordination is such that, even when flying at speed, they can turn to avoid a wire but turn to catch an insect. Proof of their extraordi-

nary powers came from an experiment in which fine wires were stretched haphazardly across a room and the room was completely blacked out. Bats were released into the room, but their echo-location systems ensured that they did not hit any of the wires as they flew about.

Bat-haters live in fear that a bat will get tangled up in their hair, but such an occurrence is extremely unlikely to say the least: the bats are far too clever at avoiding trouble.

Although we have about 14 species of bats in Britain, several of them are very local species and only six are common over large areas of the country. But even these common species will not be seen in areas devoid of suitable trees or buildings, or perhaps caves, in which they can roost. The commonest species, which is also our smallest bat, is the **pipistrelle**. It weighs no more than about 7 grams and it is only 40 or 50 mm in length, although its wings span up to 230 mm. This little bat is less fussy about its sleeping quarters than the other species and will often make use of the shelter provided by ivy or some other creeper on a wall. Large numbers very often cluster tightly together when roosting and they wedge themselves into very small cracks in walls and tree trunks.

Bats are usually born in June or July and each female normally gives birth to just one baby. The baby is blind and more or less naked at first and it may be carried around by its mother for a few days. It is then left in the roost while its mother goes out for food. The males play no part in rearing the young and often form separate roosts at this time of year. Although there may be hundreds of bats in a roost, especially in the hibernation quarters, there is never any co-operation between the animals and each goes off to hunt for itself.

Most of our bats go into hibernation in October, although some may remain active until well into November in a mild autumn. Some bats undertake regular migrations between summer and winter quarters. The bats that flit around your house may roost in neighbouring trees or buildings in the summer, but they may leave the neighbourhood altogether in the autumn and hibernate in a cave many miles away. Such a cave may contain thousands of bats, drawn from all over the surrounding countryside. Although the winter sleep is a very deep one (see page 245), the bats wake up from time to time and flutter around. They may even venture outside in mild weather and we then get the unusual sight of bats flying in daylight.

PLATE 24: **Mammals.** 1 Hedgehog 243; 2 Mole 247; 3 Common shrew 246; 4 Wood mouse 249; 5 House mouse 250; 6 Bank vole 252; 7 Brown rat 251; 8 Glis-glis or edible dormouse 254; 9 Weasel 254; 10 Grey squirrel 253.

CHAPTER 10

The Wildlife Gardener

IT will be obvious from earlier parts of this book that plants and
animals will live in a garden only if the conditions are right for them.
This is why gardens in different areas and on different soils support
rather different populations of weeds and animal guests. Many of
these guests are certainly not to be encouraged, and some should be
positively attacked, but others do much to enhance the appearance
of a garden and it is well worth while encouraging them to come and
making them feel at home when they do arrive. Indeed, perhaps we
ought to do this, for the thousands of acres of gardens could form an
immense nature reserve for animals which are being driven out
from many of their natural homes by increasing urbanisation and
industrialisation. Butterflies and birds are the main things which
spring to mind when we think about animals to brighten up the
garden, but there are several other attractive and interesting pos-
sibilities, and some of them are useful as well. They include some of
the bees and wasps and various water-loving creatures, such as frogs
and dragonflies, which may arrive if a pond can be built in the
garden.

Butterfly gardening

One often hears it said that there are far fewer butterflies around
today than there were fifty years ago. It is doubtful if this is true of
the really wild habitats, such as forest, heath, and downland, but it is
certainly true of the garden. Today's gardens tend to be too neat
and tidy for the butterflies, and there has also been a marked change
in the types of flowers being grown. Gone from most gardens are
the old-fashioned herbaceous borders with their sweet rocket and
lavender and their michaelmas daisies, and in their places we find
monstrous dahlias and chrysanthemums and assorted bedding
plants which have often been bred for size and colour at the
expense of scent and nectar. There is thus far less to attract the
butterflies in today's average garden, and the improved hygiene,
involving the regular use of herbicides, has reduced the crop of
weeds on which many of the caterpillars depend for their food. But

the situation can be remedied to a large extent by planting the right kind of plants in the garden.

Among the many useful, low-growing spring flowers are polyanthus, arabis, yellow alyssum, and aubretia. The latter is particularly attractive to the awakening brimstones and tortoiseshells, and it is also regularly visited by the striking bee-fly (Plate 17) and many early bees and hover-flies. Honesty and sweet rocket are two of the real 'cottage garden' flowers, full of butterfly-beckoning nectar and especially useful because both serve as food plants for the larvae of the orange-tip. Later-flowering species which pull in the butterflies include the little annual alyssum, so commonly used as an edging plant, ageratum, dwarf phlox, lavender, and thyme. The trumpet-shaped petunias and tobacco flowers are especially attractive to hovering moths: the day-flying hummingbird hawkmoth (Plate 12) is very common at petunias around the south coast, while tobacco flowers, with their pale colours and heavy scents, gather in a large assortment of night-flying moths. Perhaps the most famous of the butterfly-attracting plants, however, are the buddleia, aptly named the butterfly bush in many gardening catalogues, and the spectacular ice plant, which is a large pink stonecrop. Coming into flower about the middle of July, the buddleia is soon alive with whites and small tortoiseshells, and these are joined in August by the brimstones, peacocks, and red admirals, as well as by numerous moths, all of which add greatly to the enjoyment of a garden. As the buddleia sprays begin to fade in the second half of August, the ice plant is beginning to open its plate-sized heads of nectar-rich flowers, and the butterflies waste no time in moving over to this rich new source of food. Dozens of small tortoiseshells may gather on a single head, oblivious of each other and of almost everything else as they drink

Small tortoiseshell butterflies feasting on the rich nectar of the ice plant before going into hibernation for the winter

deeply from the hundreds of small, star-like flowers. They may fly up if suddenly disturbed, but, as on the buddleia, they become 'drunk' with the nectar and they are very easily approached. The probing action of the tongue can then be seen very clearly, and the butterflies can be photographed with great ease. As well as small tortoiseshells, the ice plant attracts peacocks, red admirals, painted ladies, and commas, but the most common insects are often silver Y moths (Plate 13), which are generally seen in the form of greyish blurs as they hover over the flowers in full daylight.

The best butterfly attractant for later autumn is undoubtedly the michaelmas daisy, whose abundant flowers provide a rich supper for the tortoiseshells and peacocks before they bed down for their winter sleep. Red admirals and small coppers also visit the flowers quite regularly. Some of the late-flowering dahlias are quite useful butterfly attractants as well, but they must be the single varieties, not the 'double' monsters in which the nectaries have given way to additional petals and which are not therefore particularly alluring to insects.

It is also worth encouraging some of the wild flowers around the garden for the sake of the butterflies which they attract. Brambles in the hedge, for example, will bring in ringlets and gatekeepers, and a few thistles in a sunny corner will attract all the usual garden species. A coat of ivy on an old wall will, if it is allowed to flower, draw large numbers of moths and other insects in the late autumn, and it may also provide a shelter for holly blues and hibernating brimstones.

So far we have talked only of attracting the adults, but this is, of course, only half of the story. You can plant as many butterfly-attracting plants as you like, but you will be sure of success only if there are suitable breeding sites for the insects. Small tortoiseshells, red admirals, peacocks, and commas all feed on stinging nettles in the caterpillar stage and, although it might go against the grain to spare these invasive plants, there is much to be said for leaving a bed of them in an out-of-the-way corner of the garden or on the verge outside. One can help the butterflies even more by cutting down half of the nettle patch early in June, for this will give the tortoiseshells a fresh crop of tender leaves on which to lay their eggs in July. Deadnettles and dandelions are also worth keeping here and there, especially along the bottoms of walls and hedges, for they provide food for the hairy caterpillars of the garden tiger moth and the ermines. Thistles provide food for painted lady larvae, and so do burdock plants, but one needs a very large garden to accommodate the latter and one must be prepared to pull up the innumerable seedlings which inevitably invade the tidier parts of the garden. Docks will have to be tolerated if you want to have a constant population of small copper butterflies in your garden, and you will have to go easy on the mowing if you want to see the wall brown and the other 'browns', for the larvae of all these feed on coarse grasses. The orchard-owner can ensure the survival of these butterflies by leaving the grass long everywhere except immediately around the trees.

Attracting bees and wasps

The idea of attracting bees and wasps to the garden may fill some gardeners with horror, for these insects are still regarded by many people as nothing more than 'nasty stinging insects'. Admittedly, they will sting if molested, but, left to themselves, they are both useful and interesting creatures to have in the garden. The value of the honey bee to the hive owner is well known, but the honey bees also benefit the gardener as well by pollinating his fruit trees and other crops, and in this they are aided by the bumble bees and a host of non-social bees, such as *Anthophora* (page 168) and *Andrena* (page 167). Between them, the various kinds of bees collect pollen and nectar from nearly every kind of flower, and one need not grow special flowers just to attract bees, but the greatest numbers will come to the nectar-rich flowers already mentioned as butterfly attractants. One can obviously increase the numbers of bees in the garden by keeping 'tame' honey bees in a hive, but the wild species can also be encouraged by providing them with nest sites. The bumble bees nest in or on the ground in rough, grassy places and appreciate undisturbed hedgebanks in the sun. They do not dig their own burrows, but take over old mouse holes and similar cavities. Up-turned flower pots, buried almost completely in the ground, may interest the queen bees in the spring, but the insects are rather fussy and will not usually take up residence unless some debris from an old mouse nest has been placed in the cavity.

Many of the solitary bees nest in small tunnels in the ground, in dead wood, or in masonry. They sometimes make their own tunnels, but they are more than happy to take advantage of ready-made cavities and they readily move in if we provide such sites in the garden. There is a well-known example of a red osmia bee (page 168) which made its nest in a keyhole, but this is one of the few instances in which a bee has really inconvenienced its landlord: the majority are very good tenants. They can often be encouraged to make use of the tubular cavities in ventilation bricks scattered around the garden or built up into a small wall, and they will also nest in short lengths of cane or hogweed stems plugged at one end and glued to the undersides of window sills. Some of the smaller bees will even nest in drinking straws, but, whatever kind of home we provide for them, they are more likely to take up residence if the tubes are grouped into bundles than if they are scattered singly. If they do take a liking to the artificial sites, we can sit back and watch them bringing in mud or leaves to make their cells, and later on we can watch them bringing loads of pollen, and have the satisfaction of knowing that our plants are being pollinated as well.

The wasps that can be attracted to garden nest sites are not the familiar social species (page 176) which gather to feast on fallen apples in the autumn, but the smaller, solitary species such as the mason wasps (page 175) and digger wasps (page 174). Like the solitary bees, these insects nest in holes and they can be encouraged to use the same kinds of artificial sites as the bees. An old tree stump, or a few decaying logs left in the garden will also provide nesting sites for these insects, as well as potential breeding sites for interesting flies and beetles. I knew of one decaying old stump which, when finally knocked over, yielded more than a bucketful of stag beetle larvae and pupae.

Bird gardening

There can be few households which do not put at least a few scraps out for the birds, even if the scraps are merely thrown out on to the ground. This elementary form of bird gardening is certainly of benefit to the house sparrows and some of the other common birds, but there is no doubt that a little more thought and effort makes the whole business far more interesting for birds and gardeners alike.

Table scraps may be good tum-fillers for many small birds, but you need something more than scraps if you want to attract the more unusual birds to your garden and to ensure that they visit you regularly. Taking the garden itself first, we can obviously make it more attractive to the birds by growing the types of plants which they enjoy for food and in which they can find the necessary shelter for their nests. Berry-bearing shrubs are among the most obvious things to grow, for a very wide variety of birds feed on brightly coloured fruits, and the fruit-laden bushes can also be very attractive plants in their own right. Among the most useful bird-attracting shrubs are the various forms of barberry, some of which make good hedges as well as single shrubs, and the numerous varieties of cotoneaster – the neat wall climbers as well as the more vigorous three-dimensional bushes. These plants are also very attractive to bees and wasps when they are in the flowering stage. Ivy, again very attractive to insects when it is flowering in late autumn, provides both food and shelter for birds when it is allowed to clothe old walls and tree trunks. The yew and holly both provide welcome berries, but there are drawbacks with these plants: both are rather slow growing and both are dioecious – meaning that there are separate male and female plants. As only the female plant bears fruit (the male plant contributes the pollen), you must get the sex right if you want to avoid disappointment. Other good shrubs and hedging plants include the hawthorn – possibly the best of the lot because of its rapid growth and abundant fruit – the spindle, and the blackthorn. The latter does not tempt the birds with its sour fruits, but its dense, spiky branches provide secure nesting sites for many small birds. The elder is also very good for the birds, because of its succulent berries, but it is a bit of a weed in the hedge because it tends to smother the other species. If you can find room for the odd specimen at the bottom of the garden, however, and can plant one before it plants itself, it will repay you with a wealth of berries and bird life. And what about a red currant bush just for the birds. This early fruiting species is a real favourite with the blackbirds.

If space allows, one or two larger trees will give additional pleasure. Rowans provide abundant orange fruits in the autumn, while the attractive birches yield many small seeds in their catkins. A discarded Christmas tree or some other quick-growing conifer makes a useful contribution to the bird habitats because it gives cover for roosting birds in the winter – and, of course, it will provide seeds when it matures. Poplars provide elevated concert platforms for thrushes and also support a number of interesting caterpillars – and how easy these trees are to grow from cuttings. I used a slender poplar twig to support a piece of wire netting in the garden and now, eight years later, the twig has become a trunk more than seven inches in diameter. The top was lopped when it reached about 25 feet in height and the tree was reduced to about ten feet, but the new shoots have climbed back almost to the original height within two years. Ash and willow are also useful in the garden, and the ordinary fruit trees, such as apple and pear, are also welcomed by the birds. As well as providing fruit and roosting or possibly nesting sites, the trees all provide trunks of rough bark in which the birds can probe for insect food.

Moving on to smaller plants, there are many herbaceous species which the gardener can plant for the benefit of the birds as well as for his own pleasure. The sunflower, for example, provides a wealth of oil-rich seeds for finches and other birds, while evening primroses, poppies, and most of the daisy-like flowers are also useful suppliers. Grass itself is not a bird food, although the seeds are taken by many species, but an area of lawn is a very good feeding place for some of the bolder birds. Blackbirds, thrushes, wagtails, and even woodpeckers will come down to the grass to see what they can find lurking in or under the sward. Many of our weeds also yield food for the birds, and the gardener with a small patch of thistles or plantains may well be rewarded with the sight of a couple of goldfinches swaying precariously to and fro on the stems as they peck away at the seeds. Other finches also appreciate these weeds, and they thoroughly enjoy docks and teasels as well, but the gardener must not get too carried away in this direction if he wants to grow food for himself as well.

Although the birds can obtain a great deal of food by foraging in a well-stocked garden, most bird gardeners like to provide additional food in a prominent place where the birds can actually be seen at their meals. The kitchen scraps already referred to can be put out as they are, but a more interesting method of serving them is to incorporate them into a pudding with various kinds of seeds and perhaps some cheese and porridge oats (uncooked). Mix the ingredients together in a bowl – half a coconut shell is ideal – and then pour enough melted dripping or lard over them to bind them into a mass. When set, the pudding can be turned out on to the bird table or, if it has been made in a coconut shell, it can be strung up complete. A wide variety of birds will find this dish very acceptable. Chopped bacon rind is eagerly taken, and so is pastry, either cooked or uncooked, and if you are wondering what to do with the bone from the weekend joint, string that up too. Make sure that it is out of the way of marauding cats, and the birds will delight you with their antics as they try to remove the last scraps of fat and meat from it. Even the starlings will make a valiant attempt to hover in front of it while they peck.

While many of the finches and other seed-eaters will enjoy some of the foods listed above, they will be particularly appreciative if you provide them with a variety of seeds and dried fruits. Commercially produced wild bird seed is very worth while buying because it contains a very wide variety of seeds and it thus caters for the majority of our birds' tastes, but you can also make up your own fruit and seed mixtures if you have the time. This involves collecting the seeds of plantains, thistles, knapweeds, teasels, and other wild plants and storing them until the winter. They will keep very well as long as they are dried properly and stored in a dry, airy place. Hazel nuts, acorns, and beechmast can also be added to the mixture, and so can chopped-up conkers and sweet chestnuts and, if you have the patience, the seeds shaken from pine cones and other conifers. Even juicy fruits such as elderberries can be dried and stored, together with rowan berries. Hips and haws can be dried, but they keep quite well if spread out on trays in a cool shed.

Pea-nuts are excellent value, especially if they are hung up in special feeders or unshelled in strings so that the blue-tits and other birds have to work to get them, but be sure that you do not give salted nuts, for too much salt can easily kill small birds. Desiccated coconut is also very bad for them because it swells up in their tiny stomachs and makes life very uncomfortable for them to say the least. Fresh coconut is excellent, however, although, like peanuts, it should not be given to the birds during the breeding season because it is rather indigestible for the youngsters. Fruit of all kinds is a good standby, and the birds don't mind if it is past its best: a few 'tired' apples or bananas can very often be begged from the local shop, or at least bought for a song.

A wire basket full of peanuts attracts a wide variety of birds and is a source of amusement for birds and birdwatcher alike

Insect-eating birds will often peck at the nuts and bacon rind, and the tits positively thrive on such foods, but if you want to attract the robin there is no better way than by offering it some mealworms – the larvae of a rather common black beetle. The mealworms can be bought at pet shops, and when once you have a supply it is not difficult to keep them going by breeding them in a bin of bran and bread. As well as attracting the robin, the mealworms will bring in blackbirds and possibly wrens and woodpeckers as well as other insect-eating species.

Many people merely throw their bird food out on to the ground but, although this is obviously better than not feeding the birds at all, it is not the best way to encourage them. Blackbirds and dunnocks prefer to feed on the ground, but most of the other garden-frequenting birds prefer to take their meals on a higher plane and

A simple bird table, with a roof to keep off the worst of the rain. A few drain holes in the tray prevent the food from getting waterlogged

the traditional bird table is the most common way of feeding them. The table should be at least 2 feet square, to allow for a bit of shoving and pushing, and it should have a rim around most of it to prevent the food from being blown away. A roof is not necessary, although it does help to keep the rain off the food. The table can hang from a tree, or it can stand on a post, but the essential thing is to see that it is cat-proof – too far out on a slender branch for pussy to crawl along to it, and too high for the cat to jump up to it. About six feet from the ground is a good height – although a short gardener might prefer one slightly lower so that he or she can see to put the food on – and the supporting post, if any, must be too smooth for the cat to climb. Be sure to put the food out *regularly,* because once you start the birds will become dependent on you and will turn up regularly for dinner. And don't forget that birds cannot live by bread alone – they need water just as we do, and they will appreciate a regular supply of clean water.

The Royal Society for the Protection of Birds produces a range of high quality bird tables and other feeding devices, and a free catalogue is obtainable from the RSPB at The Lodge, Sandy, Bedfordshire. Further information on bird tables and feeding wild birds in the garden can be obtained from Tony Soper's excellent guide – *The New Bird Table Book.*

Having attracted wild birds to the garden by putting out food, the keen bird watcher will want to try to get them to settle permanently by providing them with suitable nesting sites. This usually means putting up nesting boxes, although a good thick hedge is just as good for blackbirds and thrushes. A dead tree trunk in the garden may also provide a home for a family of tits or nuthatches, or even some woodpeckers. Holes in old walls are also readily taken over by the birds, and you can help with conservation by leaving a few gaps in the mortar and even by making a few extra ones.

Artificial nest boxes can be made in many ways to suit the various kinds of birds. Some species prefer a completely enclosed box with just a small entrance hole, while others require little more than a ledge, with or without a roof over it. The boxes are very easy to make, and you don't need to be a good carpenter– small gaps where you didn't cut the wood quite straight provide the essential ventilation and drainage for the box. Designs for the various kinds of nest box can be obtained from a booklet called *Nestboxes,* which is published by the British Trust for Ornithology (see page 273). Siting the boxes is very important: they must be out of the way of cats, and, unless you want fried eggs, they must be out of the full

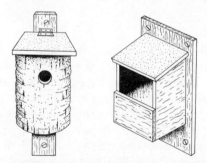

Two kinds of nestbox. The tit-box on the left will attract blue tits and other small birds, and if the entrance is no more than 30 mm in diameter it will keep out the ubiquitous house sparrow. The open-fronted box on the right is suitable for robins, redstarts, flycatchers, and several other species

sun, for it can get very hot in a small box as soon as the sun beats on to it. Fix the boxes up in autumn or early winter if possible, so that the birds get used to seeing them before the breeding season gets under way, and try to arrange for some kind of landing platform or staging post a few feet away from the entrance. Many further ideas on nest sites and boxes can be obtained from Tony Soper's book mentioned above.

A pond in your garden

Judging by the numbers of 'instant ponds' that can be seen for sale in the ever-increasing number of garden centres dotted all over the country, garden ponds are becoming very popular, and deservedly so, for they can be delightful centres of attraction and they are also valuable refuges for some of our aquatic wildlife. The common frog, for example, is no longer common in many areas as a result of the filling in of country ponds and the widespread use of pesticides

The common toad (*left*) and the common frog (*right*) will both breed in a simple garden pond, although the toad generally prefers slightly deeper water in which to lay its long strings of eggs

which seep into the remaining ponds and kill off many of their inhabitants. A network of garden ponds will do much to ensure the survival of this fascinating and useful creature and to ensure that future generations of little boys will be able to indulge in the wonderful pastime of catching wriggly tadpoles or pollywogs and keeping them (temporarily, I hope) in a jam jar.

The mere existence of the garden pond, with or without its exotic goldfish and water lilies, will attract a variety of wildlife and make the garden a much more interesting place. Many birds, for example, will come to drink and to bathe, while the wagtails and swallows will gratefully accept the swarms of small flies that flit to and fro over the water surface. Dragonflies will also hawk backwards and forwards to scoop up these little insects and, if the pond is large enough, they may breed there themselves. Water beetles will be seen hanging from the surface film as they replenish their air supplies, while the slender bugs known as pond skaters glide backwards and forwards over the surface in their search for food. Frogs, toads, and newts may all make their appearance in the spring and deposit their spawn in the water.

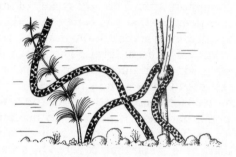

Toadspawn

There are various ways of going about the business of making a garden pond, but the site should not be overhung by trees if possible. Enough leaves will get in to the water during the autumn even in the open, and shading by overhanging trees will obviously retard plant growth in the pond and increase the risk of stagnation. Try to make the largest pond you can, but don't worry if you have only a small space available. I have had a flourishing pond in my own garden for several years and it measures only about three feet by two feet – made from an old inspection chamber in the abandoned sewage system. Several generations of newts have been reared in

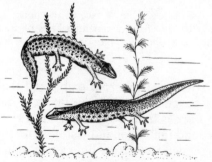

Smooth newts (male *above*, female *below*) will also breed in the garden pond. Unlike the frogs and toads, they lay their eggs singly, wrapping each one up in a folded leaf

269

The phantom larva is the young stage of a mosquito-like midge called *Chaoborus*. The phantom is abundant in ponds and water butts

this little pond, and frogs have also laid spawn in it. Nevertheless, a larger pond can support a much greater variety of life. It should be at least 15 inches deep, so that you can be sure that at least some unfrozen water will remain at the bottom in a hard winter, and there should be at least two different levels. The sides should be rather rough and sloping, for this reduces the risk of a cave-in and it also provides easy egress for newts and small froglets.

There is, unfortunately, no substitute for the hard work of digging out the pond, but there is no need to make the pond with concrete these days. The hole can simply be lined with sand or peat to cover any sharp stones and then covered by a waterproof liner.

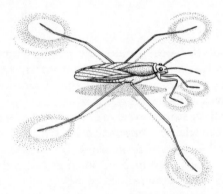

The pond skater skims over the surface of the pond, supported on the surface film with the aid of water-repellent hairs on its feet. The insect, which is a true bug (see page 119) feeds on other insects which fall on to the water

The latter can be of butyl rubber, a flexible and elastic material sold specially for the purpose, or it can be made of heavy gauge black polythene. The liner is held down with stones or paving slabs or pieces of turf around the edges and water is run slowly into it. The weight of the water will stretch the liner and mould it to the shape of the pond, and as soon as it is full of water you can start to install the plants and animals. An even quicker way of installing a pond, is to use one of the fibreglass ponds which can be bought in a variety of

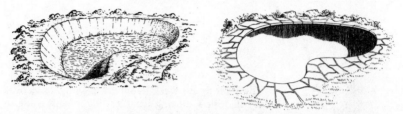

Constructing the pond. Using concrete or a polythene liner, the pond can be almost any shape you like. Ensure that the sides are sloping and, if using a liner, free from sharp-edged stones. The edge can be finished off 'formally' with paving stones or, perhaps better for wildlife, it can be turfed right to the water's edge

shapes. As long as you dig the hole to more or less the correct shape, you can lower the pond in and fill it straight away, and there is no risk of punctures. Concrete ponds involve a lot more work, but have the advantage that they can be made to any shape you like. Coated with one of the new pond-sealing paints, they should be completely water-tight and long-lasting. A large pond should have one or two rounded boulders placed in it in order to provide landing sites for both birds and aquatic creatures which like to come out and sunbathe at times.

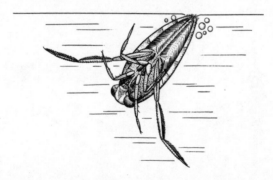

The backswimmer will probably be one of the first insects to colonise the new pond, for it flies well and often seeks a new home. It swims on its back and periodically comes up for air

You will have to introduce plants of various kinds into your new pond, and among the most suitable of the completely submerged species are Canadian pondweed, water milfoil, and hornwort. These will live quite happily floating freely in the water, although water milfoil might benefit from being planted in a flower pot of

271

The alder fly is a weak-flying insect whose larva lives
in still or slow-moving water. It will probably colonise
the new pond as soon as sufficient mud has accumulated on the bottom

soil. Arrowhead and purple loosestrife are attractive plants for the
shallow parts of the pond and are best planted in wire baskets
resting on the ledges at the margins. A variety of insects, molluscs,
crustaceans and many other creatures will find their own way to
your pond, or be brought in the mud on the feet of visiting birds.
You can then sit back and enjoy your pond, but if you add fish,
whether they be exotic goldfish or native sticklebacks, look out for
the heron. He, too, will enjoy your pond, and you may find it
necessary to put a roof of wire netting over it to preserve your fish.
Happy gardening.

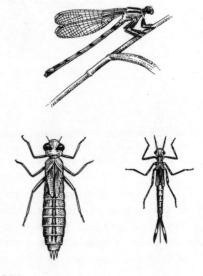

Dragonflies and the more slender
damselflies (*above right*) will appear at
the larger ponds and probably breed
there, especially if there are reeds or
other tall plants at the margin. Their
nymphs (*right*) are voracious predators in the water

Books to Read

Weeds and Other Plant Guests

Fitter, R. S. R., Fitter, A. & Blamey, M. 1974 *The Wild Flowers of Britain and Northern Europe*, Collins
Hatfield, A. H. 1969 *How to Enjoy your Weeds*, Frederick Muller
Hubbard, C. E. 1954 *Grasses*, Penguin
Mabey, R. 1972 *Food for Free*, Collins
Salisbury, Sir Edward 1961 *Weeds and Aliens*, Collins

Insects and other Invertebrates

Beirne, B. P. 1954 *British Pyralid & Plume Moths*, Warne
Bristowe, W. S. 1958 *The World of Spiders*, Collins
Butler, C. G. 1954 *The World of the Honey Bee*, Collins
Chinery, M. 1973 *A Field Guide to the Insects of Britain and Northern Europe*, Collins
Colyer, C. N. & Hammond, C. O. 1951 *Flies of the British Isles*, Warne
Eason, E. H. 1964 *Centipedes of the British Isles*, Warne
Ellis, A. E. 1926 *British Snails*, Oxford (includes slugs)
Free, J. B. & Butler, C. G. 1959 *Bumblebees*, Collins
Higgins, L. G. & Riley, N. D. 1970 *A Field Guide to the Butterflies of Britain and Europe*, Collins
Janus, H. 1965 *The Young Specialist Looks at Molluscs*, Burke
Linssen, E. F. 1959 *Beetles of the British Isles* (Vols I & II), Warne
Nichols, D., Cooke, J. & Whiteley, D. 1971 *The Oxford Book of Invertebrates*, Oxford
Savory, T. H. 1952 *The Spider's Web*, Warne
Savory, T. H. 1955 *The World of Small Animals*, ULP
South, R. 1961 *The Moths of the British Isles* (Vols I & II), Warne
Southwood, T. R. E. & Leston, D. 1959 *The Land and Water Bugs of the British Isles*, Warne
Russell, Sir E. J. 1957 *The World of the Soil*, Collins
Step, E. 1932 *Bees, Wasps, Ants, and Allied Insects of the British Isles*, Warne
Stokoe, W. J. 1948 *The Caterpillars of British Moths* (Series I & II), Warne
Sutton, S. L. 1972 *Woodlice*, Ginn

Birds and Mammals

Brink, F. H. van den 1967 *A Field Guide to the Mammals of Britain and Europe*, Collins

Bang, P. & Dahlstrom, P. 1974 *Collins Guide to Animal Tracks and Signs*, Collins

Flegg, J. J. M. & Glue D. E. 1972 *Nestboxes*, BTO, Tring, Herts.

Hartley, P. H. T. 1957 *The Bird Garden*, RSPB, Sandy, Beds.

Heinzel, H., Fitter, R. S. R., Parslow, J. L. F. 1972 *The Birds of Britain and Europe with North Africa and the Middle East*, Collins

Murton, R. K. 1971 *Man and Birds*, Collins

Nicholson, E. M. 1951 *Birds and Men*, Collins

Peterson, R., Mountfort, G. & Hollom, P. A. D. 1954 *A Field Guide to the Birds of Britain and Europe*, Collins

Soper, T. 1973 *The New Bird Table Book*, David & Charles

Soper, T. 1975 *Wildlife Begins at Home*, David & Charles

Recordings

British Garden Birds (two seven-inch records) published by Record Books and obtainable from RSPB, The Lodge, Sandy, Bedfordshire. These records are accompanied by a short explanatory booklet by Peter Conder and they give the typical songs and calls of 25 garden birds.

Index

Index

References to plates are in *italic* type

277